NGOs in International Politics

NGOs in
International Politics

Shamima Ahmed & David Potter

Kumarian
Press, Inc.

NGOs in International Politics
Published in 2006 in the United States of America by Kumarian Press, Inc., 1294 Blue Hills Avenue, Bloomfield, CT 06002 USA

The text of this book is set in 11/13 AGaramond.

Production and design by Joan Weber Laflamme, jml ediset.
Proofread by Beth Richards.
Index by Robert Swanson.

Printed in Canada by Transcontinental Gagné. Text printed with vegetable oil-based ink.

∞The paper used in this publication meets the minimum requirements of the American National Standard for Information Sciences—Permanence of Paper for printed Library Materials, ANSI Z39.48–1984

Library of Congress Cataloging-in-Publication Data

Ahmed, Shamima, 1959–
   NGOs in international politics / Shamima Ahmed, David Potter.
     p. cm.
   Includes bibliographical references and index.
   ISBN-13: 978–1–56549–230–1 (pbk. : alk. paper)
   ISBN-10: 1–56549–230–7 (pbk. : alk. paper)
 1. Non-governmental organizations. I. Potter, David M., 1961– II. Title.
   JZ4841.A36 2006
   327.1—dc22

                                            2006023642

---

15 14 13 12 11 10 09 08 07 06   10 9 8 7 6 5 4 3 2 1   First Printing 2006

Contents

Part I
Overview of NGOs in International Politics

Part II
Case Studies

Part III
Conclusion

Illustrations

Foreword

In the last three decades NGOs have emerged as an important force in the fields of development and human rights. Few countries in the world do not have indigenous NGOs, and their numbers are growing all the time. The same is true for international NGOs, whose work extends across national borders. This phenomenon has emerged in the public eye all over the world. Newspapers and other media frequently carry stories about NGOs, and government agencies and officials often call for closer interaction between the government and such organizations. Indeed, agreement that NGOs have an important place in policymaking and public life spans the political spectrum.

The Nobel prizes to The International Campaign to Ban Landmines in 1997 and to Medicins Sans Frontieres in 1999 have highlighted the emergence of these organizations as "new" forces in international politics. Yet no work to date has provided a comprehensive overview of the varieties of interaction between NGOs and states, between NGOs and international organizations, or among NGOs in international politics. This is especially true of books aimed at undergraduates; nowhere have we found a book that surveys the range of NGO activities and relationships in a manner accessible in the classroom. The scholarly work tends to be too specialized. Work by practitioners tends to be interesting to students but does not address key international relations issues. While a number of books on NGOs in international politics have been published in recent years, individual contributions tend to address one or a few aspects of the topic. Scholars, for example, have focused on NGOs' ability to provide alternative views to state policies, to promote civil society both domestically and internationally, and to deliver services to people beyond the reach of state programs.

There is, moreover, a fundamental break between the literature on NGOs and economic development in developing countries and that on NGOs in international politics. Yet clearly the two research agendas overlap. This is most apparent in the literature on foreign aid and on NGO relations between North and South; topics explored in Part II of this book.

Despite the gap in the textbook literature, NGOs are being taught about in the classroom either in theoretical terms or as components of service learning.[1] This book is designed to remedy the gap between interest in NGOs and accessible literature for use in the classroom.

Organization of This Book

This book has three parts. Part I, Chapters 1 through 5, discusses NGOs in light of international relations theories; surveys the development of NGOs; discusses how NGOs are formed and the obstacles to their development and maintenance; surveys the major roles NGOs now play in international society; and assesses their relationship with states. Despite governments' interest in reaching beyond their current capabilities, especially in areas like foreign aid, NGOs appear to be at the fringes of political and economic agenda setting in other significant areas of international politics.

Part II consists of five sets of case studies that develop issues outlined in Part I. Chapter 6 takes up the issue of NGOs and foreign aid; Chapter 7 focuses on NGO accountability as a transnational problem; Chapter 8 discusses NGO roles in international security; Chapter 9 explores the relationship between women's NGOs and the United Nations (UN); and Chapter 10 examines NGOs in international environmental politics.

Part III consists of Chapter 11, which summarizes the main themes of this book and makes the reader aware of some emerging issues on NGO performance and work.

We have, of course, benefited from the assistance and advice of numerous people and organizations. We are both indebted to Northern Kentucky University for providing summer research support and sabbatical leaves at critical times in the formulation and execution of this project. We trust that this volume will remind university colleagues and administrators that sabbaticals are time well spent taking stock, starting, reassessing, and completing scholarly endeavors. We also acknowledge gratefully the provision of a Pache I-A Research Grant by Nanzan University to support one coauthor's end of what has turned out to be a trans-Pacific writing program.

A number of colleagues have been especially helpful during the formulation and writing of this book. Our thanks to Jim Lance for his editorial advice. We also thank Enamul Choudhury, Robyn Lim, Sudo Sueo, Steven Breyman, and anonymous reviewers for their helpful comments on the manuscript.

Students have played a critical role in the creation of this manuscript. The original idea for it came out of a brace of intensive summer courses on NGOs in international politics. At the time there was no overview of the topic that covered major issues in a manner required by a three-week course format. We would like to acknowledge the work those students did, some of which laid the background for topics taken up in Chapter 2 of this book. We thank Robert Johnson and Brandon Webster for continuing their work in that course in the form of independent studies that contributed further background material.

We come to this topic from rather different perspectives. One of us comes from a background in comparative politics and international relations, with an emphasis on Japan. The other comes from a background in public administration, with an enduring interest in the problems of social, economic, and political development in the developing countries, Bangladesh in particular. The divergence of approach says a great deal about the nature of NGOs; they are not the creatures of a single academic discipline. Our collaboration has enriched our individual understandings of this dynamic new kind of international actor. Without the input of both of our respective perspectives, this book would not have the form it has taken.

Note

[1] For an example of the latter, see Amy Patterson, "It's a Small World: Incorporating Service Learning into International Relations Courses," *PS* 33, no. 4 (2000): 817–22.

Abbreviations and Acronyms

ACVFA	The Advisory Committee on Voluntary Foreign Aid
ADAB	Association for Development Agencies in Bangladesh
ADB	Asian Development Bank
AI	Amnesty International
AMKA	Export Marketing Enterprise Agency
ASA	Association for Social Advancement (Bangladesh)
BNP	Bangladesh Nationalist Party
BRAC	Bangladesh Rural Advancement Committee
CARE	Cooperative for Assistance and Relief Everywhere
CEDAW	Convention on the Elimination of All Forms of Discrimination Against Women
CIDA	Canadian International Development Agency
CITES	Convention on International Trade in Endangered Species of Wild Flora and Fauna
CONGO	Conference of NGOs in Consultative Relationships with the United Nations
CRS	Catholic Relief Services
CSO	civil society organization
CSW	Commission on the Status of Women
DAC	Development Assistance Committee
DFID	Department for International Development
ECHO	European Community Humanitarian Aid Office
ECOSOC	Economic and Social Council (UN)
EDF	Environmental Defense Fund
ELCI	Environmental Liaison Committee International

EU	European Union
G8	Group of eight industrial countries—Canada, France, Germany, Italy, Japan, Russia, the United Kingdom, and the United States—that represents about 65 percent of the world economy
GAD	gender and development
GATT	General Agreement on Tariffs and Trade
GCC	Global Climate Coalition
GNP	gross national product
GSS	Gono Shahajjo Shangstha
HRW	Human Rights Watch
ICBL	International Campaign to Ban Landmines
ICRC	International Committee of the Red Cross
IFC	International Facilitating Committee
IGO	intergovernmental organization
IMF	International Monetary Fund
INGO	international nongovernmental organization
INSTRAW	United Nations International Research and Training Institute for the Advancement of Women
ISIS	International Women's Information and Communication Service
IUCN	International Union for the Conservation of Nature
IWY	International Women's Year
JANIC	Japan NGO Center for International Cooperation
MNC	multinational corporation
NGO	nongovernmental organization
NGOAB	NGO Affairs Bureau (Bangladesh)
NNGO	Northern NGO
NPO	nonprofit organization
ODA	Official development assistance
OECD	Organization for Economic Cooperation and Development
OXFAM	Oxford Committee for Famine Relief
PVO	private voluntary organization

SLORC	State Law and Order Restoration Council
SNGO	Southern NGO
TNC	transnational corporation
UK	United Kingdom
UN	United Nations
UNCED	United Nations Council on Economic Development
UNDP	United Nations Development Program
UNDRO	United Nations Disaster Relief Organization
UNHCR	United Nations High Commissioner for Refugees
UNICEF	United Nations Children's Fund
UNIFEM	United Nations Development Fund for Women
USAID	United States Agency for International Development
WCTU	Women's Christian Temperance Movement
WEDO	Women's Environment and Development Organization
WHO	World Health Organization
WID	women in development
WRI	World Resource Institute
WTO	World Trade Organization
WWF	World Wildlife Federation

Part I

Overview of NGOs in International Politics

Chapters 1 through 5 survey the development of NGOs over the last three decades; discuss how NGOs are formed and the obstacles to their development and maintenance; survey the major roles NGOs now play in international society; and assess their relationship with states.

Chapter 1 introduces NGOs, defines them, and discusses them in terms of international relations theories. It considers the reasons why international relations theories have been slow to account for NGO activity, then discusses how new approaches can help us think about NGOs in international politics.

Chapter 2 traces the development of modern NGOs. Although they appear to be a new phenomenon in international politics, not a few NGOs have long histories. The chapter examines NGO participation in civil society and in the extension of civil society to the global level. Finally, it discusses how NGOs form and how they maintain themselves as organizations over time.

Chapter 3 discusses the main roles that NGOs play in world affairs and in different contexts. Common roles include relief and charity, economic and social development, advocacy and public education, and monitoring of international agreements and transnational actors. While NGOs historically have been seen as apolitical providers of emergency relief and technical assistance for local development, in fact many of their roles have political significance. Depending on the issue area some NGOs carry out explicitly political roles. Attention focuses on NGOs as agenda setters and shapers of international norms and policies.

Chapter 4 surveys the range of relationships that exists between NGOs and governments. In particular, it analyzes those interactions in terms of four modes: NGOs in states, NGOs as collaborators with states, NGOs as opponents of states, and NGOs as substitutes for states. The attention given to non-state actors in international relations often overlooks the persistence of the Westphalian state system. NGOs, even if transnational, are located within the confines of states and carry out their operations therein. Domestic legal and political environments have a profound impact on the existence and practice of non-state actors, NGOs included. They find themselves both in conflict and in cooperation with governments.

Chapter 5 outlines NGO interactions with intergovernmental organizations. NGOs and intergovernmental organizations like the UN and the World Bank have taken on a number of significant roles in the international system. This chapter considers points of interaction and conflict between these two sets of non-state actors. It pays particular attention to the UN and the World Bank.

Chapter 1

NGOs and
International Relations Theory

A Tale of Three NGOs

During World War II, Greece was occupied by the German army. As part of the war effort the Allies blockaded the country, which resulted in widespread hunger there. In Britain a nationwide coalition of peace and relief groups organized a campaign to petition the British government to allow humanitarian relief to Greece. Professor Gilbert Murray and the Rev. R. T. Milford of Oxford University, Edith Pye, and a few others established a relief committee in October 1942. Each of the key founders had prior experience with volunteer work in other organizations. The following year the coalition registered as a charity under the name Oxford Committee for Famine Relief (Oxfam).[1] Along with other organizations the committee approached the government to ask it to allow humanitarian relief to Greece and other blockaded countries. It also organized a famine relief fund to which citizens could donate and organized local support committees around the country. While many organizations wound up their efforts at war's end, Oxfam continued its activities.

Following the war Oxfam focused its attention outside Europe, beginning with a clothing and supplies operation to Middle East refugees in 1948. It has grown over the last half century, becoming one of the most widely recognized private relief and development organizations in the world. Today it describes itself as "a development, relief, and campaigning organization dedicated to finding lasting solutions to poverty and suffering around the world."[2] Oxfam has been active in establishing relief facilities in the wake of natural disasters and civil wars; in the latter

5

capacity it has played an instrumental role in defining proper NGO conduct in humanitarian emergencies.[3]

In 1995 Oxfam transformed itself from a British NGO into a transnational federation—Oxfam International. It now has member chapters in Australia, Belgium, Canada, Hong Kong, Ireland, the Netherlands, New Zealand, Spain, the United Kingdom, and the United States. It is one of the Big Eight federations that control about half of all NGO relief assistance.[4] Member organizations cooperate but remain formally independent of one another. While Oxfam's coordinating secretariat remains in Oxford, Oxfam International has lobbying offices in Washington, D.C., New York, Brussels, and Geneva. Its American advocacy offices lobby not only the US government but also the World Bank, the International Monetary Fund (IMF), and the UN.

In 1971 Muhammad Yunus, a professor of economics at the University of Chittagong, Bangladesh, founded the Grameen Bank. During his early days there he came to recognize the huge gap between mainstream economic theory and the actual conditions of poor citizens in the area. He became aware of the potential for poor people such as itinerant peddlers and stall vendors to improve their livelihood if financial institutions would be willing to provide loans of less than thirty dollars. Unable to obtain funding for his unconventional development ideas, Yunus started his bank with personal funds. Unlike either commercial or official development banks of the time, Grameen Bank undertook to lend to the poorest level of Bangladeshi society (*grameen* is the Bengali word meaning "village"). Such people could not borrow from traditional lending institutions because they did not own property that could be used as collateral to guarantee the loans. Yunus's approach provided small loans against no collateral to the members of bank-organized groups of five or six people (overwhelmingly women). Members of each group then decided who among its members should receive loans. The system proved surprisingly successful, with nearly universal repayment by borrowers.[5] Grameen Bank grew from a small, nearly one-man operation, to a nationwide network. Today, Grameen Bank has hundreds of thousands of members and thousands of employees. Its activities encompass not only small-scale loans, but the organization has progressively added nonprofit companies to foster poor people's skills in weaving, fishery, agriculture, information technology, communications, rural power, and venture-capital development.

Grameen's microcredit scheme has attracted international attention, with multilateral lending institutions like the World Bank publicly supporting its efforts. Grameen has become the model for micro-lending programs in thirty countries as diverse as Kenya, Ethiopia, Philippines, Malaysia, and Sri Lanka. The Good Faith Fund is one of a number of nonprofits in the United States that have emulated the Grameen model. The Grameen Trust was founded in 1989 to aid this transnational learning effort. Yunus has been honored with the Ramon Magsaysay Award; former President Clinton deemed him a worthy candidate for the Nobel Peace Prize;[6] and Yunus was in fact awarded that prize in 2006.

In 1990 Harry Wray, now a retired professor of American studies living in central Japan, founded CANHELP Thailand. On a trip to Northern Thailand to visit a former student, he had been struck by the absence of primary schools in the region despite the central government's commitment to universal education. Returning to Japan, Wray set about organizing a volunteer group that could build schools in Thailand's poorest regions. Each summer since then CANHELP Thailand has organized up to four construction projects using Japanese volunteers who spend a month at a Thai site.

The organization remained skeletal during the 1990s. While a board of directors exists to oversee finances and basic policies, board members point out that leadership was largely a one-man show until Wray's retirement in late 1998. The organization has no formal membership and collects no dues, although it is supported by a student organization on Wray's home campus. Summer volunteers are university students and area citizens. Finances have been a constant headache. Individual contributions and bazaar sales have provided an inadequate base for organizational support. The problem has eased somewhat since 1997, when CANHELP Thailand began to receive grants from the Japan Ministry of Posts and Telecommunications' International Volunteer Savings scheme. Wray expressed frustration at the organization's inability to raise long-term funds from philanthropic groups in the community. When one of us opined to a board member in early 2001 that CANHELP Thailand appeared to be continually on the edge of dissolution, the member replied that that had always been the impression. Nevertheless, it continues to function under new leadership as of this writing, one of the many thousands of small NGOs that receive little attention but undoubtedly make up the numerical majority of voluntary development organizations in the world.

What Are NGOs?

Defining NGOs turns out to be a key problem in determining what they are and what they do. Organizations are often called NGOs with little concern for clarity of meaning. Scholars tend to define them in ways that suit their particular research agendas. NGOs themselves sometimes use different definitions; for example, the International Committee of the Red Cross (ICRC) is defined as a nongovernmental humanitarian *agency*, the last word denoting an intermediate status between NGO and intergovernmental organization (IGO). PVO (private voluntary organization) is sometimes used in the United States and is synonymous with NGO used in other countries. Today, NPO (nonprofit organization) and NGO are used nearly synonymously in the United States, although that is not always the case elsewhere in the world, and this book makes a distinction between them (see Box 1–1).

This book adopts the UN definition of NGOs: "Any international organization which is not established by inter-governmental agreement shall be considered as an NGO." The only constraints are that a NGO cannot be profit-making; it cannot advocate the use of violence; it cannot be a school, a university, or a political party; and any concern with human rights must be general rather than restricted to a particular communal group, nationality, or country. This book also distinguishes between Northern NGOs (NNGOs) based in the industrial democracies and Southern NGOs (SNGOs) based in developing countries because the distinction aids clarity of meaning in some of the discussions below.[7]

For purposes of this book, then, neither government agencies nor corporations are NGOs. The definition also excludes political parties, religious groups per se, private hospitals, and schools, which better fit the broader category of nonprofit organization (see Box 1–1). It also excludes organizations such as sports clubs and fraternal organizations because they are not concerned with economic and political development issues. Finally, the term is not as broad as *non-state actor* as conventionally used in international relations. The latter term includes multinational corporations (MNCs), organized crime groups, international producer cartels like OPEC, and organizations like the Palestine Liberation Organization that are not states but are not usually understood to be NGOs.

Box 1–1. Are NGOs and NPOs Different?

The terms NPO and NGO are nearly synonymous in the United States. For practitioners, there is good reason for this. Lester Salamon and Helmut Anheier define the NPOs as follows:

NPOs . . .
- have formal organization;
- are organized independently of government;
- place constraints on redistribution of earnings;
- practice self-governance; and
- have voluntary membership.[*]

All of these conditions apply to NGOs, and they are treated in this book as an important component of the nonprofit-sector universe.

---

[*] Lester Salamon and Helmut Anheier, *The Emerging Nonprofit Sector: An Overview* (Manchester: Manchester Univ. Press, 1994).

NGOs and International Relations Theories

There has been a boom in academic studies of NGOs in recent years. Discussions now appear in many textbooks on international relations, although these tend to be short and often appended near the end under rubrics like "new trends in international politics." But there has been much less attention given to the question of how NGOs fit into mainstream international relations theory. There are two main reasons why this is so.

First, the study of these organizations crosses disciplinary and theoretical boundaries. There is no unified body of NGO literature that can be readily accommodated by mainstream theories in international relations (or elsewhere, for that matter). For example, NGOs are a subset of the domestic nonprofit sector, which makes them a concern of public administration, a sub-field removed from international relations. NGOs can also fit into the theoretical framework of social movements,[8] and they have been studied as public interest groups.[9] A common feature of these approaches is that they treat NGOs essentially in terms of domestic politics or comparative politics rather than international relations. Finally, many studies of NGOs as development organizations discuss their roles in technical terms specific to disciplines outside of the social sciences, for example, agriculture, health and epidemiology, or engineering.

Second, mainstream international relations theory has tended to ignore the emergence of these new actors in areas directly concerned with international politics. Calls for new directions in the study of foreign policy[10] and new thinking in international relations theory[11] have not compelled mainstream scholars to include the study of NGOs in those efforts.

For example, one reason NGOs have not received much attention from international relations theorists is that theories still place primary importance on nation-states. *Realism* in particular has been the dominant paradigm for the last half century, and it is a theoretical approach notoriously indifferent to non-state actors. Realism's attention to the state stems from its understanding of the bases of international politics. Realism posits an anarchic international system (that is, one without a world government) in which nation-states must rely on their own devices (self-help) to maintain their own security. International politics is therefore a power game in which military power and economic power are used to ensure state survival and in which conflict is the expected mode of state interaction. This self-help security dilemma determines state interests, with state preservation being the ultimate national interest. A statement by Kenneth Waltz, the most prominent realist scholar today, aptly sums up this approach's indifference to NGOs and other transnational actors: "States are not and never have been the only international actors. But then structures are defined not by all the actors that flourish within them but by the major ones."[12] NGOs do not qualify as objects of realist attention.

Liberalism would seem like a good starting point for studying NGOs. It posits a more peaceful world than that described by realists in which a variety of cooperative relationships is possible because security considerations do not dominate all fields of activity. Liberalism allows for more attention to transnational interactions outside the state, for example, those between sub-national governments, agencies within national governments, and MNCs. It also posits a host of cooperative international relations outside of the realist concern with security.[13]

The emergence of *interdependence theory* in the 1970s, the major strand of international liberalism, however, did not lead to greater attention to NGOs. MNCs received the bulk of scholarly attention within this school. The challenge of interdependence failed to displace realism's dominance, moreover, because the two schools have since been locked in a debate about whether or not the state remains central to the study of international relations. In either case, the state remains the major object of study in this debate.[14]

Regime theory, an outgrowth of interdependence, potentially has a great deal to suggest about how informal interactions in the international arena can promote cooperation. Regimes are conventionally defined as sets of principles, norms, and expectations that guide behavior in certain areas of international politics.[15] At their core, regimes typically consist of participating governments and international laws, but research on how regimes come about and how they are sustained repeatedly points out the contributions of non-state actors. K. J. Holsti points out that "non-state actors play critical roles in helping to launch new forms of international regulation. Interest groups, transnational coalitions, and individuals lobby governments to solve some international problem. Environmental groups, for example, have been instrumental in helping to create international regimes to protect animal species and to reduce harmful effects of industrial and other forms of pollution."[16] Attention to regimes, therefore, highlights the ways in which state and non-state actors interact in certain areas of international cooperation. (Chapter 10 illustrates NGO participation in the creation and maintenance of an international environmental regime.)

The crucial problem in studying NGOs within the framework of international relations is that they organize for action in ways that are not readily seen in traditional political-science terms. They do not possess the great resources of state-centered international politics: sovereignty, territory, and coercive capability. Nor do they enjoy economic power on a scale comparable to many MNCs, the standard non-state actor of interdependence theory and international political economy. NGOs have yet to hold sovereignty at bay, and no one states, as is often claimed of the largest MNCs, that Greenpeace or Amnesty International (AI) or the Grameen Bank command economic resources greater than the GNP of the world's smaller nations. Much of the developmental work carried out by NGOs, moreover, is not seen as specifically political. Technical assistance to increase agricultural productivity, the construction of village schools in developing countries, and efforts to immunize children against disease do not appear political, although in the long run their effects may be.

This is not to say that NGOs have no power. Many scholars argue that they do, but that such power takes nontraditional forms that do not always appear political. Indeed, one good reason NGOs have not commanded greater attention from mainstream political science has to do with their avoidance of standard political repertoires. Many do not see themselves as interest groups, although advocacy NGOs clearly are. They do not view themselves as akin to political parties. They do not contest elections (usually). Indeed, the many thousands of NGOs working in the fields of humanitarian assistance, disaster relief, and social and economic development do not define their work as political. AI, which has defined a mission of changing government policies on prisoner abuse and torture, long described its advocacy as apolitical as a means of deflecting criticism of its work.[17] Only recently has it acknowledged that human rights advocacy means engaging in politics.

New Theoretical Frameworks and NGOs

International relations theory after World War II was vitally concerned with the operations of interstate relations in the context of the Cold War. The end of the Cold War represented a serious challenge to the discipline. The result has been a fragmentation of theoretical unity in the study of international politics. Following the logic of this argument, NGOs are an object of study for negative reasons; that is, the absence of a dominant theoretical paradigm allows them a place in the field of inquiry.

Two approaches to international relations that emerged in the 1990s are more congenial to the study of NGOs. One is *transnationalism*. The other is *constructivism*. Transnationalism, an outgrowth of interdependence theory, reemerged in the 1990s. It is an effort to revive the promise of interdependence theory to broaden the study of international politics beyond the scope of the state. Thomas Risse-Kappen, a proponent of this revival, defines transnational relations as "regular interactions across national boundaries when at least one actor is a non-state agent or does not operate on behalf of a national government or international organization."[18] Similarly, Fred Halliday refers to international society as "the emergence of non-state links of economy, political association, culture, ideology that transcend state boundaries and constitute, more or less, a society that goes beyond boundaries."[19] NGOs are thus part of a larger collection of non-state actors that includes MNCs, epistemic communities of scientists and technical specialists, ethnic diasporas, cross-border terrorist and criminal organizations, and so forth.

The logic for considering such an approach is well illustrated in a comment by Edith Brown Weiss and Harold Jacobsen:

> The traditional view of the international system as hierarchical and focused almost exclusively on states has evolved into one that is nonhierarchical. Effective power is increasingly being organized in a nonhierarchical manner. While sovereign states continue as principal actors, and as the only ones that can levy taxes, and conscript and raise armies, these functions have declined in importance relative to newly important issues, such as environmental protection and sustainable development. There are now many actors in addition to states: intergovernmental organizations (IGOs), nongovernmental organizations, enterprises, other nonstate actors, and individuals. . . . Nonstate actors are performing increasingly complex tasks, especially in the newer issue areas.[20]

Although this approach does not concentrate exclusively on NGOs, it argues that there is increasing new space in international relations for actors such as NGOs, and new issues over which such organizations have influence. The transnational perspective is especially useful for thinking about a dynamic form of NGO cooperation (the transnational network is discussed in Chapter 2). NGOs have formed coalitions across borders to tackle global issues, and they often do this independent of governments.

Constructivism also has the potential to help clarify what NGOs do in international politics. This approach to international politics argues that interests, identities, and roles are socially defined. Constructivists criticize the realist assertion that anarchy necessarily creates a self-help security dilemma that drives states into conflict with each other. A key constructivist insight is that the environment—the international system—is not fixed and immutable and therefore does not determine actors' behavior. Rather, the international system is created through the repeated interactions of states and other actors. The kind of international system that exists at any one time is the result of how key players understand the system and, therefore how they understand their interests and identities, and those of others, within that system. Constructivists point out that states define their relationships with one another as competitive or cooperative depending on how they define their identities toward one another and how they are defined by their counterparts in turn. As Alexander Wendt observes:

> A fundamental principle of constructivist social theory is that people act toward objects, including other actors, on the basis of meanings that the objects have for them. States act differently toward enemies than they do toward friends, because enemies are threatening and friends are not. . . . U.S. military power has a different significance for Canada than for Cuba, despite their different "structural" positions, just as British missiles have a different significance for the United States than do Soviet missiles.[21]

There are already a number of divergent approaches within this school, but in general, constructivist analysis focuses attention on ideas, norms, epistemic communities, global civil society, and regimes—areas of international politics most conducive to the exercise of NGO influence. The approach assumes the institutions of traditional statecraft and builds beyond them, as do NGOs. Constructivist analysis allows the possibility that national interests are not fixed, that states' understandings of what is appropriate political behavior can be changed.[22] By extension, NGO attempts to change the ways in which states act and how they define themselves and their roles have the *potential* to transform the international system.

Constructivism addresses a critical issue in the discussion of NGOs in international politics: what kind of power such organizations have. It is clear that NGOs do not have the kinds of power resources that states do. They are not sovereign and therefore legally not the equals of states. They cannot make law or enter into treaties. They are observers rather than full members of the formal international organizations. They do not possess coercive power; nor do they maintain armies or police forces to compel obedience and compliance. But they do act in international politics, and they do exercise some kind of power.

Constructivism is a useful tool for thinking about how NGOs influence international politics because it is concerned with the exercise of power through communication. When people, governments, or non-state actors communicate with one another over time, that communication can create common understandings of roles and behaviors. Over time, these understandings become rules that govern behavior and further communication.[23] Thomas Risse-Kappen provocatively entitled a recent article on international politics "Let's Argue!" The article portrays international politics as a discourse, an unfinished conversation about who exercises power and why.[24]

The power of NGOs, then, is the power to persuade. Their power consists of demonstrating through persuasion and action that there are other ways of organizing social and political arrangements besides those currently in use. Consider the common activities of NGOs (discussed further in Chapter 3): educating the public, advocacy, empowering people through local economic development and network construction, and monitoring international agreements. None of these involves coercion, all take place within legal frameworks established by states either individually or collectively, and all involve persuasive communication. And all aim at building or changing understandings of how the world operates and why. It is clear from the varieties of NGO activities that they operate *as if* constitutive norms exist and are an appropriate object of the conduct of international politics.

These theories inform the understanding of NGOs in international politics throughout this book. Transnationalism and constructivism are useful tools for understanding how NGOs influence international politics and civil society because NGO interactions with one another and with other actors are *transnational* and *potentially transformative*. They are carried out above and below interstate relations and often with the aim of redefining what is appropriate in the conduct of international and interstate relations. Realism, however, reminds us that a state-centered international system still applies significant restraints on what nonstate actors can accomplish (Chapter 4, especially, notes the ways in which states frame the activities and even the existence of NGOs.)

Summary

A few years ago Gerald Clarke commented that political science has largely ignored the emergence of NGOs.[25] That can certainly be said of international relations. That neglect is unfortunate. First, NGOs have an impact on international as well as domestic politics, as we shall see. Second, political science's concern with the organization and use of power in the public sphere inevitably involves voluntary organizations like NGOs. Third, the tools of political science, including study of the organization and activities of public-interest groups and civil society, provide useful means for studying NGOs. That said, critical problems remain. For one thing, the confusion about what NGOs are makes it hard to understand clearly their roles and contributions to international politics. For another, their activities are not always defined in political terms (an issue examined in Chapter 3).

Discussion Questions

1. What is an NGO? Does al-Qaeda qualify as one?
2. Why have NGOs had such a low profile in international relations theory? Should international relations take them more seriously? Why or why not?

Notes

¹ Oxfam became the organization's official name in 1965.

² Oxfam GB, *A Short History of Oxfam*. Available on the oxfam.org.uk website.

³ Deborah Eade and Suzanne Williams, *The OXFAM Handbook of Development and Relief*, vols. 1–3 (Oxford: Oxfam UK and Ireland, 1995).

⁴ Peter J. Simmons, "Learning to Live with NGOs," *Foreign Policy* 112 (Fall 1998): 82–96.

⁵ For accounts of Grameen Bank's approach, successes, and limitations, see David Bornstein, *The Price of a Dream: The Story of the Grameen Bank* (Chicago: Univ. of Chicago Press, 1996); and Muhammad Yunus, *Banker to the Poor: Micro-lending and the Battle against World Poverty* (New York: Public Affairs, 1999).

⁶ S. Kamaluddin, "Banking: Lending with a Mission," *Far Eastern Economic Review* 156 (March 18, 1993): 38–40.

⁷ The terms *Northern NGO* and *Southern NGO* to describe organizations in the developed and developing countries, respectively, may strike the reader as outdated. This book retains the usage, however, for lack of better shorthand terms and to alert the reader to the fact that NGOs in various regions of the world differ in basic organization and purpose.

⁸ Sidney Tarrow, *Power in Movement: Social Movements and Contentious Politics*, 2nd ed. (Cambridge, MA: Cambridge Univ. Press, 1998).

[9] Alan Rix, *Japan's Foreign Aid Challenge: Policy Reform and Aid Leadership* (London: Routledge, 1993).

[10] Charles Hermann, Charles Kegley, and James Rosenau, eds., *New Directions in the Study of Foreign Policy* (Boston: Allen and Unwin, 1987).

[11] Michael Doyle and John Ikenberry, eds., *New Thinking in International Relations Theory* (Boulder, CO: Westview Press, 1997).

[12] Kenneth Waltz, "Political Structures," in *Neorealism and Its Critics*, ed. R. Keohane (New York: Columbia Univ. Press, 1986), 88.

[13] Robert Keohane and Joseph Nye, *Power and Interdependence*, 2nd ed. (Glenview, IL: Scott, Foresman and Co., 1989).

[14] Miles Kahler, "Inventing International Relations: International Relations Theory After 1945," in *New Thinking in International Relations,* ed. Michael Doyle and G. John Ikenberry, 20–53 (Boulder, CO: Westview Press, 1987).

[15] Stephen Krasner, ed., *International Regimes* (Ithaca, NY: Cornell Univ. Press, 1982).

[16] K. J. Holsti, *International Politics: A Framework for Analysis,* 6th ed. (Upper Saddle River, NJ: Prentice Hall, 1992), 388.

[17] Ann M. Clark, *Diplomacy of Conscience* (Princeton, NJ: Princeton Univ. Press, 2001).

[18] Thomas Risse-Kappen, ed., *Bringing Transnational Relations Back In* (Cambridge, MA: Cambridge Univ. Press, 1995), 3.

[19] Fred Halliday, *Rethinking International Relations* (London: Macmillan, 1994), 94.

[20] Harold Jacobson and Edith Brown Weiss, "A Framework for Analysis," in *Engaging Countries: Strengthening Compliance with International Environmental Accords,* ed. Edith Brown Weiss and Harold Jacobson (Cambridge, MA: MIT Press, 1998), 3.

[21] Alexander Wendt, "Anarchy Is What States Make of It: The Social Construction of Power Politics," *International Organization* 46, no. 2 (1992): 396. Reprinted in Andrew Linklater, ed., *International Relations: Critical Concepts in Political Science* (London: Routledge, 2000), 2:619.

[22] Jeffrey Checkel, "The Constructivist Turn in International Relations Theory," *World Politics* 50, no. 1 (1998): 324–48.

[23] Nicholas Onuf, *World of Our Making* (Columbia: Univ. of South Carolina Press, 1989); Maya Zehfuss, "Constructivisms in International Relations: Wendt, Onuf, and Kratchowil," in *Constructing International Relations: The Next Generation,* ed. Karin Fierke and Knud Jorgensen (Armonk, NJ: M. E. Sharpe, 2001), 54–75.

[24] Thomas Risse, "'Let's Argue!': Communicative Action in World Politics," *International Organization* 54, no.1 (2000): 1–39.

[25] Gerald Clarke, "Non-governmental Organizations (NGOs) and Politics in the Developing World," *Political Studies* 47 (1998): 36–52.

Chapter 2

NGO Evolution

NGO evolution
Origins and maintenance
NGOs and civil society

This chapter introduces and explains the nature and emergence of NGOs as a worldwide phenomenon. First it considers how these organizations fit into broader societal patterns. Next it charts the reasons for the growth of NGOs all over the world in the last thirty years. It finishes with the puzzle of how individual NGOs organize and sustain themselves.

How Many NGOs Are There?

The issue of definition outlined in Chapter 1 has important implications for how NGOs are perceived. In fact, the ambiguity of definition complicates even the basic task of counting NGOs. How many NGOs exist in the world? The short answer is that we are not sure. It is fairly certain that the numbers are growing. The Union of International Associations estimates that the number of NGOs doubled between 1978 and 1998 and is now twenty times greater than the number of NGOs in 1951; in 2000 there were 45,674 international NGOs (INGOs) of all types.[1] This estimate is probably the best available, but it only includes INGOs known to the Union of International Associations.

Problems also occur at the national level. In many countries official counts of NGOs underestimate their actual numbers. Japan provides a case in point. Throughout the 1990s the Japan NGO Center for International Cooperation (JANIC), a national clearinghouse dedicated to fostering communication and cooperation among Japanese NGOs, estimated the number of such organizations at around two hundred. That

Figure 2–1. INGOs Headquarters by Region

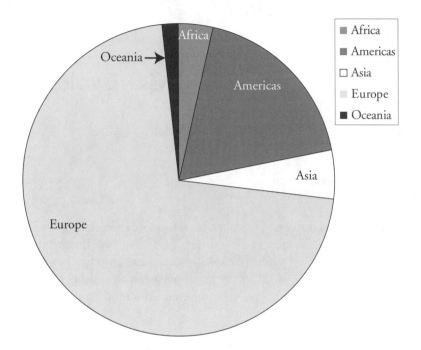

number reflected the number of voluntary organizations that were registered as NPOs, were involved in international cooperation, and had responded to JANIC surveys. The estimates did not reflect the actual number of voluntary organizations that fall within the definition of NGOs used in this book. In fact, CANHELP Thailand, whose founder certainly saw it as an NGO, was not included in the JANIC directory until the 2000 edition.

The case applies even more so in developing countries, where communication between the capital and the regions is not always easy and government statistics are often unreliable. Peter Uvin estimates the number of national NGOs in the Third World at around fifty thousand, with heavy concentrations in countries like India and Bangladesh.[2] The immense majority of NGOs are grassroots organizations based in local communities, which often makes them difficult to count.[3]

NGO Evolution

The development of NGOs and why they command so much attention now requires some explanation. This section examines the topic from two perspectives. The first considers how NGOs *in general* have developed over time. It looks to changes in the international system that have provided room for NGOs to pursue their activities. The second considers the problem of how individual NGOs establish themselves and then maintain their activities over time.

Historical Evolution of NGOs

At first glance NGOs appear new. They are closely associated with the phenomenon that Salamon has described as a "global associational revolution" that has swept the world in the last three decades.[4] "New" depends on how one wishes to think about NGOs. The term *NGO* was first used in the UN Charter in 1946, which means such voluntary organizations already existed. Indeed, private citizens' organizations were an important spur to the creation and shape of the UN itself. A look at the Organization for Economic Cooperation and Development's (OECD's) directories of NGOs shows that there are some much older than that. For example, the earliest German NGOs active now were established in the 1830s, although at the time of their founding the term *NGO* would not have made sense to them. In many developed countries it is safe to say that private charitable organizations established in the nineteenth and early twentieth centuries have recently taken on the mantle of NGO as their activities and self-definition have evolved.

It is useful to think about the historic development of NGOs in terms of two time frames. The first encompasses the nineteenth and twentieth centuries; the second comprises the last thirty years. As noted above, we have no accurate estimates of the total number of NGOs in the world today—or in any prior period. Some inferences, however, can be made about their incidence over time. John Boli and George Thomas used the *Yearbook of International Organizations*, an annual survey, to measure the growth of INGOs over the last 150 years.[5] Their research found a steady increase in the establishment of these organizations over time, with a marked upturn after World War II. In this light we should see the development of NGOs as part of a broader pattern of the development of social movements like labor unions, professional associations, and other civic groups. Significantly, Boli and Thomas found that INGOs steadily expanded in number despite world wars, economic downturns, and the rise of antidemocratic states all over the world in the 1930s.

Regional and national NGO development reveals some differences from the general pattern Boli and Thomas found. In particular, a country's political and social histories seem to affect the growth of NGOs. Consider the data for Germany and Japan presented in Table 2–1.[6]

Table 2–1. NGO Establishment in the Federal Republic of Germany and Japan

Period	Germany (N=148)	Japan (N=168)
To 1870	6	0
1871-1900	6	4
1901-1910	2	1
1911-1920	3	0
1921-1930	5	5
1931-1940	2	1
1941-1950	10	3
1951-1960	14	13
1961-1970	33	18
1971-1980	36	69
1981-1990	30	54

Source: OECD, *Directory of Non-governmental Development Organizations in OECD Member Countries* (Paris: OECD, 1990)

The two countries' histories suggest the following trends in the development of NGOs. National unification and government-led modernization, the turn to fascism in the 1930s, and democratization after World War II clearly affected NGO formation. While the earliest German organizations predate the earliest Japanese by decades, there is an upsurge in both countries after 1870, the founding date of both the Second Empire in Germany and the Meiji government in Japan. Both of these new nation-states had authoritarian governments dedicated to catching up with rival powers through the deliberate promotion of industry and military capability. As these governments gradually allowed limited democracy in the 1890s, the number of citizen-organized groups rose. This process accelerated with the introduction of parliamentary democracy after World War I.

Fascism in the 1930s and World War II in the early 1940s dealt serious blows to citizen organizations. In both countries the state banned, severely restricted, or attempted directly to control private groups. Allied occupation and the reintroduction of parliamentary democracy (at least in the western half of Germany) corresponded to a resurgence of NGO formation. Finally, the sharp upsurge in NGO establishment since the 1960s suggests, along with international features discussed below, that industrial maturity and affluence have acted as spurs to public interest activity. This last point should not surprise the reader, because it was during this period that new social movements in general, organized around issues of environment, gender equality, opposition to nuclear power and weapons, and social equity, emerged across the industrial democracies.

The developing countries of Africa and Asia offer a different perspective on the origins of NGOs. Boli and Thomas found that colonialism was a significant impediment to the development of INGOs based in colonial territories. They found that indigenous INGOs—in other words, organizations with headquarters in developing countries—expanded rapidly once the countries of Africa and Asia gained independence. They conclude that a national state is a prerequisite for a vigorous NGO sector, a point to which we will return later in this book. It supports the argument, moreover, that NGOs in developing countries have developed over the last forty years in response to issues and demands germane to the developing countries themselves. The global associational revolution is not headquartered in the North.

Global Factors in NGO Evolution

While NGOs have developed over the last century or so, their increase worldwide over the last thirty years is striking. On this point the data in Table 2–1 are clear. That the increase has occurred nearly everywhere is likewise noteworthy. Lester Salamon provides three broad reasons for this dramatic trend.[7] The first is the global communications revolution. The ease of international travel and the development of telephone, facsimile, and Internet technologies have greatly reduced the cost and effort of communicating and organizing among voluntary organizations.

For example, the International Campaign to Ban Landmines (ICBL) was able to coordinate the activities of hundreds of organizations in dozens of countries over several years through these technologies, activity that previously would have been prohibitive in terms of time and expense. The ability of thousands of NGO activists to travel to international summits in Rio de Janiero (1992) and Beijing (1995), and to stay in close contact with one another and official delegations when they got there, testifies to the power of new methods of communications. Indeed, it may not be too much to argue that email, the Internet, and the World Wide Web make up the means for new repertoires of collective action.[8]

A second factor is the retreat of the state worldwide. Jessica Mathews argues that a "power shift" is occurring in which governments are increasingly giving up responsibilities to other actors in society. This is evident in the scaling back of the welfare state in Western Europe, North America, and Japan. The change is even more far-reaching in the former communist countries of Eastern Europe and Russia. Over the last two decades citizens and political and social leaders have increasingly expressed dissatisfaction with the operation of a broad array of government programs put into place in the first half of the twentieth century. In many cases this dissatisfaction has been linked to what policymakers and academics term the failure of government. The retreat has been accompanied by strong calls for governments to reinvigorate private markets (essentially, Anglo-American style capitalism) and to delegate welfare functions to NPOs.[9] In this environment NGOs stand out for their presumed ability to combine public service with private action. This is, of course, linked closely with the revived interest in civil society.

Economic failure in the developing countries has also provoked searches for new ways to achieve social development. Third-world government programs, it is argued, have failed to produce economic growth, so that economic levels in many developing countries have stagnated over the last three decades. At the same time, traditional foreign aid programs, based on transfers of economic resources from Northern to Southern governments, have come under criticism for failing to help rectify that stagnation. A new emphasis on channeling aid through private organizations, referred to in some circles as the New Policy Agenda, reinforces the retreat of the state from welfare provision. Wars and other disasters in places ranging from the former Yugoslavia to Rwanda to Iraq have prompted private relief efforts alongside official interstate action.

Salamon's third reason has to do with the link between the general level of economic growth worldwide in the 1960s and 1970s and the formation of new citizen attitudes. Material affluence created a middle class whose values increasingly changed from emphasis on material and economic stability to concern with social equity and quality of life. The emergence of these post-material values all over the world gave rise to new concerns such as human rights, environmental protection, and promotion of citizen empowerment. NGOs address all of these concerns.[10]

NGO Origins and Maintenance

The transnational factors that explain the broad evolution of NGOs worldwide leave aside the question of how and why any particular NGO forms and develops. NGOs are social organizations. They have histories with starting dates and, in more than a few cases, ending dates. If NGOs expect to participate in and possibly transform international politics, they must be organized to do so. At a minimum they must organize themselves around an issue or issues of concern to them and then maintain that organization over time. Neither is an automatic process. Groups often fail to form around common interests. They also disband. How groups come into existence and how they persist is a critical first problem for understanding why some groups are politically influential and others are not. Not all problems get represented, and groups that cease to exist can hardly articulate interests on behalf of their members. So, how do NGOs form?

Theories about interest group formation and maintenance provide helpful insights. Jeffrey Berry defines a public interest group as "one that seeks a collective good, the achievement of which will not selectively and materially benefit the membership or activists of the organization."[11] This definition addresses squarely the key feature of NGOs: their purposes are not tied to narrow considerations of self-interest. This presents such organizations with a serious problem: how to organize when potential members cannot expect to derive a specific benefit from participating in the organization.

Origins

Two explanations of public interest group formation are especially useful when looking at how NGOs organize. The first is the *entrepreneur model* of group formation. The second explanation notes that many interest groups grow out of *other groups*. The entrepreneur model proceeds from the assumption that groups do not form naturally. Rather, they form because an individual (or a small group of individuals) identifies a problem, decides something needs to be done about it, then mobilizes other people to achieve that purpose. The entrepreneur plays a key part in defining the organization's goals and leading it through the initial stages of establishment. That person must be willing to commit the energy and time to start the organization and keep it operating. Without an entrepreneur who is willing to take on the burden of organizing and defining the goals of a group, many public interest groups will not form.

Many NGOs arise because entrepreneurs identify an issue and mobilize political, economic, and social resources around it. This is the case with Oxfam, Grameen Bank, and CANHELP Thailand. In each case one person or a small group of people can be identified as core founders. These people defined the group's original goals and began the work of creating an organization. Entrepreneurship is especially important because of the issues NGOs address. Unlike issues that lead to the formation of classic interest groups (economic well-being) or citizens' movements (local quality of life), NGOs tend to address low salience issues that will tend not to arouse intense citizen participation on their own. Many NGOs in the industrial democracies organize around issues of livelihood and well-being of people in the developing countries, or, even when domestically oriented, the well-being of people outside their national mainstreams.

Not all NGOs begin from scratch, however. NGOs can develop out of other organizations. Many NNGOs began in the nineteenth and twentieth centuries (sometimes even earlier) as charities organized by religious organizations.[12] Some of the largest NGOs active today—the Aga Khan Foundation, CAFOD, Catholic Relief Services (CRS), Christian Aid, Lutheran Relief Services, Miserior, World Vision—were organized out of established religious organizations. In the developing countries the state turns out to be a significant source of organizational talent. The New Policy Agenda's emphasis on reducing the size of government led to the displacement of a professional public-management class that became available to organize NGOs and other voluntary associations.[13]

Another organizational innovation involves what Sidney Tarrow calls *franchising,* by which organizations lend their names to organizations in other countries.[14] Many of the largest NNGOs employ this organizational style. Greenpeace, Oxfam, World Wildlife Fund, and World Vision International, for example, are composed of national chapters that are more or less independent of one another.[15] This strategy provides important advantages for entrepreneurs who wish to establish

NGOs. A franchise brings with it a recognizable name, technical and administrative expertise from other member organizations, and often financial assistance from overseas chapters.

Transnational advocacy networks provide a way for NGOs to cooperate with one another without having to create new permanent organizations. Networks of small inter-linked organizations allow NGOs to mobilize people and share resources while at the same time avoiding the costs of traditional organizational maintenance. Tarrow argues that transnational networks are "light, inexpensive to maintain professional organizations" that spend less effort on maintaining membership and more on mobilizing people for activities of short duration and specific intent. He goes on to argue that there is an emerging international pattern of social movement organization that consists of "small professional leaderships; large but mainly passive support; and impersonal network like connective structures. In this pattern, members of the organization communicate by mail, fax, or e-mail with leaders; they participate in large but rare demonstrations; and they take part by 'proxy' in small . . . demonstrative strikes by cadres of militants."[16]

The ICBL (discussed in Chapter 8) is a representative transnational advocacy network. The ICBL organized thousands of groups worldwide around a specific issue. NGOs in each country were free to lobby governments and organize information campaigns as they saw fit while sharing information, ideas, and strategies with one another worldwide. When the network's primary goal, inducing governments to create an international treaty banning anti-personnel landmine use and production, was achieved in 1999, many NGOs ceased their activities. A core group of NGOs continues to monitor treaty implementation in a successor network. While this description does not fit all NGOs, it suggests one important innovation in the classic organizational dilemma.

Maintenance

Once groups have formed, the problem becomes how to maintain them. Two key resources are especially important if a group wants to influence public policy: members and money. Membership turns out to be a thorny problem for group maintenance because NGOs are voluntary associations. No one has to join an NGO. This raises a collective action problem first outlined by economist Mancur Olson. Think of a typical NGO. Its purpose is to provide a benefit to people who are not necessarily its members. Olson pointed out that especially in a large group a single individual's contribution to the organization—in the form of dues, activity, or whatever—will be quite small. So small, in fact, that a single individual's lack of participation may not materially damage the organization. On the other hand, the organization will provide the benefit because that is its mission. It is rational for individuals not to join organizations if they can receive the benefit without effort, what is called the free-rider problem. This is doubly the case for public interest groups because, by definition, they provide public benefits—benefits that accrue to people outside the organization as well as inside.[17]

So what incentives can group leaders provide to induce people to join? The public interest group approach outlines three: *material benefits, solidary benefits*, and *purposive benefits*. Material benefits are tangible benefits that are available only to members. Solidary benefits are essentially those that derive from participation: citizens derive satisfaction from playing a part in the political process and from spending time with other like-minded individuals. Finally, purposive benefits are those that derive from a sense of being involved in an activity that achieves a goal beyond the pursuit of individual interests. Organizations can satisfy ideological goals, such as working to achieve justice or a better environment. Berry argues purposive benefits are characteristic of public interest groups.

Berry points out that any organization will provide a mix of these benefits, but that public interest groups tend to offer a mix of the latter two predominantly. While these two kinds of benefits are important to the maintenance of public interest group membership, they are likely to be weaker inducements than material and selective benefits, compounding the problem of membership/donations for NGOs.

Interest groups have gotten around this collective action problem in part in two ways. First, the "members" of many interest groups are actually other organizations. Corporations, churches, foundations, and charities are often affiliates with interest groups. This reduces the membership problem by reducing the number of members. Olson points out that small groups very often have resources to enforce member participation, thereby limiting or even preventing the free-rider problem. For example, group leaders can apply peer pressure to induce members to live up to their commitments because all of the members know one another.

Berry found out that many public interest groups are in fact memberless, or nearly so. Many have small professional staffs at headquarters. "Members" are individual donors whose participation in the organization is limited to the act of donation, prompting the appellation "checkbook membership."[18]

NGOs have solved the membership problem in these ways. Many, especially in the developing countries, still emphasize membership. Grameen Bank and Shapla Neer, a Japanese NGO that operates in Bangladesh, require local people to participate formally in certain activities in the organization in order to receive benefits. Other NGOs are essentially memberless. Most of the largest INGOs are run by professionals. Indeed, professionalism has become one of the hallmarks of the NGO sector. AI and Greenpeace are typical of NGOs organized around cadres of committed activists. Greenpeace's direct actions against polluting companies and governments that conduct nuclear testing are carried out by full-time activists who may be in the field (or at sea) for weeks or months at a time. Most people cannot afford the time or money to participate in this kind of campaign, so most members contribute through donations or letter-writing campaigns mobilized by the activist core.

Professionalization has advantages. Many NGOs are created through voluntary effort, but maintaining organizations often requires commitments and skills not readily found in a volunteer-based organization. Grameen Bank again provides an example. It began as a volunteer effort. Over time, expansion of the organization's scope and membership, as well as Yunus's desire to run it as a bank, began to require professional commitments. Today, Grameen Bank has a two-tiered structure: a paid, professional staff and a large body of member-clients who receive its services. As another example, Greenpeace's campaign activities, in particular its confrontations with MNCs and national governments, require a great deal of time from activists. Volunteer membership is simply not viable.

Financing is a key problem as well. The availability of large, stable budgets separates the established INGOs like Oxfam and Grameen from the likes of CANHELP Thailand. To the extent that an NGO has a professional staff and a global reach, budgets become critical. In general, NGOs have three sources of income: contributions from individuals, foundations, and businesses; public subsidies; and fees and sales.[19] The proportion from each source varies from organization to organization, and among countries, of course. Two general conditions, however, usually obtain. First, private contributions tend not to be the main source of NGO income, especially for NGOs that are major transnational players. Voluntary contributions are simply too small and inconsistent a base on which to build sustained assistance efforts or campaigns. Second, government subsidies are an important source of income. The largest NGOs in the United States—Catholic Relief Services, Save the Children, and World Vision—rely on government support for upward of two-thirds of their annual income. Governments can therefore act as significant contributors to NGO maintenance, supplying finance and professional expertise.

NGOs and Civil Society

NGOs are considered by many social scientists to be an important component of civil society. Rita Maran reflects a widely held view when she states, "NGOs are an embodiment of civil society: they serve to fill in societal gaps and failures with respect to disparate issues ranging from environment and sustainable development, to women's human rights, health and nutrition, and civil and political rights, among many others."[20] The term *civil society*, however, is ambiguous; its meaning has changed dramatically across western history and even now is assumed rather than carefully thought out.[21]

For purposes of this book, it is important to understand civil society in contrast to the state. Authority, coercion, and control of a given territory characterize the state. As such, power relations within the state are vertical. Law and constitutional order are the mechanisms by which control and authority are utilized and defined. In contrast, civil society constitutes the arena outside the state and above the individual. Political scientist Paul Wapner, following the Prussian philosopher Friedrich Hegel, defines it as an arena of individual needs, private interests, and conflict, but as also a sphere in which citizens can come together to achieve common purposes. He goes on to define it as the arena above the individual in which "people engage in spontaneous, customary and nonlegalistic forms of association" with the intention of pursuing common goals.[22]

Civil society need not be specifically political. Private associations in a society could as easily be corporations, business associations, sports clubs, churches, sororities, or labor unions as interest groups or political parties. Nevertheless, civil society has important implications for politics. To the extent that interest groups and political parties are part of that sphere, the connection to politics is obvious. Yet beyond that, civil society comprises a key component of the public sphere—that sphere where individual opinions become public opinion and individual goals and needs become collective goals and needs. Consider Harold Lasswell's classic definition of politics: who gets what, when, and how in a society. In this case it is possible to conceive of politics outside the realm of the state completely and within the realm of civil society exclusively.

Indeed, most liberal conceptions of democracy consider that a public sphere that is independent of state control—but not necessarily completely separated from it because the state is also part of it—is a necessary condition for democracy to exist.[23] Civil society, by supporting the independence of the public sphere, contributes to democracy. Or at least, that is what one school of social scientists avers (see Box 2–1).

Box 2–1. Civil Society and Democracy

In his landmark study of democracy and government performance in Italy, *Making Democracy Work* (1993), Robert Putnam found that the presence and incidence of civic associations was a major predictor of government performance. Regions that have long histories of civic associations—ranging from sports clubs to political parties—have government that is responsive to citizen demands and innovative in policymaking. Citizens in those regions also display high levels of trust in their fellow citizens and in government. In contrast, regions that lack civic associations tend to have less democratic, less trustful political cultures, and government that is unresponsive to citizen demands.

Putnam found that the presence of civic associations also tended to be a major predictor of economic performance. Northern Italy, with a high level of civic community, has had better economic performance than southern Italy, which has low incidence of civic community. Francis Fukuyama, in his book *Trust* (1996), elevated these two propositions (which he called "spontaneous sociability") to a global level, arguing that civic associations are a key indicator of democratization and economic development in societies ranging from Italy to France to China to Japan.

Within the sphere called civil society a basic distinction can be made within the generic term *private sector*. At its broadest the private sector can be said to comprise all organizations that are not part of the government or public sector. Within the private sector, however, a distinction needs to be made between corporations and other kinds of private organizations. Corporations are essentially organizations of the capitalist market, which has important consequences for their composition and goals. Pursuit of profit, the enforcement of property relations through contract, and professional specialization are hallmarks of the private sector in a capitalist economy. A second private sector is properly called the voluntary sector. This sphere, in which NGOs belong, comprises private organizations that are not organized specifically to conduct business in the market. The voluntary sector exists between states and markets, or, perhaps, alongside states and markets is a better description. As Marc Nerfin poetically describes it, the voluntary sector is "neither prince nor merchant."[24]

The discussion of civil society has largely been conducted within the confines of domestic society. Nevertheless, there is a growing understanding that the globalization of economic activity, the transnational nature of information flows, and the emergence of global governance mechanisms trying to manage them have created the space, and the need, for a global civil society. International relations is no longer (if it ever was) made up simply of a society of states; it includes the activities of economic, social, and non-state political actors.[25] Recent works on this topic carry provocative titles like *Constructing World Culture, Global Citizen Action,* and *The Third Force: The Rise of Transnational Civil Society.*[26] Just as civil society in the domestic arena exists alongside the state and the market, and interacts with both, global civil society does the same at the transnational level. NGOs' transnational linkages and activities make up an important part of international society.

Summary

NGOs are not new. Depending upon how they are defined, they are as old as the origins of modern missionary organizations. What is new is their spectacular growth. In the last thirty years there has been an explosion of NGO formation around the world. The growth of global civil society, technological innovations, and the reemergence of democracy have all contributed to this trend. The growing presence of NGOs has challenged assumptions of traditional international relations theory.

As voluntary organizations dedicated to assisting other people, NGOs face special problems in organizing themselves and then persisting over time. They are voluntary organizations, which means that they face membership and budgetary fluctuations that in some cases can threaten the existence of individual NGOs. NGOs can go bankrupt. This, of course, makes it hard to know how many NGOs are in operation at any given time. This is especially the case with the small NGOs like CANHELP Thailand. Finally, how well they are organized in terms of staff, members, and finance has a great deal to do with how powerful they are perceived to be by other actors in the international system.

Discussion Questions

1. Why and how have NGOs developed in the last three decades? Why are they prominent today?
2. How do NGOs fit into domestic and international civil society?
3. What are key problems that face NGOs when they form? How do they continue to operate once they are established?

Suggestions for Further Reading

For an extensive account of global civil society and how NGOs fit into it, see Helmut Anheier, Marlies Glasius, and Mary Kaldor, eds., *Global Civil Society* (Oxford: Oxford Univ. Press, 2001).

Notes

[1] Union of International Associations, ed., *Yearbook of International Organizations: Guide to Global Civil Society Networks, 2000–2001*. Vol. 1B (Munich: K. G. Saur Verlag, 2002), 2407.

[2] Peter Uvin, "From Local Organizations to Global Governance: The Role of NGOs in International Relations," in *Global Institutions and Local Empowerment: Competing Theoretical Perspectives,* ed. Kendall Stiles, 9–29 (New York: St. Martin's Press, 2000).

[3] Michael Cernea, *Nongovernmental Organizations and Local Development* (Washington, DC: The World Bank, 1988), 9.

[4] Lester Salamon, "The Rise of the Nonprofit Sector," *Foreign Affairs* 73, no. 4 (1994): 109–22.

[5] John Boli and George Thomas, eds., *Constructing World Culture: International Nongovernmental Organizations since 1875* (Stanford, CA: Stanford Univ. Press, 1999).

[6] The OECD's 1990 *Directory of Non-governmental Organizations in OECD Countries* covers organizations in existence at the time of the survey that responded

to the OECD's request for information, and therefore should be treated as an indicator rather than an actual number. Germany means West Germany in this case.

[7] Salamon, "The Rise of the Nonprofit Sector."

[8] See Sidney Tarrow, *Power in Movement: Social Movements and Contentious Politics,* 2nd ed. (Cambridge, MA: Cambridge Univ. Press, 2000).

[9] Jessica Mathews, "Power Shift," *Foreign Affairs* 76, no. 1 (1997): 50–66. For a highly readable account of these trends, see Daniel Yergin and Joseph Staninslaw, *The Commanding Heights* (New York: Simon and Schuster, 1997).

[10] See Paul Abramson and Ronald Inglehart, *Value Change in Global Perspective* (Ann Arbor: Univ. of Michigan Press, 1995).

[11] Jeffrey Berry, *Lobbying for the People* (Princeton, NJ: Princeton Univ. Press, 1977).

[12] Brian Smith, *More than Altruism: The Politics of Private Foreign Aid* (Princeton, NJ: Princeton Univ. Press, 1990).

[13] John Farrington and Anthony Bebbington, eds., *Reluctant Partners: Nongovernmental Organizations, the State, and Sustainable Agricultural Development* (London: Routledge, 1993).

[14] Tarrow, *Power in Movements.*

[15] Paul Wapner, *Environmental Activism and World Civic Politics* (Albany: State Univ. of New York Press, 1996).

[16] Tarrow, *Power in Movement,* 133.

[17] Mancur Olson, *The Logic of Collective Action* (New York: Schocken Books, 1971).

[18] Jeffrey Berry, *The Interest Group Society* (New York: Scott Foresman, 1984).

[19] The following discussion draws heavily from the research on NPOs carried out by the Johns Hopkins University Comparative Non-Profit Research Project. See Lester Salamon and Helmut Anheier, eds., *The Nonprofit Sector in Comparative Perspective* (Manchester: Univ. of Manchester Press, 1997); and Lester Salamon and Wojciech Sokolowski, eds., *Global Civil Society: Dimensions of the Nonprofit Sector* (Bloomfield, CT: Kumarian Press, 2004).

[20] Rita Maran, "The Role of Non-governmental Organizations," in *An End to Torture: Strategies for Its Eradication,* ed. B. Duner, 222–24 (London: Zed Books, 1998).

[21] See John Ehrenberg, *Civil Society: The Critical History of an Idea* (New York: New York Univ. Press, 1999).

[22] Wapner, *Environmental Activism and World Civic Politics,* 5.

[23] We use the term *liberal* in its classical sense, not its contemporary American sense. Liberalism, then, is the general predisposition to keep government from intervening overmuch in private life.

[24] Marc Nerfin, "Neither Prince nor Merchant—An Introduction to the Third System," *IFDA Dossier* 56 (1986): 3–29.

[25] The term *society of states* was coined by Hedley Bull (1984) and has come to be associated with the so-called British School of international relations.

[26] Boli and Thomas, *Constructing World Culture*; Michael Edwards and John Gaventa, eds., *Global Citizen Action* (Boulder, CO: Lynne Rienner, 2001); and Ann M. Florini, ed., *The Third Force: The Rise of Transnational Civil Society* (Tokyo: Japan Center for International Exchange; Washington, DC: The Carnegie Endowment for International Peace, 2001).

Chapter 3

NGO Roles
in International
Politics

Relief
Social and economic roles
Political roles

For most of the twentieth century what we now call NGOs were usually identified with charity and relief. The historical image of today's NNGOs in particular is that of Christian missionary groups performing good works to save (in both senses of the word) people in the non-European parts of the world. What started as missionary roles, followed by an emergency relief role, have taken new shapes and directions since the 1970s. In the parlance of current scholarship, NGOs engage in naming, framing, blaming, and shaming. These organizations "have acted as complements to official development assistance, as supplements, and sometimes as critics and watchdogs. However they have been viewed, they have added to the vibrancy of the development debate and have become an important part of North interaction with the South."[1]

This chapter discusses the major roles that NGOs play in international relations and politics. The traditional role, disaster and famine relief, continues to occupy an important place in the repertoire of NGO transnational action. In recent years, however, other roles—roles centered around economic and social development; political roles such as advocacy (including lobbying), agenda setting, and public education; monitoring of international agreements; and interacting with intergovernmental organizations—have greatly expanded the opportunity for the voluntary sector's influence in international politics.

Relief

Charitable and community organizations can be traced back throughout history. Individuals in different societies have founded these organizations to meet community needs, defend or advocate interests, ensure justice, or promote new policies. For example, the anti-slavery movement, founded in England in the eighteenth century, gave rise to organizations that eventually led to the World Anti-Slavery Convention in 1840.

Until the 1970s NGOs were mostly seen as playing an active role during emergency situations. INGOs in Europe and North America have roots in Christian missionary organizations that date back, in some cases, to the sixteenth century. During the colonial period missionary organizations combined religious work with education, relief from famine and disaster, and introduction of Western medicine in indigenous societies across the globe. The Christian notion of charity toward the unfortunate was a powerful moral stimulus to the creation of an early kind of private aid. By the late nineteenth century religious groups had established a repertoire of collective action involving private donations from parishioners channeled to missions in Asia, Africa, and Latin America for the twin goals of saving souls and relieving hunger and disease. As one English missionary enjoined his countrymen in the late nineteenth century, "Mighty England, do good."[2] With somewhat different wording, this formula can still be found among private relief organizations today.

The modern secular NGO got its start with the creation of the Red Cross in the 1860s. Like the Red Cross, several of today's most widely known NGOs grew out of war. Save the Children was founded in 1920 during the dislocations that followed World War I; Foster Parents Plan during the Spanish Civil War; Oxfam and CARE (Cooperative for Assistance and Relief Everywhere) during or just after the Second World War. As with their religious counterparts, the early work of these organizations tended to focus on short-term relief, an emphasis that was understandable given the circumstances in which they were founded.

Charity and relief aid remain key NGO roles today. The award of the Nobel Peace Prize in 1999 to Medecins Sans Frontieres (Doctors without Borders), an organization dedicated to quick humanitarian intervention in behalf of victims of natural and manmade disasters, highlights

---

Box 3–1. NGOs in Focus: Oxfam

Oxfam is one of the most widely known NGOs. Its original purpose was to provide relief to wartime Greece. Since its establishment, its various national branches have expanded well beyond the initial relief role to include funding for long-term development projects and campaigns for social and economic justice. Relief work remains, however, a major component of Oxfam activities. Its activities focus on providing clean drinking water and food; promoting hygiene in refugee camps and centers; and distributing items like blankets, clothing, and shelter materials. Immediate relief work is supplemented by long-term development work on livelihoods, disaster preparedness, and community organizing in order to allow victims of disaster to start returning to normal lives. For example, Oxfam agencies have helped 1.8 million people in several countries affected by the tsunami disaster rebuild their lives by providing clean water and sanitation, rehabilitating agricultural lands, and assisting in other reconstruction activities. The agencies received US$278 million in donations for the disaster.

   Another Oxfam current activity is providing clean water to thirty-two villages (150,000 Palestinians) across the West Bank.

Source: oxfam.org website

---

the continuing relevance of this kind of work. The tasks themselves display a great deal of continuity across the last century. Consider Japan at the beginning and end of the twentieth century. In the first quarter of the twentieth century, foreign relief organizations acted as important conveyors of social technology to philanthropic Japanese organizations. While some Buddhist organizations provided charity, Christian missionary organizations were also active. The names are familiar: several YMCA groups, the Red Cross, a mission sponsored by the American Episcopal Church, and the Foreign Auxiliary of the Women's Christian Temperance Union (WCTU). In the early part of the century the WCTU operated school and dormitory facilities for transient workers from the countryside.[3] Today HELP, an organization that grew out of the WCTU, provides shelter facilities for foreign women in Yokohama.

This conception of the NGO role suits Northern foreign aid donor governments. Brian Smith notes that "one reason for this increase in private involvement in foreign aid has been the growing reputation of nonprofit institutions in the United States, Canada, and Europe for being efficient and cost-effective channels of help in disasters."[4] He notes as well that NGOs are perceived as impartial providers of disaster aid. By the early 1990s, 75 percent of British food aid was being channeled through NGOs and 40 percent of Swedish spending on emergencies and refugees was going through Swedish NGOs. By 1996, 46 percent of French emergency funding was being spent through NGOs. Between 1992 and 1997 the United States Agency for International Development (USAID)—which has the biggest emergency budget in the world—spent over 60 percent of its budget, not counting food aid, through NGOs.[5] Today, about two-thirds of the European Union's (EU's) European Community Humanitarian Aid Office (ECHO) funding is spent the same way.

Social and Economic Development

Despite relief's long pedigree among transnational voluntary activities, NGOs have come to realize that relief and charity work by itself addresses short-term needs but does nothing about long-term issues of development. Increasingly, they are exploring the so-called relief-development continuum, considering ways in which communities visited by disaster or conflict can be rehabilitated in the long run. Others have moved wholesale from narrow relief efforts to support of economic and social development in developing countries as they have become concerned with long-term issues of poverty and economic inequality. Numerous NGOs, both Northern and Southern, provide services—intangible technical services as well as more tangible resources for development and for other purposes. Several operate their own development programs. For example, CARE's development programs include a variety of agricultural projects such as building irrigation systems, establishing farmer cooperatives, and fighting deforestation. Similarly, Catholic Relief Services (CRS) offers loans for small businesses, builds water projects, and promotes new farming technologies in addition to its relief work. Discussing the active role of Palestinian NGOs, Allam Jarrar reports: "It is believed that the share of the NGO sector in service provision covers over 60 percent of all health-care services, 80 percent of all rehabilitation services, and almost 100 percent of all preschool education."[6]

Box 3–2. NGOs in Focus: CARE International

CARE International consists of eleven member organizations whose goal is to fight poverty. Its mission is to serve individuals and families in the poorest communities of the world. It provides economic development opportunities, strengthens local capacities for self-help, delivers relief in emergencies, and attempts to influence government policy decisions. For example, CARE Australia's recent work in Cambodia includes:

- De-mining and development: CARE is working closely with the Cambodian Mine Action Centre in de-mining different areas of Cambodia.
- HIV/AIDS and STDs: Through its Community Caring and Prevention Project, CARE works closely with the Ministry of Health and other related agencies to further peer education and to distribute birth-control devices and other preventatives to control the escalating rate of HIV/AIDS cases in Cambodia. It also provides different types of caring services, such as medicines and blankets, to HIV patients and their relatives.

Source: careaustralia.com.au website

There is increasing governmental interest in INGOs because of their claim to be able to reach the poorest groups in developing countries, populations that often do not receive government services. In 1973 the US Congress mandated a "new directions" approach for US bilateral aid that would focus more directly on the needs of the poorest majority in the Third World. It also urged that foreign aid "be carried out to the maximum extent possible through the private sector, particularly those institutions which already have ties in the developing areas, such as educational institutions, cooperatives, credit unions, and voluntary agencies."[7] Congress felt that these agencies could reach the rural poor through means not available to USAID and thus could help fulfill the spirit of the "new directions" mandate. Canadian and other European government agencies voiced similar as well as unique reasons for expanding their own subsidies to NGOs. As an example, the Canadian International Development Agency (CIDA) began matching grants to Canadian NGOs in 1968 in an attempt to utilize the wide range of expertise and experience of the Canadian nonprofit sector.

NNGOs have also helped propel the meteoric growth of SNGOs. Most SNGOs are funded by foreign governments, NNGOs, or by private donors from the developed world. Indigenous NPOs in developing countries at the national and regional levels act as intermediaries in channeling this international assistance to the poor in their own societies. "It is estimated that there are now at least 30,000 to 35,000 intermediary nonprofit development organizations at the national and regional levels in Asia, Africa, and Latin America."[8] These intermediary NGOs sometimes carry out projects, but more frequently they act as brokers among local groups at the grassroots level who have formed their own smaller counterparts. The intermediary NGOs offer these smaller grassroots organizations both technical assistance in drawing up project proposals for foreign NGO funding and advice in the implementation and evaluation of the actual projects that receive funding from abroad.

Enterprise support activities and income-generation support projects are widespread among the SNGOs. Some have developed their enterprise activities to such an extent that they are seen as specialists in this area, particularly those focusing on the provision of microfinance. Organizations such as the Kenya Rural Enterprise Program and Kenya Women's Finance Trust; Independent Business Enrichment Centres and Get Ahead in South Africa; AMKA in Tanzania; Zambuko in Zimbabwe; and Grameen Bank in Bangladesh are recognized internationally in this respect. Other NGOs have incorporated enterprise-oriented activities into their broad portfolio of development work. Examples include the Bangladesh Rural Advancement Committee (BRAC), PROSHIKA, and the Association for Social Advancement (ASA) in Bangladesh; and the Self-Employed Women's Association in India.

Political Roles

Relief and development works tend to be regarded as nonpolitical by governments and the public alike. Many NGOs tend to see their work as specifically technical and therefore not aimed at challenging existing political, economic, or social arrangements beyond their projects' target groups. Increasingly, however, NGOs are coming to define their development objectives in political rather than economic terms. At the same time there is a growing realization that numerous NGOs (both Northern and Southern) engage in a variety of advocacy, lobbying, and agenda-shaping activities, all of which are intended to influence the policies of governments, corporations, or IGOs. That is to say, they engage in politics.

Advocacy and Lobbying

Advocacy is increasingly understood as a key NGO role in international affairs. Margaret E. Keck and Kathryn Sikkink observe that a new type of NGO actor, the transnational advocacy network, has emerged in the global arena:

> Networks are forms of organization characterized by voluntary, reciprocal, and horizontal patterns of communication and exchange. . . . We call them advocacy networks because advocates plead the causes of others or defend a cause or proposition. Advocacy captures what is unique about these transnational networks: they are organized to promote causes, principled ideas, and norms, and they often involve individuals advocating policy changes that cannot be easily linked to a rationalist understanding of their "interests."[9]

The ICBL and Jubilee 2000 (discussed in Part II) are examples of successful transnational advocacy networks that have brought together hundreds of NGOs to address specific global problems. NGOs are credited for driving the anti-trafficking movement. According to the US State Department, anywhere between 600,000 to 800,000 persons, mostly women and girls, are traded annually across international borders. The Vital Voices Global Partnership is one major INGO that directly engages in advocacy activities to promote strong anti-trafficking laws. It engages in several strategies and activities, including publishing an electronic newsletter *(Trafficking Alert)* that not only gives updated information but also engages in debates and discussion on best practices to address human trafficking worldwide.[10]

Keck and Sikkink explain that advocacy networks engage in four kinds of politics: (1) information politics, in which networks provide and reinterpret information on issues of concern; (2) symbolic politics, involving the use of symbols to raise awareness of issues; (3) leverage politics, in which networks attempt to gain moral or material leverage over more powerful actors (states and IGOs); and (4) accountability politics, in which networks try to compel states to live up to norms to which they have formally agreed. They argue that networks influence international politics by (1) creating new issues and setting international agendas; (2) changing the discursive positions of international actors; (3) influencing institutional procedures; (4) promoting policy change in states, IGOs, and MNCs; and (5) affecting state behavior.[11]

Lobbying is a closely related activity. It is no surprise that NGOs lobby their governments, other governments, and different powerful international organizations. Environmental protection (taken up in Chapter 10) represents an important issue area in which NGOs are very active. Although the vast majority of environmental groups remain rooted in specific project-based activities and focus at the local, regional, or national levels, many NGOs attempt to exert influence in global politics. In international environmental politics the main representatives of civil society are the various NGOs active in lobbying national governments and international organizations. The composition of these agencies varies from large, well-known NGOs like Greenpeace and the International Union for the Conservation of Nature (IUCN) to varying grassroots environmental groups. Of environmental NNGOs Paul Wapner writes: "It makes sense . . . to see transnational environmental activists foremost as pressure groups that try to persuade governments to work for environmental well-being."[12]

NGOs frequently lobby governments on behalf of certain causes either at home or abroad. American NGOs regularly testify in support of increased foreign assistance at congressional hearings and are among the most reliable lobby groups the State Department has to support foreign aid. In fact, the law in the United States is generous when it comes to nonprofit agencies' lobbying activities. According to the 1976 Lobbying Act, most charities can spend up to 20 percent of their budget on lobbying activities. For advocacy organizations there is no spending ceiling; they can engage in unlimited lobbying. US NGOs thus actively serve as lobbyists for their Southern partners and work to influence their own government's policies and priorities.

NGOs sometimes act as lobbyists for their home governments. The *stiftungen*, political organizations affiliated with each of the main political parties in Germany, are a good example. They have an overtly political mission: to promote the institutions of parliamentary democracy in developing countries. They often have acted as informal channels of communication between the German parties, including those in coalition in the cabinet, and their counterparts in Asia, Africa, and Latin

America. On occasion they have acted as informal representatives of the governing parties.[13]

An innovative transnational form of such lobbying can be found in what Keck and Sikkink call the "boomerang pattern." NGOs that find their claims of rights blocked by their own governments bypass them to locate allies in the international system—other NGOs, especially those who are willing to approach their own governments or IGOs to put pressure on the original governments in behalf of the domestic NGOs. Networks thus provide NGOs in many states with indirect leverage over their own governments.[14]

A recent example of the boomerang pattern comes from Asia. In the 1990s the government of Indonesia constructed the Koto Panjang Hydroelectric Dam in Western Sumatra with foreign aid from the Japanese government. Completed in 1997, the dam has never operated anywhere near its planned capacity. Moreover, typical of many large development projects, dam construction resulted in the displacement of thousands of local residents. The Indonesian government's promises of property compensation and relocation were not fully met. Opposition by residents emerged during dam construction, and Indonesian NGOs lent their support to the movement. Pleas to halt dam construction and provide adequate redress to residents, made both to the Indonesian and Japanese governments, fell on deaf ears. Finally, in September 2002, a group of about thirty-eight hundred residents filed a civil lawsuit in Tokyo District Court against the Japanese government and contractors that had been involved in constructing the dam. The suit argued that by funding the Koto Panjang Dam the Japanese government and the private contractors were responsible for the project's failure.

Japanese and Indonesian NGOs have used the occasion of the lawsuit to publicize the claims of those who oppose the dam. Activists and journalists have written newspaper articles and editorials for the Japanese press. In December the Foundation for Human Rights in Asia, a Japanese NGO, gave its Asia Human Rights Award to Arun Muhammed, an Indonesian who heads the Taratak Foundation. The Taratak Foundation has opposed the Koto Panjang Hydroelectric Dam for years. Significantly, alongside the Tokyo suit, NGOs have called upon Japan to pressure the government of Indonesia to destroy the dam and restore the area to its original condition, and to pressure Indonesia to live up to its compensation promises to residents. They have also called for suspension of Japanese foreign aid until Jakarta discloses the details of aid funds.

Public Education and Consciousness Raising

Public education and consciousness raising are two related activities with political implications. Lacking many of the tools of influence used by states and MNCs, NGOs often rely on the presentation of information to make their case. NGO mandates cover a broad spectrum and usually include outreach activities to educate local, national, or international governments and institutions.[15] Indeed, NGOs' most important work may lie in the area of political socialization. For example, one of the strategies of Greenpeace is to bring instances of environmental abuse to the attention of people throughout the world. It does so through television, radio, newspapers, and magazine stories. The antipersonnel landmine issue (taken up in Chapter 8) exemplifies the significant role that NGOs have played in disseminating information about the scope of landmine use and its effects. In fact, the civil society and international organizations are given more credit than the states for identifying and politicizing the situation as a crisis issue on state agendas.[16] NGOs thus educate the public; in fact, public opinion is a commonly cited object of NGO advocacy. NGOs also educate one another; one of Grameen Bank's signal successes as an alternative style of people-centered banking has been its replication outside of Bangladesh. The Philippines provides a case of successful transplantation, to the point that Grameen's founder, Muhammad Yunus, recently stated: "Today the Philippines is at a stage where many other countries could come here and learn from it."[17]

Finally, many NGOs educate their own members. "As their workforce is often composed of volunteers, NGOs educate members as well as stimulate public consciousness about the concern central to their formation."[18] Oxfam International and Grameen Bank have expanded their activities from their initial focus on disaster relief and microfinance, respectively. As they have matured, each has passed on its experience to other members of the transnational NGO community. Oxfam Great Britain, for example, now publishes books on subjects of concern to NGOs under its own label. In 1995 it published *The Oxfam Handbook of Development and Relief*, designed to serve as a manual for practitioners in those fields. The handbook provides information on practical issues NGOs confront in the field and also provides a code of conduct NGOs are enjoined to follow during human and natural disasters (see Chapter 8).

Grameen's experiment with microcredit has sparked interest around the world. We noted in the introduction to this book that organizations

---

Box 3–3. NGOs in Focus: Amnesty International (AI)

AI is a worldwide campaigning movement that works to promote all human rights embodied in the Universal Declaration of Human Rights and other international standards. Specifically speaking, AI campaigns to free all prisoners of conscience; to ensure fair and prompt trials for political prisoners; to abolish the death penalty, torture, and other cruel treatment of prisoners; to end political killings and "disappearances"; and to speak out against human rights abuses by opposition groups.

AI has approximately 1.8 million members and supporters in over 150 countries and territories. Its activities range from public demonstrations to letter writing, from human rights education to fund-raising concerts, from individual appeals on a particular case to global campaigns on a particular issue.

AI's current campaigns include efforts to

- Stop violence against women: This includes a campaign against genital mutilation, domestic violence, rape, and other forms of prevailing violence against women and girls.
- Control arms: AI, along with Oxfam and the International Action Network on Small Arms, is calling on governments to toughen up arms control. The groups are also calling for a global arms trade treaty.
- Stop torture and ill-treatment in the "war on terrorism": A current focus is on prisoners at the US detention center in Guantanamo.

AI uses a variety of strategies to promote its campaign activities including publicizing stories, reports, videos, and monitoring states' policies in relevant areas.

Source: amnesty.org website

---

in over thirty countries have tried to reproduce its success. In 1989 Grameen set up the Grameen Trust to facilitate that process. The Grameen Trust holds training seminars in Dhaka (the capital city of Bangladesh) for interested organizers. It also publishes a newsletter, *Grameen Dialogue* (available on the Internet), and maintains a library of materials related to its mission.

Public education has proven to be a significant resource for voluntary organizations that champion human rights. One of the best-known NGOs in the field of human rights is Amnesty International (AI). AI's actions in defense of political prisoners rely heavily on publicity. Kathryn Sikkink points out that AI's reports on disappearances in Argentina in the 1970s brought worldwide attention to the problem, forcing that country's government to change its human rights practices.[19] AI sends international observers to trials where the rights of the accused are likely to be abrogated or where human rights violations are raised. These visits can have a substantial impact on fair treatment being accorded the defendant. Similarly, the ICRC visits political detainees to provide them with international visibility and protection from abuse while imprisoned. AI and other human rights groups have succeeded in placing human rights on the international political agenda. Before AI began its work in the early 1970s, the idea of a human rights regime did not exist.[20]

Agenda Setting

Through public education and advocacy and lobbying activities NGOs participate actively in the agenda-setting process. Agenda setting involves putting issues on the political agenda, the list of issues or problems that policymakers pay attention to at a given time. At some point problems and proposals for their solution get onto the political agenda because someone in government picks up those problems and/or their solutions and attempts to deal with them.[21] Agenda setting, therefore, means advocating certain issues to policymakers so at least they will pay attention to them. Note that agenda setting is high on Keck and Sikkink's list of NGO advocacy roles outlined above. There are wide-ranging policy domains where the main issues have only been considered because of the work of NGOs; women's rights and individual rights, along with other issue areas, have been led by NGOs.

Issue framing—rendering an issue understandable to a target audience—represents a significant public education activity.[22] From environmental protection to human rights to bans on certain kinds of warfare and weaponry, NGOs have often succeeded spectacularly when they convince publics and governments that a new way of viewing problems opens up opportunities for resolution of those problems. Framing also involves the process of convincing states and civil society actors that a problem exists at all.

Greenpeace serves as an example of an NGO that engages in framing activity. Since almost all parts of the world are vulnerable to the environmental consequences involved, Greenpeace seeks to persuade people to care about and take actions to protect the earth. Today millions of people know and care about environmental threats and have undertaken significant practices to protect the earth. Greenpeace engages in direct nonviolent actions and advertises them through the media worldwide. The long-term objective in all of these activities is to create an ecological sensibility that makes states and citizens aware of the impact of their actions on the natural environment and willing to change behavior to accommodate that realization.[23]

Along with activist NGOs like Greenpeace there are numerous think-tank NGOs, whose specialty lies in collecting information, and who concentrate on action research or media for public education and advocacy. Examples include the Institute for Agriculture and Trade Policy and the Rural Advancement Foundation International. A growing number of think tanks, including the Trilateral Commission and the Institute of South East Asian Studies in Singapore, operate beyond their home states. Many of the think-tank NGOs also act as policy entrepreneur in both domestic and international policy domains on cross-national problems of pollution, trade, and so forth. Think tanks provide input to international conferences, monitoring of international agreements, and project development in international organizations like the World Bank. There are significant sources of demand at the global and regional levels for such think-tank services. International organizations such as the UN and the World Bank are contracting think tanks to provide expert evaluations of their programs. Many think-tank organizations provide expert knowledge and advisory services to different NGOs who do not have the resources to have such in-house support systems.

Think-tank entrepreneurs also initiate international meetings to exchange views on policy issues or management concerns. The Atlas Foundation, for example, organizes an annual international conference for free-market policy institutes to help promote their spread and consolidation. The World Bank in 1998 sponsored a number of regional and international meetings of think-tank executives as part of its broader agenda of promoting knowledge development. "These factors have helped create a transnational community of think tank experts. These experts interact in think tank networks but also in other transnational policy networks."[24]

Many SNGOs have come to articulate *explicit* roles in the political process as well. Recent examples can be seen in NGO activities in Bangladesh. A group of NGOs expressed solidarity with the democratic movement of 1990, which overthrew the autocratic regime of General H. M. Ershad and reestablished the democratic process in the country. In 1996 an NGO alliance played a crucial role in the mass movement that arose because of doubts that the 1996 elections would be fairly managed by the ruling Bangladesh Nationalist Party (BNP). Before the election NGOs had implemented a countrywide voter-awareness education program that contributed significantly to raising voter awareness. It also contributed to a very high voter turnout—73 percent.[25] In Chile, NGOs helped other citizens' organizations to contest the 1992 local elections and subsequently to participate in local government. In Brazil, NGOs supported the Partido dos Trabalhadores (Workers Party) and its candidate Luis Inacio Lula da Silva in the 1990 presidential elections.[26]

A contentious area of consciousness-awareness activities is also evident in the work of NGOs in the developing countries. For example, empowering the poor (social empowerment) is a major goal for most of the prominent NGOs working in Bangladesh (for example, BRAC and ASA). Such goals are reflected in the different adult education/literacy programs and in the microcredit programs. A major target population for these programs is poor women living in villages and in the poverty-laden sections of urban areas. Such consciousness-raising goals have political implications because they seek to help target populations at least to start the process of reevaluating their rights and situation in a tradition-bound societal context.

Monitoring Other Transnational Actors

NGOs engage in a wide range of activities designed to ensure that states comply with laws they have made and international treaties that they have signed. As examples, the IUCN oversees the implementation of the World Heritage Convention; the Women's Environment and Development Organization (WEDO) monitors women's status and violation of rights; and AI monitors the treatment of political prisoners. As Ramesh Thakur points out, "The world needs NGOs so that they can operate outside the framework of the states-systems in order to put pressure on states on a variety of fronts, such as human rights (AI) or the environment (Greenpeace). It would be difficult to dispute the claim that the world would be a less pleasant place to live in today had there been no NGOs holding governments to account over the past 50 years."[27]

Box 3–4. NGOs in Focus:
Women's Environment and Development Organization

WEDO, an international advocacy network whose goal is to increase women's equality in global policy, "seeks to empower women in decision making to achieve economic, social and gender justice, a healthy peaceful planet and human rights for all." It was established in 1990 by Bella Abzug (a former US Congresswoman) and Mim Kelber (a feminist activist and journalist).

WEDO has three program areas: gender and governance, sustainable development, and economic and social justice. The gender and governance program focuses on three strategies: consciousness building regarding the under-representation of women in decision-making positions and the potential impact that women in such positions can make; spreading a global campaign, "50/50 by 2005: Get the Balance Right"; and developing information resources and strategies to achieve equal representation in decision-making bodies. The sustainable development program promotes development policies and programs that are environmentally sound, economically viable, and socially just. It focuses on developing, maintaining, and strengthening networking among women's and environmental groups in order to promote and foster sustainable development projects. The economic and social justice program's goals are to promote women's economic and social rights, to develop awareness of the effects of development programs on women, to promote gender analysis of such projects, to advocate gender sensible sustainable development projects and policies, and so on.

Source: wedo.org website

NGOs also monitor MNCs and IGOs. For more than a decade nongovernmental environmental and development organizations have formed various transnational advocacy coalitions, both within the Northern industrial countries and across the developing South, to pressure different multilateral banks to be more transparent and accountable. As Peter Uvin explains: "NGOs have been faster and more active in lobbying international organizations than governments. These institutions are relatively easy to influence, and pose no danger: they have no power to imprison or torture NGO staff. Moreover, in the case of the Bank, they possess great financial and intellectual resources as well as a strong capacity to modify government policies."[28]

The process of building such global networks is also occurring in relation to the institutions of the market. Besides lobbying and calling for transparency and accountability from multilateral development banks, including the World Bank and the IMF, strong associations of consumer groups are also acting at the global level. Consumers International, for example, has contributed significantly to ensuring greater public account-ability of market enterprises. Advocacy groups have been key players in convincing companies and industry associations to develop corporate codes of conduct that commit multinationals to appropriate environ-mental practices and equitable treatment of workers in developing coun-tries.[29] Corporate Watch in the UK and Multinationals Resource Center in the United States are examples of NGOs that specifically monitor transnational corporations.

Box 3–5. NGOs in Focus: Consumers International

Consumers International supports, networks, and represents consumer groups around the world. It acts in a concerted way to promote con-sumer groups' rights. Founded in London, it now has more than 250 member organizations in 115 countries. It maintains regional offices in London, Kuala Lumpur (Malaysia), Harare (Zimbabwe), and Santiago (Chile). The network defines its mission as promoting a fairer society by defending the rights of consumers, supporting and strengthening member organizations and the consumer movement in general, and campaigning at the international level for policies that respect consumer concerns.

The organization was founded in 1960 as the International Organiza-tion of Consumers Unions by a group of national consumers' organiza-tions that realized that they could have a stronger effect by joining to-gether across national borders. It now acts as the voice of the interna-tional consumer movement and focuses on a variety of issues such as product and food standards, patients' rights, the environment, regula-tion of public utilities, and others.

Source: consumersinternational.org website

Agenda Setting in the Global Decision-Making Arena

Thousands of NGOs attend conferences and present information to different UN agencies, commissions, and field offices. International agencies like the International Fund for Agricultural Development, the United Nations Development Program, the World Health Organization (WHO), the UN's Office of the High Commissioner for Human Rights, and the World Bank all have regular NGO consultation meetings. Often NGOs play a leading role in promoting the various dedications of "days," "years," and "decades" that the UN system regularly proclaims.

NGO agenda setting now occurs at the international level, particularly in the deliberations that take place at the UN. UN Charter article 71, issued in 1945, empowered the Economic and Social Council (ECOSOC) to "make suitable arrangements for consultation with non-governmental organizations which are concerned with matters within its competence." Since then, NGOs' influence has grown steadily, to cover all the work of the ECOSOC, along with operational programs in developing countries, the specialized agencies, and the UN conferences. They have access to all UN documents, once these have been officially released. In addition, they are able to attend different meetings and proceedings. This means that they can gain high levels of information about the political process. NGOs with consultative status have security passes that give them access to all the buildings, including the lounges, bars, and restaurants used by the diplomats. This gives them access to the delegates. This, in turn, gives them the opportunity to obtain more information through informal discussion, including hearing about what happened at the private meetings.

Finally, being awarded consultative status gives NGOs a legitimate place within the political system. This means that the NGO activist is seen as having a right to be involved in the process. As a result, in the informal contacts with delegates, it is possible to express views about issues on the agenda and to lobby for particular decisions to be taken.

The above exposure to information gives NGOs the opportunity to influence agenda-setting processes at the UN. There are wide-ranging policy areas (protection of the environment, women's rights, individual rights) where the main issues have been seriously considered because of the work of different NGOs at different UN conferences. (In Chapter 9 we focus on the influence of women's NGOs at the UN in the agenda-setting process.)

Summary

NGO roles are multifaceted and far reaching, directed at influencing individuals, states, IGOs, and other non-state actors. From traditional relief activities they have become important agents of development. Increasingly they have become significant political actors in international politics: advocating policies to states and IGOs, setting political and social agendas, educating the public, and monitoring international agreements and national policies. At the public level they help mobilize support for particular policies, widen participation in international policy, focus attention on critical global problems, frame issues, and set policy agendas. At the individual level they provide information, consciousness-raising education, and resources to individuals to support them in their efforts to live a better life. At both levels the significance of NGO activities lies in their ability to influence—and that makes them very much political actors.

Discussion Questions

1. What are the major roles NGOs play in international politics?
2. Are some of these roles more controversial than others? Which?
3. Are there roles NGOs should not play? Why?

Suggestions for Further Reading

Many of the largest international NGOs regularly report their activities. For example, students can find annual reports for Oxfam, CARE, Grameen Bank, and others posted on the organizations' websites.

Notes

[1] Ian Smillie, "At Sea in a Sieve? Trends and Issues in the Relationship between Northern NGOs and Northern Governments," in *Stakeholders: Government-NGO Partnership for International Development,* ed. Ian Smillie and Henny Helmich, 7–35 (London: Earthscan, 1999), 8.

[2] Steven Maughan, "'Mighty England Do Good': The Major English Denominations and Organisation for the Support of Foreign Missions in the Nineteenth Century," in *Missionary Encounters: Sources and Issues,* ed. R. Bickers and R. Seton, 11–37 (Richmond, Surrey: Curzon Press, 1996).

[3] Sally Hastings, *Neighborhood and Nation in Tokyo, 1905–1937* (Pittsburgh: Univ. of Pittsburgh Press, 1995), 54.

[4] Brian Smith, *More than Altruism: The Politics of Private Foreign Aid* (Princeton, NJ: Princeton Univ. Press, 1990), 3.

[5] Smillie, "At Sea in a Sieve?"

[6] Allam Jarrar, "The Palestinian NGO Sector: Development Perspectives," *Palestinian-Israel Journal of Politics, Economics, and Culture* 12, no. 1 (2005): 43–44.

[7] Smith, *More than Altruism,* 5.

[8] Brian Smith, "Nonprofit Organizations in International Development: Agents of Empowerment or Preservers of Stability," in *Private Action and the Public Good,* ed. W. Powell and E. Clemens, 212–27 (New Haven, CT: Yale Univ. Press, 1998), 217.

[9] Margaret E. Keck and Kathryn Sikkink, *Activists beyond Borders* (Ithaca, NY: Cornell Univ. Press, 1998), 8–9.

[10] Wenchi Yu Perkins, "NGO Watch," *UN Chronicle,* no. 1 (2005): 54–55.

[11] Keck and Sikkink, *Activists beyond Borders,* 19–25.

[12] Paul Wapner, *Environmental Activism and World Civic Politics* (Albany: State Univ. of New York Press, 1996), 3.

[13] Veronica Forrester, "The German Political Foundations," in *Pressure Groups, Policies, and Development: The Private Sector and EEC-Third World Policy,* ed. C. Stevens and J. V. Van Themaat, 40–60 (London: Hodder and Staughton, 1985).

[14] Keck and Sikkink, *Activists beyond Borders,* 12–13.

[15] Rita Maran, "The Role of Non-Governmental Organizations," in *An End to Torture: Strategies for Its Eradication,* ed. B. Duner, 222–44 (London: Zed Books, 1998).

[16] Richard Price, "Reversing the Gun Sights: Transnational Civil Society Targets Landmines," *International Organization* 52, no. 3 (1998): 613–44.

[17] Muhammad Yunus, quoted in Alkman Granitsas and Deirdre Sheehan, "Grassroots Capitalism," *Far Eastern Economic Review* 39 (July 12, 2001).

[18] Maran, "The Role of Non-Governmental Organizations," 222.

[19] Kathryn Sikkink, "Human Rights, Principled Issue Networks, and Sovereignty in Latin America," *International Organization* 47, no. 3 (Summer 1993): 411–41.

[20] Ann M. Clark, *Diplomacy of Conscience* (Princeton, NJ: Princeton Univ. Press, 2001).

[21] John Kingdon, *Agendas, Alternatives, and Public Policy* (New York: Harper Collins, 1995).

[22] Keck and Sikkink, *Activists beyond Borders*, 3.

[23] See Wapner, *Environmental Activism and World Civic Politics*.

[24] Richard A. Higgott, Geoffrey R. D. Underhill, and Andreas Bieler, eds., *Non-State Actors and Authority in the Global System* (London: Routledge, 2000), 215.

[25] Mahbubul Karim, "NGOs, Democratization, and Good Governance: The Case of Bangladesh," in *New Roles and Relevance: Development NGOs and the Challenge of Change*, ed. David Lewis and Tina Wallace, 99–108 (Bloomfield, CT.: Kumarian Press, 2000).

[26] Gerald Clarke, "Non-Governmental Organizations (NGOs) and Politics in the Developing Countries," *Political Studies* 47 (1998): 36–52.

[27] Ramesh Thakur, "Human Rights: Amnesty International and the United Nations," in *The Politics of Global Governance: International Organizations in an Interdependent World*, ed. Paul Diehl, 247–68 (Boulder, CO: Lynne Rienner, 1997), 265.

[28] Peter Uvin, "From Local Organizations to Global Governance: The Role of NGOs in International Relations," in *Global Institutions and Local Empowerment: Competing Theoretical Perspectives*, ed. Kendall Stiles, 9–29 (New York: St. Martin's Press, 2000), 19.

[29] See Marina Ottaway, "Reluctant Missionaries," *Foreign Policy* (July-August 2001): 44–54; Gary Gereffi, R. Garcia-Johnson, and E. Sasser, "The NGO-Industrial Complex," *Foreign Policy* (July-August 2001): 56–65.

Chapter 4

NGO Relations with States

NGOs in states
NGOs as collaborators with states
NGOs as opponents of states
NGOs as substitutes for states

As we saw in Chapter 1, the study of international relations still takes the state as its starting point. Realism champions that approach; interdependence has come to accommodate it;[1] even transnationalism cannot avoid it.[2] We start this chapter from the understanding that NGOs operate in a world polity fundamentally ordered by states. That is, we acknowledge that states remain the basic actors in international systems, even as we consider the behavior of a certain kind of non-state actor.[3] Non-state actors have not replaced sovereign governments as the primary players in international politics. Neither are they independent of those governments. This is a situation often overlooked by the more exuberant champions of NGO roles in international politics. Like it or not, NGOs must live with and operate within a system established by and for the interests of sovereign, territorial states.

How NGOs interact with governments, then, is a crucial aspect of understanding what NGOs do. How those interactions occur is equally important. Observing Japanese NGOs, Lori Forman made a distinction between NGOs as "watchdogs and working dogs." In the former case, she argues, NGO-state relations tend to be antagonistic; in the latter they tend to be cooperative.[4] Most scholars and activists see NGOs in the latter capacity. What distinguishes NGOs from other social movements, they argue, is that NGOs tend not to confront governments directly (and often violently), preferring to cooperate with official agencies in the pursuit of common goals.

This chapter explores NGO relations with states at two levels: at the domestic level, as NGOs engage their home governments; and at the transnational level, as NGOs engage other states or groups of states in international issue areas. It points out that relationships between states and nongovernmental actors are neither static nor homogeneous. It is useful to think about those interactions in terms of four modes: NGOs in states, NGOs as collaborators with states, NGOs as opponents of states, and NGOs as substitutes for states.

NGOs in States

NGOs, even if transnational, are located within the confines of states and carry out their operations therein. Domestic legal and political environments have a profound impact on the existence and practice of non-state actors, NGOs included. Why this is so stems from a commonly overlooked aspect of the international legal system: NGOs do not enjoy anything like the legal status enjoyed by nation-states and their representatives under international law. "Except for a regionally-limited Convention of the Council of Europe, there is no international, global convention granting NGOs a single legal personality and capacity over the territory of all states where they have staff and activities."[5] They are thus subject to the laws of the nation-state in which they reside and operate. This legal inferiority is not limited to the relationship between NGOs and national governments. The former are also subject to the legal jurisdictions of sub-national governments as well; NGOs whose representatives haunt the halls of UN headquarters in pursuit of international goals still have to pay their New York City parking tickets.[6]

This legal superiority is anything but trivial. In the extreme case the legal authority of sovereign states confronts private organizations with the problem of whether they will be allowed to exist in open society and on what terms. To cite an example from Southeast Asia, Asia Watch, in its investigation of prostitution in Thailand and Burma, found that "in Burma, no indigenous NGOs are allowed to operate. At most, religious institutions attempt to discreetly offer services to assist poor communities, but they are under considerable pressure to maintain a low profile and are often themselves victims of abuse by SLORC [State Law and Order Restoration Council] authorities. Very few independent international NGOs have been willing to work in Burma for fear of giving legitimacy to SLORC, even if they could obtain access."[7] Another study concludes that in the case of the People's Republic of China the government "has been omnipresent and overbearing for four decades and has left virtually no room for private voluntary organizations."[8] NGOs are beginning to find room to engage in certain types of activity in that country, a change brought about in no small part by liberalization of the economy, but the Chinese legal system still does not recognize private voluntary organizations per se.

Even in societies in which the government recognizes the right and benefits of voluntary organizations' existence, official policies can place limitations on those organizations. Fisher observes that in governments across the political spectrum certain agencies will promote NGO activities while other agencies will oppose them. While NGOs in authoritarian political systems often find some sympathetic ears among officialdom, their counterparts in democratic political systems find bureaucracies unwilling to cooperate with them even in areas in which the government formally acknowledges a role for voluntary organizations. Security agencies tend to be especially suspicious of NGOs because the latter's work often brings them into contact with people outside the law.[9]

Asia Watch, for example, found that while Thailand has one of the strongest NGO movements in Asia, few are engaged in women's and children's rights and fewer still work on prostitution issues. Because of inconsistencies in legal statutes and agency mandates covering prostitution and the people involved in it (four separate and contradictory laws applied at the time of the study), NGOs sometimes find themselves in violation of one or another statute when they engage in rescue and repatriation operations for Burmese girls (for example, the law against harboring illegal immigrants). As a rule, Thai NGOs engaged in prostitution issues do not have formal contacts with law-enforcement agencies, nor are they consulted by officialdom on issues of concern to them.[10]

This problem is not limited to NGOs as we define them, and it is useful here to think of them in the context of the broader nonprofit sector. The state-centered nature of nonprofit determination is clear in many governments' approach to NPOs. Nonprofit status is a valuable resource for NGOs because it typically confers tax advantages on such organizations and, in some cases, provides tax incentives to encourage private donations. Most governments require citizen organizations to register with a government agency in order to obtain nonprofit status. Many developing-country governments, of course, require NNGOs to register with government agencies in order to operate within the country. Establishing a relationship with the appropriate authorities is often time consuming, and agency approval is not necessarily automatic. Governments may also require that voluntary organizations have high levels

---

**Box 4–1. Key Concept:
German NGOs and Interest-Group Politics**

Germany provides an excellent example of how states can shape NGO activities. Germany has a two-tier NGO community: a few large NGOs and many smaller ones. The largest NGOs are typically affiliated with the Catholic Church, the Lutheran synods, or Protestant evangelical churches, or with the political parties in the case of the *stiftungen.* These NGOs enjoy frequent access to government policymakers and official development funds. They participate regularly in government policymaking processes. In contrast, smaller NGOs complain that they are excluded both from policymaking influence and official funding.*

Students of German politics will readily identify the corporatist elements in this scenario. The German government has fostered close, formal relations with key interest groups throughout its postwar history. The major labor, business, and religious interest groups have been given a recognized place in the formal policymaking process and preferential access to state resources. In return, the government controls conflict between major parts of society and can act as honest broker when conflicts break out. Access to the pinnacles of power, however, is closed to all but a few large interest groups. In the 1970s and 1980s social movements that eventually formed the Green Party made the same kinds of arguments about unequal treatment that small NGOs make today. In sum, then, the German government has gone about organizing its relationship with NGOs in the same way it does with societal groups in general.

---

* Judith Randel and Tony German, "Germany," in *Stakeholders: NGO-Government Partnerships for International Development,* ed. Ian Smillie and Henny Helmich, 114–22 (London: Earthscan, 1999).

---

of capitalization or maintain budget surpluses in order to retain their legal status. The government may also limit voluntary organizations' ability to raise money from private sources. Some developing-country governments place limitations on the amount or sources of funds from international donors. Such limitations may be inadvertent, as was the case until recently in Japan. Until 2000, charitable contributions made by individuals to voluntary organizations were not tax deductible, effectively closing off a significant avenue of fund raising to NGOs in that country.

Tax-exempt status is critical to the development of NGOs because it serves as an enabling device for agenda setting. Not only does it augment material resources such as donations and budgets, but it gives an organization visibility with the government. Not surprisingly, those NGOs that have frequent contact with the government, especially those that receive subsidies, tend to be those with nonprofit status. In many countries official statistics about NGOs reflect only such organizations.

Nonprofit status, however, can itself cause problems. For example, a 1998 bill passed by the Japanese parliament eased financial restrictions on nonprofits while at the same time preventing them from engaging in electoral activity. The federal government in the United States also forbids nonprofits from engaging in overt political activity. As Jeffrey Berry has pointed out, the line between legitimate nonprofit activities and political action is ambiguous, with the result that tax authorities have considerable room to threaten withdrawal of tax-exempt status.[11] Some Northern governments prohibit NGOs based in their countries from carrying out development work in third-world countries deemed politically unacceptable due to diplomatic conflict and/or type of political regime.[12]

A world formally organized around sovereign states poses problems for transnational NGO activities as well. Not only do NGOs face the problem that different sets of laws about private organizations face them when they operate in more than one country, but also national laws and policies mean that international NGOs cannot simply duplicate their activities from one country to the next. Indeed, global strategies can prove counterproductive in specific countries.

Consider the case of environmental NGOs engaged in wildlife protection. Environmental NGOs play an important role in creating and monitoring international wildlife-protection agreements such as the Convention on International Trade in Endangered Species of Wild Flora and Fauna (CITES). Thomas Princen notes that environmental NNGOs were instrumental in establishing an Ivory Trade Control System under CITES auspices in the mid-1980s. Transnational environmental NGOs attempted in the late 1980s to promote an international ban on ivory trade. The effects of the ban on producer states in Africa varied depending on national policies already in place. Kenya, for example, was experiencing a severe elephant-poaching problem. An international ban was expected to help Kenya's elephant population because it would remove the market for illegal ivory, which in fact appears to have happened. The same ban, however, directly undercut Zimbabwe's policy of herd man-

agement and managed ivory production, a conservation policy also conducted by several other African states. The impact on elephant conservation was significant because sales of culled ivory were used to pay for
herd management. NGO lobbying for a CITES ban, Princen concluded,
was by definition a "blunt instrument" because it did not account for
differences in national policy.[13]

NGOs as Collaborators with States

Many NGOs, both Southern and Northern, find it expedient and proper
to cooperate with government. Cooperation is the preferred mode for
many state agencies as well, which see NGOs as organizations capable of
implementing official policies. This is a common view of NGO-state
relations in foreign aid provision. NGOs provide social and other services on behalf of states, supposedly for the comparative advantages
the former enjoy in terms of flexibility, efficiency, and proximity to
target populations. The popularity of this formulation can also be at-
tributed to the effects of the New Policy Agenda, mentioned in Chapter 2; that is, in an environment in which government is expected to
be smaller and to intervene less in society, the state is "looking for new
partners to help implement and fund social and development
programmes."[14]

The Philippines provides an outstanding example of formal government-NGO cooperation. The 1987 constitution provides NGOs with
formal legal status and enjoins all government agencies to consult with
them on social and economic development issues. Article II goes so far
as to declare that "the state shall encourage non-governmental organizations, community-based, or sectoral organizations that promote the
welfare of the nation." While this does not guarantee that official agencies and NGOs will see eye to eye on issues of common concern, the
constitution certainly provides a legal environment in which communication and cooperation are expected and normal.

Collaboration between government and NGOs has potential benefits for both parties. Cooperation provides legitimacy to NGOs. It also
affords them access to public funding through state subsidies and grants.
This is no small inducement to collaborate with government, since funding is a constant worry for most voluntary organizations. For their part,
governments find NGOs can be useful providers of public welfare services as well as mediators between the state and populations it cannot

reach through other means. In some cases NGO activity strengthens the state or otherwise promotes broader development goals. Smillie has argued that in Zimbabwe, for example, where NGOs provide 40 percent of the health services and are paid to do so, the government has been strengthened through its effective management of improved services.[15] In Bangladesh, BRAC and CARE/Bangladesh (two large NGOs) worked very closely with the Ministry of Public Health and Family Planning staff and representatives of WHO and UNICEF to plan and implement the national Expanded Program of Immunization.

NGOs also bring expertise that often is not available or is in short supply among government agencies. In certain cases such cooperation extends to the international level. NGO representatives are sometimes invited to attend international negotiations as members of national negotiating teams. Canadian NGO leaders representing the ICBL, for example, attended the 1997 Ottawa negotiations as members of the official Canadian delegation.

Finally, NGOs can sometimes act as surrogate foreign-policy actors. From time to time governments find it useful to maintain contacts with governments with which they do not have formal relations; NGOs provide one way of maintaining communication. The German *stiftungen,* mentioned in Chapter 3, have sometimes served as informal channels of contact with developing country counterparts whose government policies make it difficult for the German government to maintain overtly friendly relations. In the 1970s the Social Democratic Party in power in Bonn used its *stiftung* to maintain contact with social democratic organizations in Latin America operating under military dictatorships. This informal contact allowed the German government to assist grassroots organizations working for democracy while maintaining a formal ban on official development assistance to the military governments.[16] During the Cold War the CIA and the KGB supported some INGOs through covert actions. Iran, Libya, and Syria have also assisted private organizations that support national liberation struggles, although whether they meet the usual definition of NGO is problematic.[17]

Ann M. Clark outlines four factors that foster a healthy collaborative relationship between states and NGOs. First, she argues that governments and NGOs must want to pursue such a relationship. This is not always possible. States are frequently suspicious of NGO intentions, sometimes seeing them as rival sources of power. NGOs frequently resent what they see as interference in their work. Moreover, the basic aims of official agencies and voluntary organizations may be in conflict.

Second, as a corollary to the first, states must provide "good governance," by which Clark means the use of social and political policies to encourage civil society and government accountability. Third, government must try to strike a balance in the use of regulation that promotes NGO growth while ensuring that they remain free of corruption and mismanagement. Such regulations, she argues, must be impartial. Finally, government can afford opportunities for NGOs to cooperate with official agencies, including participation in fostering public debate on important issues and encouraging NGOs to help formulate policy. In sum, government must present itself as an interested yet fair player that can be trusted to cooperate with NGOs over time. This is a tall order indeed in many societies.[18]

There are, of course, potential problems with cooperation between NGOs and government. For one thing, *collaboration* may simply mean that the state dominates the NGO sector or uses voluntary organizations to carry out public functions that it is either unwilling or unable to implement on its own. Activists and others worry that state support for official aims undermines NGO independence of action, a common theme that runs through the literature on voluntary organizations.

Even if states are willing to cooperate with NGOs, the way government agencies tend to look at the world can hamper efforts to facilitate cooperation with NGOs. Government agencies are arranged vertically, with decisions taken at the top disseminating down to the implementation levels. They tend to favor rule-based activity according to standardized procedures. NGOs are organized voluntarily and therefore tend to be organized horizontally, allowing at least the possibility of bottom-up decision making. They tend to emphasize flexible adaptation to particular circumstances. The difference in operating styles can hamper effective cooperation. In the case of agricultural development in Asian and African countries, the state has often inherited its agricultural world view from the colonial period. Colonial agricultural schemes were based on European practices and did not necessarily have anything to do with local social, environmental, or even climatic conditions. Colonial agricultural policy favored large-scale cash-crop production, with single-crop plantations seen as the ideal. This perspective is based on a rationalist, scientific, and industrial world view that, when coupled with authoritarian government, produces a tendency to simplify agricultural development planning to the point where local populations and their needs are comprehensively ignored. Even when this extreme case does not obtain, government-sponsored development tends to assume that the state and its managers occupy the center and top of a hierarchical model of organization.[19] The organizational difficulties that confront NGOs representing and promoting the interests of specific groups of people who confront local issues of social and economic development are obvious.

NGOs as Opponents of States

NGOs, of course, may choose not to cooperate with government. In certain areas, such as human rights, states and NGOs often come into conflict. Many non-state actors define their political role as watchdogs over state actions. These organizations view independence from state control as the sine qua non of effective criticism of state policy. Sometimes NGO opposition is of the government's own making. Authoritarian governments in Latin America in the 1970s and early 1980s often outlawed opposition political parties and fired academics and government officials who held leftist views. With no other means of employment, many of these people founded private think tanks and other organizations that came to serve as the nucleus of opposition to military rule.[20]

Box 4–2. Case Study:
Human Rights and Opposition to States

Human rights NGOs often find themselves confronting governments about their human rights policies. The 2002 war in Afghanistan brought AI and the US government into conflict over American military treatment of captured Taliban prisoners. AI and the ICRC have criticized the Bush administration's refusal to designate Taliban captives as prisoners of war, which would give the prisoners internationally recognized rights while in captivity. In an April 2002 report, AI argued that the US government "has not only violated the rights of those individuals, but threatens to undermine the rule of law everywhere."*

---

* Katharine Seelye, "U.S. Is Said to Erode Rule of Law," *International Herald Tribune* (April 16, 2002), 3.

Perhaps the outstanding example of NGO opposition to state poli-cies can be found in the kind of direct action campaign that is Greenpeace's hallmark. Greenpeace has come to symbolize the dramatic nonviolent confrontation between citizens' organizations and states and MNCs. While Greenpeace's ultimate target is public opinion, educating the public through direct action relies on overt opposition to govern-ment policies because it creates sensational media coverage. The extent of the divide between states and oppositional NGOs can be seen in events in New Zealand in 1985. Greenpeace was in the middle of a campaign opposing the French government's testing of nuclear weapons in the South Pacific, in which it relied on a well-used strategy of occupying the area of a test site to prevent the intended official action. Greenpeace's ship, the *Rainbow Warrior*, was docked in Auckland, New Zealand, when agents of the government of France's security service boarded it and deto-nated a bomb that destroyed it. The incident brought international op-probrium down on France, provoked a diplomatic protest from the government of New Zealand, and highlighted France's continuation of a controversial policy.

A second kind of opposition, undermining the authority and func-tions of the state, is more subtle but equally of concern to governments. Indigenous NGOs in Zambia, for example, have been more effective than the government in building roads and latrines, and in teaching women and poor villagers basic skills in agriculture. This level of in-volvement has also led to the development of a strong network with the poor. "The net effect is the steady erosion of state hegemony and cred-ibility and the strengthening of grassroots consciousness which would strengthen civil society and provide a basis for challenging the state."[21] Alison Van Rooy argues that in the extreme case of Mozambique, for example, support to civil society organizations has undercut key func-tions left to the state. Relief agencies and NGOs in particular, some of which have programs larger than those of the largest bilateral donor, have become the chief provider of public welfare and important sources of employment. They also further weakened government's capacity by attracting trained and competent local professionals from the govern-ment to the NGO sector. Jobs in the NGO sector are much more attrac-tive, in part because salaries are higher.[22] A similar situation is found in Bangladesh where BRAC has siphoned off competent personnel from the official primary school system in order to run its own thirty-three thousand schools, albeit through the weakening of the state system.

Finally, NGOs can undermine state authority by redefining key international norms that buttress state sovereignty. We agree with Stephen Krasner that sovereignty does not mean that states are free to do as they like.[23] The fact remains, however, that many governments have used the notion of sovereignty to argue that other international actors have no right to interfere in domestic affairs. As Kathryn Sikkink contends, the argument made by human rights organizations, that human rights are universal, has led to changes in international law that reduce the ability of governments to claim that state sovereignty allows a free hand in treating their citizens as they wish, including denying basic human rights.[24] Humanitarian intervention in civil wars, often championed by NGOs as necessary to preserve human life and civil rights, is quite often interpreted as a diminution of state sovereignty.

NGOs as Substitutes for States

Rather than merely complementing official policies and agencies, in some cases NGOs act as substitutes for state agencies. This is true in complex political emergencies, such as those in East Africa since the 1980s. It can also be the case where state authority—even in those states that have not "failed"—is so limited that large sections of society are ignored by the state and traditional civil society mechanisms are too weak to link state to society.[25]

Grameen Bank illustrates a kind of substitution at the domestic level. Grameen's entire approach to microfinance involves a repudiation of traditional development attitudes. Its clientele, poor people, are those whom the state does not reach and traditional banks refuse to serve. Its hallmark, creation of a system of credit allocated for people who have no collateral and who decide among themselves who is creditworthy nonetheless, has created a style of development finance that is beyond the state. In essence, Grameen-style microfinance acts in parallel to established state–private sector finance, but at a different level of society.

A striking example of NGOs attempting to substitute for civil authority comes from Lima, Peru, in the 1970s. NGO leaders concluded that the government was uninterested in addressing issues of concern to poor people. In response, NGOs established a centralized grassroots organization that led a self-contained squatter community of almost 300,000 people. The organization functioned as "the governing body of that territory or activity and the legitimate authority that should have control of the resources in the design and implementation of policies."[26] The project never fully reconciled the tension between the aim of autonomous development and ultimate state authority (incorporation of the community into the Lima metropolitan area led to duplication of functions between the organization and the municipal government), but the attempt by NGOs to create a formal community at least partly independent of official authority is striking.

A second kind of substitution occurs at the transnational level, when global citizen networks attempt to create a global civil society outside the bounds of the traditional interstate system. Increasingly, networks among voluntary organizations across national boundaries are creating what many scholars see as a global civil society that exists outside the traditional society of states and that is arguably creating a global civil culture.[27] There are several benefits to this kind of international contact. First, organizations can provide NGOs with what Sally Hastings calls social technology[28] or what sociologists call repertoires of collective action. Foreign organizations can teach organizational and other skills to local groups. Second, these organizations can provide organizations themselves. Oxfam International, Greenpeace, the World Wildlife Fund, and other NGOs can provide local activists with ready-made organization, advocacy techniques, and a "brand name" that can help a fledgling group publicize its existence and activities. Networking flows not only North to South but across borders everywhere. About one-tenth of the Japanese NGOs listed in a recent directory, for example, are branches of foreign NGOs.

Third, they can apply pressure in behalf of indigenous organizations' goals. The boomerang pattern of NGO networking presented by Keck and Sikkink enables NGOs that find their claims of rights blocked by their own governments to bypass them and locate allies in the international system—IGOs or other NGOs especially—who are willing to pressure their own governments in behalf of the domestic NGOs. Networks thus provide NGOs in many states with indirect leverage over their own governments.

Networks also give NNGOs legitimacy in their support of SNGOs.[29] Such legitimacy is important for NNGOs. For example, in April 1990 AI issued a memorandum urging Japanese officials to investigate allegations of mistreatment of prisoners and called special attention to those cases being publicized by the Japan Federation of Bar Associations.[30] Missions from INGOs can sometimes get audiences with political leaders inaccessible to domestic protestors. Foreign affiliations can be called upon to try to influence public opinion. The Association to Stop Racism against Blacks, a tiny group based in Osaka, Japan, relies on its affiliates overseas to help organize letter-writing campaigns in behalf of its efforts. One member acknowledged that without the support of such organizations neither the Japanese government nor the corporate sector would even pay attention to its concerns.[31]

Finally, foreign contacts can provide a sense of solidarity for organizations operating at the margins of society. Identification with other people in similar situations is probably an important morale booster and source of identity.

Some activists and observers argue that NGOs are not merely creating their own networks across national boundaries but are assuming international roles historically the preserve of states. Diplomacy is one such role. Some NGO leaders certainly see themselves in that light. Rosiska Darcy de Oliveira, Brazilian activist at the Global Forum NGO Summit that occurred alongside the 1992 Rio Summit proclaimed: "Now we are beyond government. There are new actors and NGOs are among them. There is a new kind of diplomacy, and another kind of representative—they are the NGOs."[32] Philip Shabecoff observes that the NGOs at the Global Forum crafted thirty alternative "treaties" designed to complement the treaties being made at the official summit but also notes that the NGO agreements had no legal standing.[33] These documents represented at best statements of ideals. Ann M. Clark has entitled her recent book on AI *Diplomacy of Conscience,* clearly meaning something different from the traditional statecraft of Kissinger, Bismarck, and Metternich.

How seriously are we to consider these claims? Is this simply loose use of terminology, or are non-state actors taking formal places in the international society of states? Clearly, NGOs engage states in international contexts. Consider Greenpeace's open ocean interference in French nuclear testing and plutonium shipments to Japan. Non-state actors have quite actively established alternative summits when UN and other IGO summits occur. They enjoy observer status at the UN. Activists sometimes have been invited to join official delegations to interstate conferences and summits.

Yet, many international relations scholars would point out that these activities do not make them diplomats. Diplomacy in the mainstream international relations literature remains a state-centered activity. Hedley Bull's definition, "the conduct of relations between states and other entities in world politics by official agents and by peaceful means,"[34] gives primacy of place to nation-states and their representatives. Geoffrey Stern lists seven functions of diplomacy:

1. representation: the classic diplomatic function and the origin of diplomatic immunity;
2. communication between governments;
3. negotiation between governments;
4. ingratiation: maintenance of good relations between governments;
5. intelligence gathering;
6. protection of a state's citizens abroad; and
7. recommendation (by which he means "tendering advice to the home government on the basis of the diplomat's appreciation of the situation in the country to which he or she is accredited").[35]

Here again, state functions are given priority.

NGOs do not enjoy the privileges states extend to one another's representatives. They do not carry official credentials unless states provide them that privilege when they accompany official delegations. They do not enjoy diplomatic immunity. They may represent new actors in international politics, but they are not classed as equals with their diplomatic counterparts because they do not represent sovereign entities. Their treaties have no binding effect on law, domestic or international. Unlike states, NGOs are not subjects of international law. They may not accede to treaties, nor may they opt out of them in any legal sense. Observer status at the UN is not the same as member status.

Transnationalist scholars, on the other hand, allow for the possibility that NGOs and other non-state actors might engage in an unofficial form of diplomacy including NGO participation in international conferences and other activities that have led to changes in international law or interstate behavior.[36] Indeed, if we consider diplomatic functions instead of formal status, the case for NGOs as agents of unofficial diplomacy looks somewhat stronger. While Stern's list focuses on state-to-state interactions, NGOs are transnational actors; in that capacity they communicate, negotiate, ingratiate, gather and disseminate intelligence, and recommend with states, with one another, and with other transnational actors.

Summary

This chapter outlined four modes that capture most NGO-state interactions. These modes, however, are not exclusive categories. Depending on circumstances, NGOs and governments engage each other in different modes at different times. Greenpeace, for example, is well known for its opposition to official policies that affect the environment. The infamous 1985 bombing of the organization's ship *Rainbow Warrior* by agents of France's security service suggests the depth of division that can exist between governments and specific NGOs. Greenpeace has also opposed the Japanese government's policy of shipping spent nuclear reactor fuel to France and then importing the recycled fuel. Its opposition has included highly visible attempts to intercept cargo ships en route between Japan and Europe. Yet, the same organization was also responsible in 1993 for informing the government of Japan that Russian naval vessels were planning to dump spent reactor fuel in the ocean off the Japanese coast.

Similarly, human rights NGOs have often engaged states in different modes. Governments interested in humanitarian foreign policies have collaborated with human rights NGOs and have regarded the latter as a valuable source of information. These same NGOs may also condemn other governments for their human rights records.

Discussion Questions

1. In what ways do NGOs interact with states? Are some ways more problematic than others?
2. In what ways do NGOs support or inhibit state action?
3. In what ways do states support or inhibit NGO action?

Suggestions for Further Readings

Shigetomi Shinichi, ed., *The State and NGOs: Perspective from Asia* (Singapore: Institute of Southeast Asian Studies, 2002); and Lester Salamon and Wojciech Sokolowski, eds., *Global Civil Society: Dimensions of the Nonprofit Sector* (Bloomfield, CT: Kumarian Press, 2004).

Notes

[1] Miles Kahler, "Inventing International Relations: International Relations Theory After 1945," in *New Thinking in International Relations,* ed. Michael Doyle and G. John Ikenberry, 20–52 (Boulder, CO: Westview Press, 1987).

² Peter Newell, "Environmental NGOs and Globalization: The Governance of TNCs," in *Global Social Movements,* ed. Robin Cohen and Shirin M. Rai, 117–33 (London: The Athlone Press, 2000).

³ See Robert Gilpin, *Global Political Economy* (Princeton, NJ: Princeton Univ. Press, 2000); Kenneth Waltz, "Political Structures," in *Neorealism and Its Critics,* ed. Robert Keohane, 70–97 (New York: Columbia Univ. Press, 1986).

⁴ Lori Forman, "NGOs as a Catalyst for Environmental Cooperation," *CGP Newsletter* 9 (Summer 1995): 5–6.

⁵ Yves Beigbeder, *The Role and Status of International Humanitarian Volunteers and Organizations* (Dordrecht: Martinus Nijhoff Publishers, 1991), 327.

⁶ Such constraints are not limited to NGOs, of course. MNCs face essentially the same legal environment. Toyota Motor Manufacturing North America, for example, must pay not only federal tax but state and local taxes on receipts processed through its Erlanger, Kentucky, headquarters. It pays local tax, moreover, at the rate set by the City of Erlanger (David Potter, "State and Local Government Negotiation with Japanese Multinational Corporations," in *Japan in the Bluegrass,* ed. P. P. Karan, 58–79 [Lexington: Univ. Press of Kentucky, 2001]).

⁷ Asia Watch and the Women's Rights Project, *A Modern Form of Slavery: Trafficking of Burmese Women and Girls into Brothels in Thailand* (New York: Human Rights Watch, 1993), 124.

⁸ Quoted in Julie Fisher, *Nongovernments: NGOs and the Political Development of the Third World* (West Hartford, CT: Kumarian Press, 1998), 48.

⁹ Ibid.

¹⁰ Asia Watch and the Women's Rights Project, *A Modern Form of Slavery,* 120–21.

¹¹ Jeffrey Berry, *Lobbying for the People* (Princeton, NJ: Princeton Univ. Press, 1977).

¹² Brian Smith, *More than Altruism: The Politics of Private Foreign Aid* (Princeton, NJ: Princeton Univ. Press, 1990).

¹³ Thomas Princen and Matthias Finger, *Environmental NGOs in World Politics* (London: Routledge, 1994).

¹⁴ Anthony Bebbington and Graham Thiele, with Penelope Davies, Martin Prager, and Hernando Riveros, eds., *NGOs and the State in Latin America: Rethinking Roles in Sustainable Agricultural Development* (London: Routledge, 1993), 200.

¹⁵ Ian Smillie and Henny Helmich, *Stakeholders: Government-NGO Partnership for International Development* (London: Earthscan, 1999).

¹⁶ Veronica Forrester, "The German Political Foundations," in *Pressure Groups, Politics, and Development: The Private Sector and EEC-Third World Policy,* ed. C. Stevens and J. V. Van Themaat, 40–60 (London: Hodder and Staughton, 1985).

¹⁷ Brian Smith, "Nonprofit Organizations in International Development: Agents of Empowerment or Preservers of Stability," in *Private Action and the*

Public Good, ed. W. Powell and E. Clemens (New Haven, CT: Yale Univ. Press, 1998), 13–14.

[18] Ann M. Clark, "Non-governmental Organizations and Their Influence on International Society," *Journal of International Affairs* 48, no. 2 (1995): 507–26.

[19] Anthony Bebbington and John Farrington, eds., *Reluctant Partners? Nongovernmental Organizations, the State and Sustainable Agriculture Development* (London: Routledge, 1993); and James Scott, *Seeing Like a State* (Princeton, NJ: Princeton Univ. Press, 2000).

[20] Clark, "Non-governmental Organizations and Their Influence on International Society"; and Smith, *More than Altruism.*

[21] Julius O. Ihonvbere, *Economic Crisis, Civil Society, and Democratization: The Case of Zambia* (Trenton, NJ: Africa World Press, 1996), 196.

[22] Alison Van Rooy, ed. *Civil Society and the Aid Industry* (London: Earthscan, 1998).

[23] Stephen Krasner, "Sovereignty," *Foreign Policy* (January-February, 2001): 21–29.

[24] Kathryn Sikkink, "Human Rights, Principled Issue Networks, and Sovereignty in Latin America," *International Organization* 47, no. 3 (Summer 1993): 411–41.

[25] Jose Diaz-Albertini, "Nonprofit Advocacy in Weakly Institutionalized Political Systems: The Case of NGDOs in Peru," *Nonprofit and Voluntary Sector Quarterly* 22, no. 4 (Winter 1993): 317–37.

[26] Ibid., 327.

[27] See Paul Wapner, *Environmental Activism and World Civic Politics* (Albany: State Univ. of New York Press, 1996); and John Boli and George Thomas, eds., *Constructing World Culture: International Nongovernmental Organizations since 1875* (Stanford, CA: Stanford Univ. Press, 1999).

[28] Sally Hastings, *Neighborhood and Nation in Tokyo, 1905–1937* (Pittsburgh: Univ. of Pittsburgh, 1995).

[29] Margaret E. Keck and Kathryn Sikkink, *Activists beyond Borders* (Ithaca, NY: Cornell Univ. Press, 1998).

[30] Amnesty International, *Amnesty International Report* (New York: Amnesty International, 1991).

[31] David Potter, interview with Yasue Kuwahara, Association to Stop Racism against Blacks (ASRAB) member, Cincinnati, Ohio, April 20, 1996.

[32] Rosiska Darcy de Oliveira, quoted in Philip Shabecoff, *A New Name for Peace: International Environmentalism, Sustainable Development, and Democracy* (Hanover, NH: Univ. Press of New England, 1996), 171.

[33] Shabecoff, *A New Name for Peace,* 170.

[34] Hedley Bull, quoted in Michael Palliser, "Diplomacy Today," in *The Expansion of International Society,* ed. Hedley Bull and A. Watson (Oxford: Claredon Press, 1984), 371.

[35] Geoffrey Stern, *The Structure of International Society,* 2nd ed. (London: Pinter, 2000), 186.

[36] Maureen Berman and Joseph Johnson, *Unofficial Diplomats* (New York: Columbia Univ. Press, 1977); and Ann M. Clark, *Diplomacy of Conscience* (Princeton, NJ: Princeton Univ. Press, 2001).

Chapter 5

NGOs and IGOs

History of NGO-IGO relations
Modes of interaction
Issues and points of conflict

The UN Charter was signed on June 26, 1945. Though mostly un-known, the fact is that a group of private American consultants played a key role in drafting and lobbying its adoption. The consultants repre-sented public and civic organizations invited by the State Department to assist the government delegation at the founding conference of the UN in San Francisco in April 1945. Under the leadership of Professor T. Shortwell, a renowned historian at Columbia University, the consult-ants drew up a proposal recommending that the new ECOSOC estab-lish a formal system of consultation with NGOs. The shared understanding was that such a system would help the UN get expert advice and information from key NGOs. Article 71 of the UN Charter, adopted in 1947, institutionalized the relationship between NGOs and the UN.

NGOs also made their mark in the Preamble of the Charter. The Preamble states, "We the Peoples of the United Nations determined . . . to reaffirm in fundamental human rights, in the dignity and worth of the human person, in the equal rights of men and women." Earlier drafts of the Charter did not start out that way. The passage outlawing discrimination based on sex was introduced later, at the insistence of women delegates and representatives of the forty-two NGOs accred-ited to the founding conference.[1] NGOs were also instrumental in securing the establishment of the UN Human Rights Commission, which drew up the Universal Declaration of Human Rights with NGO input in 1948.[2]

We saw in the last chapter that NGO coalitions are carving out a sphere of transnational civil society that crosses national boundaries. They

75

are also assuming roles traditionally identified with national states. These activities are made easier by the existence of IGOs.[3] As the vignette above makes clear, the two sets of organizations have grown together to form important components of the community of non-state actors that inhabit international society alongside states.

This chapter examines the relationship between two sets of transnational actors—NGOs and IGOs. This relationship in some ways parallels that between states and NGOs, but it has its own characteristics as well. We examine the kinds of relationships between the two and consider the benefits and issues NGOs and IGOs face when collaborating with each other. We pay particular attention to NGO interactions with the UN and the World Bank,[4] not only because they have been widely studied, but also because they demonstrate the potential and limitations of NGO-IGO relations.

History of NGO-IGO Relations

Early Relations

IGOs are creatures of the twentieth century. While there were international conferences before then, the idea of permanent international organizations created by states, but formally independent of them, did not gain currency until the end of World War I or later. Practically all of the 110 or so IGOs in existence today date their foundations after 1940.[5]

NGOs' interactions with IGOs began with relief efforts in Europe during World War I (see Box 5–1). The League of Nations, established in 1919, provided a permanent forum for communication between the two. Relief NGOs and women's international organizations had informal relationships with the League (see Chapter 9). From the beginning, NGOs took on the roles outlined in Chapter 3. The ICRC and other NGOs engaged in agenda setting on the question of refugees, asking the League Council to take up the issue soon after its founding. The League Council responded by appointing a High Commissioner for Russian Refugees in 1921.[6] Women's rights organizations timed their international congresses with League activities, in the process establishing the technique of parallel conferences widely practiced by NGOs today (see Box 5–2).

Box 5–1. The Commission for the Relief of Belgium

The Commission for the Relief of Belgium, organized in 1914 by Herbert Hoover, was a mix of IGO and NGO. In its relief operations in German-occupied Belgium, it undertook neutral humanitarian assistance for civilians that was in the tradition of the Red Cross and, today, the NGOs that provide relief in complex political emergencies (see Chapter 8). Unlike NGOs, however, the commission was authorized to negotiate with belligerent states and even issued its own passports. The Commission for the Relief of Belgium was dissolved with the end of hostilities in 1918.

Postwar Trends

There has been parallel growth between IGOs and NGOs since the end of World War II. There is a great difference in magnitude of growth, of course, since there are far fewer IGOs today than there are NGOs, but the upward trend across the postwar era is clear for both sets of transnational actors.[7] In general, interactions between NGOs and all IGOs have increased, especially in the last three decades. The degree and quality of interaction, however, has varied depending on the IGO. Overall, the UN has been most accessible to NGOs; the World Bank, the IMG, and the World Trade Organization (WTO) have been less so. This chapter begins, therefore, with a discussion of UN-NGO relations and then proceeds to the World Bank and IMF. It considers other IGOs in specific instances.

The UN has developed the longest relationship with NGOs. That relationship also serves as the model for other IGOs. As mentioned early in the chapter, the UN Charter provided for formal interactions between the UN and NGOs. Article 71 of the UN Charter empowered the ECOSOC to make "suitable arrangements for consultation with non-government organizations which are concerned with matters within their competence." That wording has appeared repeatedly in other IGO charters since then. For example, Article V of the Marrakesh Agreement, which established the WTO in 1994, allows the General Council to make "appropriate arrangements for consultation and cooperation with non-governmental organizations concerned with matters related to the WTO."

Originally, NGOs were accorded consultative status at the UN under three different categories: A, B, and C. Category A included organizations with broad economic and social scope; Category B included those organizations with more specialized interests; and Category C included organizations primarily interested in information dissemination. With the growing realization of NGOs as strong pressure groups, this latter category was abolished in 1950 and was replaced by a register of organizations that might be consulted on an ad hoc basis. In 1968, Resolution 1296 changed the labels to category I, category II, and the roster. It also emphasized that NGOs seeking consultative status with the UN must be representative and international.

Category I NGOs have the broadest access to ECOSOC. They may propose agenda items, send observers to all meetings and submit brief written statements. Category II NGOs can also send observers to all meetings. The council has the right to ask for written statements from any of the consultative NGOs and in rare situations has invited Category I and II NGOs to attend hearings. The process of admission to consultative status is supervised by the Committee on Non-Governmental Organizations, which is a permanent standing committee of the council. The nineteen members of the committee are elected each year by ECOSOC from among its member governments.

In 1996 a major revision was made to NGO accreditation. Resolution 1996/31 made national NGOs, those based in a single country, eligible to apply for special status or a place on the roster. It also provides for NGO participation in major conferences, including those convened by ECOSOC and by the General Assembly.

Under the current arrangement NGOs can be granted association with the UN Department of Public Information, which permits access but not participation in UN meetings or deliberations The UN also provides one-time NGO accreditation for a specific event, such as a conference, which does not imply an ongoing affiliation.

The number of NGOs formally accredited to ECOSOC has grown tremendously. In 1948 there were forty-one groups; in 1968 the number increased to 377; and by 1998 there were 1,350 NGOs accredited to the council.[8] As of 2005, there are 2,719 NGOs in consultative status with the council. There are another 400 (approximate) NGOs accredited to the Commission on Sustainable Development, a subsidiary body of the council. The original meaning of consultative status implied that these NGOs could attend ECOSOC's meetings, submit written statements, testify before meetings, and in limited cases propose items for the agenda. However, over the years NGOs' participation has moved far beyond the original meaning and scope of Article 71.

Other IGOs have taken longer to recognize NGOs. Unlike the UN, many IGOs' founding charters did not make specific provision for NGOs. The World Bank and the regional development banks did not begin to pay attention to NGOs until the late 1970s or later. For example, the World Bank began to cooperate with NGOs in the 1970s but did not develop an official policy or a forum for formal collaboration until 1989.

What caused the change in the World Bank's attitude toward NGOs? In the late 1970s and early 1980s the bank rethought its basic development philosophy. Previously, it had emphasized funding for large-scale infrastructure projects, such as dam and highway construction, on the assumption that this supported economic development. By the 1970s it was clear that infrastructure construction by itself was insufficient to stimulate and maintain growth. Along with the IMF, World Bank officials began to pay much more attention to countries' policy environments, especially the ways that governments facilitated or blocked the development of free markets. The result was the introduction of structural adjustment lending, aimed at helping governments make more effective economic policy. Typically, governments were asked to remove barriers to free domestic and international economic transactions and to reform their legal and bureaucratic systems to make them more responsive to free market functioning. In order to ensure that governments actually made necessary reforms, World Bank and IMF loans were to depend on how much progress a country made toward economic reform.

Structural adjustment programs tended to focus on macroeconomic policy reform. They therefore overlooked the side effects of these programs, including growing poverty and economic slowdown during the reform period. NGOs, many of which were working with local communities in the countries undergoing reform, quickly perceived these effects, and civil society networks organized to oppose World Bank and IMF policies. Some NGOs have gone so far as to argue that structural adjustment does not simply hurt the poor by raising poverty and unemployment levels; rather, these policies are inherently anti-poor, offering economic and political elites the opportunity to cut welfare and other social benefits in the name of reform. These are harsh criticisms, indeed, and the World Bank and the IMF found themselves uncomfortably aware of the potential power of NGOs operating in their advocacy roles. Policy engagement with NGOs was initially a reaction to these criticisms.

The New Policy Agenda, of which structural adjustment is a key component, downplays the role of the state, in economic development and in provision of social welfare. This forced national policymakers and development bank experts to look to civil society and the market for alternatives; NGOs were one of the rapidly developing centers of civil society at the time. Thus, the shift in World Bank attitudes toward greater appreciation of NGO contributions to development mirrored the changes in attitudes about development itself.

James Wolfensohn, World Bank president since 1994, is widely credited with opening dialogues with NGOs around the world. Cooperation now includes a modest grant program to support NGO projects (predominantly made to SNGOs); the NGO–World Bank Committee, which includes NGO representatives from every region of the world; collaboration on project implementation; and dialogue on World Bank policies. Since 1997 an annual Structural Adjustment Participatory Review Initiative has included NGOs both as members of the steering committee and as review participants. Somewhat like the UN's three-category division of NGOs, the bank distinguishes two types: operational and advocacy organizations.[9] Roughly, the first type is made up of relief and development NGOs; the second comprises those engaged in advocacy, agenda setting, and public education. The World Bank typology, however, has not been formalized in the way that the ECOSOC categories have been.

The WTO, founded in 1995 as the successor to the General Agreement on Tariffs and Trade (GATT), established a formal policy toward NGOs in 1996. As seen above, WTO relations with NGOs are structured on the UN model: NGOs may ask to register with the IGO, provided that they can prove they are "concerned with matters related to those of the WTO."[10] Acceptance of registration entitles NGOs to observe plenary sessions and ministerial conferences. Because trade affects so many other economic and social issues, in practice NGOs representing environmental, economic development, labor, business, and agricultural issues have successfully claimed to be "concerned with matters related to those of the WTO." At the Fourth Ministerial held in Doha, Qatar, in November 2001, for example, the organization's External Relations Division counted 365 NGOs attending the conference. Church groups; business, labor, farmer, and consumer associations; and human rights, environmental, and development groups from every inhabited continent registered with the conference. In addition, the WTO Secretariat (which organizes the actual conferences) has initiated symposiums and briefings to maintain day-to-day contact with NGOs during conferences. NGOs have also submitted position papers on issues of concern, which are posted on the WTO's website.

Other IGOs have recognized NGOs but do not actively encourage interaction with them. Points of contact with the IMF have increased since the 1980s: the board of directors, the External Relations Department, and other departments have developed contacts with NGOs and other civic groups. These contacts remain mostly ad hoc, however, and determined by the IMF organs. The IMF, moreover, is reluctant even to supply NGOs with information on its internal policy proceedings because it defines its primary counterparts as national governments.[11] A great deal of NGO attention, therefore, has been aimed at opposing IMF policies while at the same time arguing for greater openness on the part of the IMF. One author characterizes the relationship between the IMF and NGOs as still "problematic" compared to relations between NGOs and other IGOs.[12] This has not stopped NGOs from commenting on IMF policies or insisting that they be included in IMF policymaking, of course.

Like the IMF, the International Tropical Timber Organization, founded in 1994, is explicitly intergovernmental. Its founding document, the International Tropical Timber Agreement, clearly lays out the organization's heavy emphasis on representing governments. NGOs are nowhere mentioned.

Modes of Interaction

In some ways the interactions between IGOs and NGOs are less complex than those between NGOs and states. The "NGOs in States" category explored in Chapter 4 has no counterpart in NGO relations with organizations like the UN or the WTO. IGOs are not sovereign, territorial entities, so they cannot force NGOs to obey laws and regulations in the same way that national governments can. NGOs can simply avoid IGO restrictions by not working with them at all, something that they cannot do with governments (which are everywhere, after all).

In other ways, however, some relationships between NGOs and IGOs resemble those between NGOs and governments. Lori Forman's distinction between NGOs as "watchdogs and working dogs" applies to NGO interactions with IGOs as well as with states. While NGOs can be seen as new partners with IGOs, relations between the two can range from cooperation to conflict. In part, this reflects different NGO roles. Project-oriented development NGOs will tend to find points of collaboration with IGOs; advocacy NGOs will tend to come into conflict with them.

Points of Engagement

The UN has been positive about NGO cooperation for longer than any other major IGO. As a result, relationships have developed across a number of policy fields. We use that organization's experience as the centerpiece of our study of NGO-IGO cooperation. The roles that NGOs currently engage in with the UN are very different compared to the ones in the founding period. In contrast to their nonpolitical status, NGOs are now recognized as active political actors in shared partnership with states. Political roles can be found in all three stages of the policymaking process: agenda setting, policy formulation, and policy implementation.

Agenda Setting

IGOs are responsible first to the nation-states that have created them. A consequence of this is they tend to look to their member states, particularly the major ones, before creating policy. They also tend to be reluctant to take up new issues if there is the possibility that key members may object. IGOs, therefore, tend to be conformist and status quo–oriented.[13] A major reason why NGOs exist is their ability to promote issues that are not currently being undertaken by governments or to challenge the way an issue is being considered by the government.[14] Through information dissemination, media attention, mobilization, and lobbying, NGOs routinely bring issues to the agenda-setting process. Their image as volunteers, experts, and non-state actors gives them the power to influence the process because these identities convey a sense of neutrality. It is now widely recognized that issues like human rights, women's rights, and environmental protection that have dominated the UN meetings/platforms did so mostly because of the active role of influential NGOs.

Policy Formation

NGOs regularly provide information, ideas, and advice, and at times have shared in drafting UN policies and resolutions. They can mobilize public opinion in support of a draft policy or against it. They can put pressure on governments to sign a treaty. Numerous NGOs have significantly contributed to international policymaking, as found at the San Francisco Conference in April 1945, where NGOs played a pivotal role in securing inclusion of human rights language in the final draft of the UN Charter. The International Planned Parenthood Federation drafted resolutions on the right of access to family-planning information passed by the 1968 International Conference on Human Rights. Similar examples abound in the history of the relationship between NGOs and the UN.

Along with making their marks strongly felt in ECOSOC, NGOs are gradually encroaching on other UN organs too, including the General Assembly and the Security Council. There are also instances in the past when non-state organizations that were involved in conflicts were allowed to present their views before the General Assembly. For example, Peter Willetts points out the UN resolution in 1947 that provided for the First Committee to grant hearing to the Jewish Agency for Palestine and the Arab Higher Committee.[15] Since the 1970s NGOs have addressed special sessions on disarmament and on development. The UN Special Committee against Apartheid and the UN Special Committee on Palestinian Rights have extensive and ongoing relations with relevant NGOs. In addition, a few NGOs have even been granted recognition to become observers in the General Assembly. The ICRC was granted such recognition in 1990, the first time an NGO was given such status.

Recently, NGOs have engaged the Security Council too. In informal sessions CARE and Medecins Sans Frontieres have briefed the different committees of the Security Council. In 1997, for example, CARE representatives reported on the situation in the Great Lakes region of East Africa, a region that had been destabilized by a series of civil wars and in which relief NGOs were active in providing refugee assistance.

Policy Implementation

Many of the UN's development and relief agencies act as authorizing agencies in the field. WHO, the UN High Commission for Refugees (UNHCR), and the UN Disaster Relief Organization (UNDRO) are examples. In this capacity they coordinate operations and channel funds to counterparts that actually carry out projects on the UN's behalf.[16] NGOs are regularly involved in implementing different development programs, like family planning or sex education. NGOs monitor UN treaties and policies. As Peter J. Simmons points out, "Where governments have turned a blind eye, groups such as Amnesty International and the Committee to Protect Journalists call attention to violations of the UN Declaration on Human Rights."[17] On a few occasions relevant NGOs have been given access to committees of the Security Council to report violations of sanctions resolutions.

What gives NGOs the opportunity or access to the policymaking process? The UN's organizational structure is one answer. Agency missions overlap with many of the activities NGOs engage in. Collectively, their purview covers the range of policy areas associated with social and economic development. The specialized development and relief agencies have found it useful to cooperate with NGOs within their fields of expertise. This cooperation, in turn, gives NGOs the chance to speak not only to project implementation but also to formulation and the broader issues of the UN agencies' objectives.

Second, a major venue for NGO influence lies in UN-sponsored conferences and NGO forums. Major specialized conferences focus attention on particular issues and bring them to the global agenda-setting process. NGOs participate actively in the preparatory phases of conferences, submit information, and at times prepare reports at the request of the UN Secretariat or governments. They attend different conference committees, lobby delegates, draft resolutions, and offer suggestions. A UN-sponsored conference is preceded by a series of preparatory committees, or "prepcoms," where the official document of the upcoming conference is discussed and refined and where most of the significant changes are made. NGOs unfamiliar with such UN procedures often ignored these prepcoms and then became frustrated in the world conference when they realized the limitations placed on substantive changes only at that time.[18]

NGOs also organize unofficial conferences, known as forums, through the Conference of NGOs in Consultative Relationship with the United Nations (CONGO).[19] These forums typically include seminars, panels, films, and field trips, all meant to reflect the debates and disagreements among the diversified body of stakeholders. Sometimes a forum is conveniently placed close to the conference site; sometimes it is in a different part of the city. The significance of such forums is that they bring diplomats and NGO representatives into proximity; diplomats often attend NGO-organized sessions. Journalists also attend such forums, which give them more media coverage. Official UN conferences are frequently constrained by prior consensus and compromises. NGO forums,

---

Box 5–2. The Beijing Conference

The Fourth UN Conference on Women, held in Beijing in 1995, witnessed a classic demonstration of the boomerang pattern. As host of the official UN conference, the Chinese government found itself the reluctant host of the unofficial NGO parallel conference. The Chinese government provided facilities for the NGO conference in Huairou, a suburb at some distance from the official conference. Nevertheless, the NGO delegates managed to attend and monitor the official conference proceedings. Moreover, a coalition of human rights NGOs (including AI and Human Rights Watch) took advantage of the situation to publicize a detailed criticism of the Chinese government's shabby treatment of the NGO parallel conference. The report also documented incidences of Chinese government interference in NGO participation, including denial of visas to opponents of government policy toward Tibet, refusal to allow Chinese organizations to participate, and surveillance and harassment of NGO representatives and journalists. It called upon the government of China and future UN conference hosts to provide NGOs with better access to official conferences.

Note that Human Rights Watch's criticisms were not about the status of women in China, but rather that the NGOs used the opportunity to comment on government policies in a high-profile way.

---

unconstrained by such limitations, have been found to be livelier in terms of the coverage of the topics and the debates.

UN conferences provide a useful resource because they allow NGOs to overcome some important collective-action problems. The NGO community by itself is diverse, small scale, and geographically widespread. It is impossible for NGOs to organize the events that a major IGO can. This is especially true of the smaller NNGOs and most SNGOs. NGOs, in effect, "piggyback" on the organizational and financial resources of IGOs. They rely on the latter for agenda-setting venues and the accompanying media and public attention. Because the IGO absorbs the overhead costs of organizing the official event, cash-strapped voluntary organizations do not incur expenses that are beyond their means in normal circumstances. The international conferences themselves provide NGOs with significant internal resources. In particular, meetings of like-minded NGOs can reinforce feelings of solidarity and common purpose, providing individual organizations with the intangible benefits on which voluntary organizations rely. They also provide a venue for NGOs to share information among themselves.

Parallel conferences have become a tool in NGOs' repertoire of collective action.[20] While the parallel conferences organized around UN conferences and the demonstrations that accompany meetings of the G8 or the World Economic Forum may look new, they are not. NGO predecessors have been organizing parallel conferences around IGO meetings since the time of the League of Nations.[21] Parallel conferences also provide effective forums for using the boomerang pattern of advocacy (see Chapter 3). IGOs stand outside of states, allowing NGOs a platform from which to criticize national policies or support domestic NGOs.

Boomerangs, of course, fly in both directions. NGOs have found that appeals to key national governments can influence IGOs. NGO coalitions headquartered in Washington, D.C., understand that the US government's position as the World Bank's and IMF's principal member and funder gives it leverage over IGO policy. Congress, which is accessible and habitually suspicious of multilateral organizations, has proven to be a good place for NGO lobbying to change World Bank policies. The Fifty Years Is Enough coalition used the occasion of the fiftieth anniversary of the World Bank and the IMF in 1994 to call for a "profound transformation" of both institutions (see Box 5–3). The campaign's launch in Washington, D.C., occurred one day before the House of Representatives Appropriations Committee was due to report its proposals to fund the two institutions for the following year.[22] In 1995, US environmental NGOs successfully lobbied Congress to stipulate that its World Bank subscription was contingent on establishment of an environmental inspection panel that would oversee World Bank projects.[23] Appeals to Congress to place policy or other conditions on the US's membership subscription to the World Bank have forced bank policymakers to take NGO demands seriously.

Interactions with IGOs have also allowed NGOs to influence policy through participation in global policy networks. Less than a decade old in most cases, global policy networks are loose associations of IGOs, concerned national governments, NGOs, and other private-sector actors. Typically, they emerge around a specific technical issue that transcends national boundaries, such as malaria control, agricultural research, water resources management, or dam construction. These networks have the advantage of pooling expertise from a wide array of actors. IGOs provide convenient centers for policy discussion and formulation.[24] Moreover, they institutionalize the participation of non-state actors like NGOs and research centers, ensuring that policies do not simply reflect the views of governments and specialized international agencies.

Points of Conflict

Not all interactions are cooperative. From time to time organizations are bound to come into conflict. Different identities, development objectives, and operational styles are likely to contribute to those conflicts.

The World Bank has experienced both cooperation and conflict with NGOs. As Smillie puts it, "Contacts have ranged from collaborative arrangements on project planning and delivery, to policy dialogue and some of the most vituperative criticism in the history of development assistance."[25] The sources of discord in this case illustrate the potential problems IGOs are likely to confront when interacting with the voluntary sector. Some of the issues are ideological because development banks and many NGOs understand development quite differently. But the potential for conflict also derives from the nature of the organizations themselves. The characteristics that set NGOs apart from IGOs like the World Bank—flexibility, attention to grassroots development, and small scale—can make it difficult to cooperate with large organizations that carry out official development programs in the name of national development.

Unlike the UN in general, NGOs were not involved with the international financial institutions from their inception. Interactions began only in the 1970s, and then only fitfully. The NGO–World Bank Committee was established only in 1982. The World Bank did not establish an independent NGO unit within its organization until 1988, and since then it has migrated around various bureaus.[26] NGO-IGO cooperation, then, is not as deep in the case of the international financial institutions.

Moreover, the development banks tend to define interaction with NGOs in more restrictive terms. The World Bank, for example, values NGOs primarily for their role in the implementation of World Bank projects. The 1989 Operational Directive that established basic policy toward NGOs emphasizes that aspect. Because the World Bank in principle lends only to governments, its willingness to provide grants to NGOs remains limited (the bank disbursed about US$5 million in grants to NGOs in 1998). Nelson found that the most common form of World

Bank–NGO collaboration involved NGOs carrying out a project, or part of one. He found also that bank staff resisted NGO attempts to redefine development agendas or cooperate in designing programs beyond specific projects.[27] To the extent that NGOs are involved at all in structural adjustment policies, the suspicion exists that their projects are only tools to alleviate the adverse economic effects of World Bank–led adjustment policies.

In general, it is safe to say that NGO interactions with the World Bank have been more contentious than with the UN. NGOs have been especially critical, for example, of World Bank program lending because its narrow focus on macroeconomic policy reform leads it to overlook the environmental and social consequences of the reforms it urges on developing country governments. As the World Bank moved from project

---

Box 5–3. NGOs in Focus: Fifty Years Is Enough

The year 1994 marked the jubilees of two of the postwar international system's key economic IGOs: the World Bank and the IMF. The occasion was marked by controversy, with supporters arguing for their relevance in an increasingly globalized economy, and their detractors calling either for their abolition or for fundamental reform. The Fifty Years Is Enough Network, composed of over 200 US NGOs and 185 partner organizations worldwide, is one of the latter. Founded in 1994, it defines its primary objective as "transforming the international financial institutions' policies and practices, to ending the outside imposition of neo-liberal economic programs, and to making the development process democratic and accountable." Its platform includes

- calls for public accountability by the Bank and the IMF;
- a shift in those institutions' economic policies from structural adjustment lending to sustainable and participatory development;
- an end to environmentally destructive economic policies;
- scaling back of Bank and IMF roles and financing; and
- the reduction of developing country debt owed to them.

It is difficult to see how the World Bank and the IMF could accommodate these demands without completely transforming themselves in the process, an unlikely prospect.

lending to structural adjustment lending in the 1980s and 1990s, NGOs responded by demanding that its policies consider the broader effects of the new policies. They have engaged both the World Bank and the IMF on issues such as environment destruction as a consequence of donor-prescribed economic-growth strategies; the rights of indigenous peoples displaced by large-scale development projects; the impacts of macroeconomic reforms on the poor, especially women; and the development of democratic civil societies.

At times IGOs and NGOs come into conflict because they represent different constituencies. IGOs are established by international treaties, agreed upon by national governments that then make up the organizations' members. They represent the interests of nation-states. Voting rules, basic policies, and organizational structures all reflect that fact. In the case of the development banks, their members are also their clients.

NGOs and transnational advocacy networks, on the other hand, represent non-state actors. As the Narmada Dam case below demonstrates, many of those beneficiaries either operate below the national level (in the case of indigenous populations) or across national boundaries (in the case of transnational activist networks). This means that they do not fit neatly into a world organized into sovereign, territorial states; neither, then, do the interests of the NGOs that claim to represent them.

NGO opposition to the World Bank's support for India's Narmada Dam highlights some of the conflicts that arise between NGOs and IGOs. The Narmada protest has been one of the longest and most powerful of all the campaigns against the World Bank and illustrates the evolving alliances between NGOs and grassroots groups. An unprecedented grassroots and international NGO campaign against India's Narmada Dam (also known as the Sardar Sarovar Dam) severely damaged the World Bank's international credibility.[28] Approved by the World Bank in 1985 with a loan of US$450 million, the project was fraught with environmental and resettlement problems from the outset. Although the project would displace more than 150,000 people from their homes and villages, most of these people did not have access to the most basic information about their impending resettlement—such as basic entitlements, timetables, or locations where they would be resettled. Many were not even informed that they had to move.[29]

Concerned with the World Bank's and the Indian government's neglect of these concerns, different NGOs and activists started to form coalitions with individuals who would be affected by this project and demanded access to information about resettlement plans and timetables, results of environmental studies, and project appraisals. Information, collected mostly through informal sources, points to the project's devastating impact both environmentally and socially. As Udall points out, the Indian activists also discovered that a comprehensive resettlement and rehabilitation plan, which according to bank policy was supposed to be completed before project appraisal, had not been finished even five years *after* project approval.[30] The activists later contacted and formed coalitions with international NGOs for support in targeting both the World Bank and the Japanese government for their involvement in the project. Activists traveled to important international meetings to argue against the project and to inform the international community.

By 1988 an informal network of individuals and NGOs in the major donor countries was working to influence legislators, ministries, and executive directors on Narmada. A turning point in the international campaign was when the World Bank's involvement in the project became the subject of a special US Congressional oversight hearing. Various activists and NGO leaders testified. In 1990, Japanese NGOs held the first International Narmada Symposium, in which several Indian activists participated. After unprecedented media exposure, within a month the Japanese government withdrew from the project. Amid vehement local opposition and international opposition, the World Bank formed the Morse Commission to conduct an independent review of the project. After a year of intensive investigation, the commission recommended that the World Bank take a "step back" to consider how to improve the situation. The new president of the World Bank, Lewis Preston, decided not to stop the loan, but the bank finally withdrew in June 1993, nominally at the request of the government of India.

The leverage INGOs used over donor governments in the Narmada Dam case resulted in structural changes within the World Bank, including the 1993 information policy reform and the establishment of an inspection panel to investigate complaints about bank project procedures. The former gave more public access to project information; the latter worked as an appeal mechanism for project-affected people. It is widely acknowledged that environmental NGOs played a pivotal role in the reform process.

The Narmada Dam represents a broader protest by NGOs about the nature of economic development. In the 1990s, criticism of large-scale development projects pitted NGOs and the World Bank against each other on a range of issues. Dams were at the center of this confrontation, as they were visible symbols of the official commitment to large-scale development. Significantly, the newly created Inspection Panel took up a World Bank–funded dam project in Nepal as its first case.[31] In the case of dam construction, conflict led to searches for common ground where cooperation between the bank and NGOs might be possible. In 1997 an informal workshop organized by the World Bank took up the issue, paving the way for the creation of the World Commission on Dams the following year. The commission was charged with developing new standards for dam construction worldwide.[32] The commission consisted of IGO staff and representatives from governments and the private sector. The NGO community was represented by members of the Philippine Tebtebba Foundation (Philippines), the Environmental Defense Fund (United States), Oxfam International Australia, and Ms. Medha Patkar, who had founded the Narmada Bachao Andolan (Struggle to Save the Narmada River). The commission's work was funded by IGOs, national aid and foreign affairs agencies, MNCs, and major environmental NGOs.

The Narmada Dam case suggests a number of sources of conflict between IGOs and NGOs. First, note that opposition reached critical proportions after the project had been approved by the World Bank, the government of India, and other bilateral aid donors. In this case the NGOs were engaging in one of their well-recognized roles—monitoring. NGOs take their watchdog role seriously, especially since IGOs like the World Bank have been slow to engage in dialogue with NGOs at the design stages of projects.

Second, the problem of representation abetted the conflict. As an IGO, the World Bank understood its client to be the government of India, which had accepted the dam. The claim against the World Bank was made by organizations that represented Indian citizens—precisely the people the World Bank assumed would be represented by the Indian government!

In part, conflict between NGOs and the World Bank stem from very different understandings of economic development. IGOs tend to be vertically organized and bureaucratic. Projects tend to be large scale and complex. The Narmada Dam, for example, was the centerpiece of a larger development program in which the World Bank and several bilateral aid donors had agreed to take responsibility for different parts. It is difficult to change such programs once plans have been approved and work started. NGOs, on the other hand, take pride in their flexibility, willingness to experiment, and concern with the local and individual consequences of development projects. The two are likely to come into conflict not only over the specifics of development projects, but with their very structure.

The Narmada Dam protest was part and parcel of a broader protest against World Bank development policies in general.

NGOs have engaged in adversarial relations with the WTO, too. WTO rules and agreements have become targets of NGO protests, and the 1999 Seattle protests against the WTO brought the contention to a heightened level. The protests and the ensuing chaos at Seattle ultimately led city officials to declare a state of emergency.

International trade is a flashpoint because it affects so many parts of society. According to Gillian Hughes Murphy: "Perhaps the most publicized contested aspect of the WTO's trade rules is its requirements that member nations maintain nondiscriminatory trade relationships with all other members. This has the effect of disallowing historical trade relationships with all other members . . . based on longstanding preferences and agreements, trade (or trade bans) based on environmental considerations, and many other aspects that are not specifically related to the good being traded."[33] Murphy cites the issue of hormone-fed beef as an example. The United States had challenged an EU ban on the sale

---

Box 5–4. Grameen Assesses the IGOs

In *Banker to the Poor* (1999), Muhammad Yunus gives his views on the consequences of the different organizational perspectives between IGOs and NGOs:

> I find multilateral donors' style of doing business with the poor very discomforting. I can cite one example of my experience in the island of Negros Occidental in the Philippines. Because hunger was so bad there, one of our replicators started Project Dunganon back in 1988. More than half the island's children were malnourished, and so in 1993 Dr. Cecile del Castillo, the replicator, still innocent about the nature and work habits of international consultants, asked the International Fund for Agricultural Development (IFAD), a Rome-based UN agency created to assist the rural poor, for money to expand her successful programme quickly. IFAD responded by sending four missions to investigate her proposal, spending thousands of dollars in airline tickets, per diems and professional fees. But the project never received a single penny. (14)

of such beef. The EU justified the ban on the grounds of public health. However, since the ban would go against US interests in marketing the product, the United States brought a challenge to the WTO. The WTO eventually ruled that the public-health measure was an illegal barrier to trade under the WTO agreements. Activists, before and during the Seattle protests, actively publicized issues like these to portray the organization as undemocratic and anti-environmental.

Protests organized by civil society organizations have become widely publicized features of subsequent WTO meetings. Despite the media image of rioting, these protests have been organized by activist groups including labor unions; student and civic associations; and environmental, developmental, and human rights NGOs. While the NGO activists have been criticized as having no focus,[34] the strength of the protests has made it clear that IGOs like the WTO and others cannot avoid recognizing that NGOs are a force to be reckoned with.

Summary

NGOs and IGOs have grown in tandem over the last half century. Increasingly, INGOs and transnational advocacy networks find that IGOs provide important partners for their development and advocacy activities. This trend is an important confirmation of the transnational approach to international relations because significant transactions take place between two kinds of non-state actors. Cooperation with IGOs affords NGOs a number of critical resources, including access to organizations with global reach, venues for NGO public education and advocacy, and access to expertise.

In turn, IGOs have recognized the importance of NGOs. The UN has recognized NGOs since its founding and a wide range of interactions have developed between the two. Although other IGOs were slower to recognize NGOs as dialogue partners, most IGO charters now contain wording stating the organization's relationship with NGOs. As Jessica Mathews argues: "Until recently, international organizations were institutions of, by, and for nation-states. Now they are building constituencies of their own and, through NGOs, establishing direct connections to the peoples of the world."[35] Receptivity to NGO participation, however, varies from one IGO to another. Even in the UN, the Security Council has been reluctant to countenance what it sees as unwarranted public invasion of its jurisdiction. The World Bank has been reluctant to allow full NGO participation in its policymaking processes beyond limited implementation of projects it designs itself. The IMF and International Tropical Timber Organization have been uninterested in close interaction with NGOs. In these cases NGOs have been the driving force in engaging IGOs.

Even when NGOs and IGOs agree to cooperate on issues of common concern, problems remain. NGOs and IGOs are organized quite differently, answer to different constituencies, and do not always speak the same "language." For example, what the World Bank and NGOs mean by *development* is not the same thing.

Discussion Questions

1. In what ways do NGOs interact with IGOs?
2. What advantages do NGOs receive by engaging IGOs? Are there benefits for IGOs, too? Are there drawbacks for either party?
3. Why is NGO interaction with some IGOs easier than with others?

Suggested Further Reading

Jonathan A. Fox and L. David Brown, eds., *The Struggle for Accountability: The World Bank, NGOs, and Grassroots Movements* (Cambridge, MA: Cambridge Univ. Press, 1998); Kerstin Martens, *NGOs and the United Nations: Institutionalization, Professionalization, and Adaptation* (New York: Palgrave Macmillan, 2005).

Notes

[1] United Nations, *The United Nations and the Advancement of Women, 1945–1996,* Blue Book Series 6, rev. ed. (New York: UN Department of Public Information, 1996), 10.

[2] Thomas Risse, "The Power of Norms Versus the Norms of Power: Transnational Civil Society and Human Rights," in *The Third Force,* ed. Ann Florini, 177–210 (Tokyo: Japan Center for International Exchange; Washington, DC: The Carnegie Endowment for International Peace, 2000).

[3] The term *intergovernmental organization* is used in its conventional sense as a non-state organization created by agreement among states. IGOs are thus one kind of international organization.

[4] The World Bank and the IMF are officially part of the UN system. They were established separately, however, and in practice they have taken on very different roles in managing international relations in the last fifty years. The World Bank and the IMF reflect the economic concerns of their main contributors, notably the United States. The two institutions have been champions of the New Policy Agenda and the diminution of the role of the state in managing national economies. In contrast, the UN economic councils, notably the United Nations Council on Economic Development (UNCED), have tended to reflect the economic concerns of developing countries. Thus, the two components of the same UN system have often come into conflict over the direction of economic development.

[5] John Rourke and Mark Boyer, *World Politics: International Politics on the World State, Brief,* 2nd ed. (New York: Dushkin/McGraw-Hill, 1998).

[6] Yves Beigbeder, *The Role and Status of International Humanitarian Volunteers and Organizations* (Dordrecht: Martinus Nijhoff Publishers, 1991).

[7] For data on foundation rates for IGOs in the twentieth century, see Rourke and Boyer, *World Politics.*

[8] Karen A. Mingst and Margaret P. Karns, *The United Nations in the Post–Cold War Era* (Boulder, CO: Westview Press, 2000).

[9] Robert O'Brien, A. M. Goetz, J. Aart Scholte, and M. Williams, *Contesting Global Governance: Multinational Economic Institutions and Global Social Movements* (Cambridge, MA: Cambridge Univ. Press, 2001).

[10] WTO, "Agreement Establishing the World Trade Organization," Article V (Extract), Available on the wto.org website.

[11] Jan Aart Scholte, "The IMF and Civil Society: An Interim Progress Report," in *Global Citizen Action,* ed. Michael Edwards and John Gaventa, 87–103 (Boulder, CO: Lynne Rienner, 2001).

[12] Ibid., 102.

[13] Paul J. Nelson, *The World Bank and Non-Governmental Organizations* (New York: St. Martin's Press, 1996).

[14] Peter Willetts, ed., *"The Conscience of the World": The Influence of Non-Governmental Organizations in World Politics* (Washington, DC: Brookings Institution, 1996).

[15] Peter Willetts, "From 'Consultative' Arrangements to 'Partnership': The Changing Status of NGOs in Diplomacy at the UN," *Global Governance* 6, no. 2 (2000): 191–213.

[16] Beigbeder, *The Role and Status of International Humanitarian Volunteers and Organizations.*

[17] Peter J. Simmons, "Learning to Live with NGOs," *Foreign Policy* 112 (Fall 1998): 87.

[18] Irene Tinker, "Non-Governmental Organizations: An Alternative Power Base for Women," in *Gender Politics in Global Governance,* ed. Mary K. Meyer and Elizabeth Prugl, 88–104 (Boulder, CO: Rowman and Littlefield, 1999).

[19] Similar to a trade union, CONGO works primarily to protect the rights of NGOs in consultative status with ECOSOC.

[20] On repertoires of collective action, see Sidney Tarrow, *Power in Movement: Social Movements and Contentious Politics,* 2nd ed. (Cambridge, MA: Cambridge Univ. Press, 1998).

[21] See Nitza Berkovitch, "The Emergence and Transformation of the International Women's Movement," in *Constructing World Culture: International Nongovernmental Organizations since 1875,* ed. John Boli and George Thomas, 100–126 (Stanford: Stanford Univ. Press, 1999).

[22] Pratap Chatterjee, "'Fifty Years Is Enough' Launch," *Inter Press Service* (May 17, 1994). Available online.

[23] Ngaire Woods, "The Challenges of Multilateralism and Governance," in *The World Bank: Structure and Policies,* ed. J. Gilbert and D. Vines, 132–56 (Cambridge, MA: Cambridge Univ. Press, 2000).

[24] Wolfgang Reinicke, "The Other World Wide Web: Global Public Policy Networks," *Foreign Policy* 117 (Winter 1999–2000): 44–57.

[25] Ian Smillie, "The World Bank," in *Stakeholders: Government-NGO Partnership for International Development,* ed. Ian Smillie and Henny Helmich (London: Earthscan, 1999), 278.

[26] Ibid., 280.

[27] Nelson, *The World Bank and Non-Governmental Organizations.*

[28] Jonathan Fox and L. David Brown, eds., *The Struggle for Accountability: The World Bank, NGOs, and Grassroots Movements* (Cambridge, MA: Cambridge Univ. Press, 1998).

[29] Lori Udall, "The World Bank and Public Accountability: Has Anything Changed?" in Fox and Brown, *The Struggle for Accountability,* 391–436.

[30] Ibid., 395.

[31] Gilbert and Vines, *The World Bank.*

[32] Reinicke, "The Other World Wide Web."

[33] Gillian Hughes Murphy, "The Seattle WTO Protests: Building a Global Movement," in *Creating a Better World: Interpreting Global Civil Society,* ed. Rupert Taylor, 28–42 (Bloomfield, CT: Kumarian Press, 2004), 29.

[34] Naomi Klein, "Does Protest Need a Vision?" *New Statesman* (July 3, 2000). Available online.

[35] Jessica Mathews, "Power Shift," *Foreign Affairs* 76, no. 1 (1997): 58.

Part II

Case Studies

P art II consists of five sets of case studies that develop issues outlined in Part I. Chapters 6 and 7 examine NGO roles in the provision of development assistance. Ideally, they should be read as a
set. Chapter 6 takes up the issue of NGOs and foreign aid, one of the
most significant arenas of NGO-state interactions in international relations. Here the main issues are: the degree of NGO independence from
official donor programs; official development assistance (ODA) and other
official finance to private voluntary actors; and effectiveness and efficiency of service delivery by NGOs in developing countries. Chapter 7
looks at the issue of NGO accountability using Bangladesh as a case
study. The phenomenal growth of NGOs in both North and South has
brought the issue of accountability to the forefront. Bangladesh is considered a laboratory for the study of NGOs because of the large number
of NGOs there and their dependence on foreign funding. This chapter
argues that accountability is not only a problem that exists between
NNGOs and their governments but is a transnational issue that involves
governments and NGOs in both the developed and developing countries.

Chapter 8 deals with NGO activities in international security. Despite governments' reluctance to acknowledge NGOs' role in defining
and maintaining the bounds of international security, NGOs nevertheless concern themselves with this key issue area in international politics.
The chapter examines the ICBL and complex humanitarian emergencies to assess NGO roles and influence. The ICBL may represent the
high water mark of NGO influence in traditional security politics,
since its effect was to induce states to give up what many military
experts considered to be an important conventional weapon. The ICBL
has also served as the model for NGO attempts to influence international security norms in other policy areas. This chapter explores two
key challenges that face NGOs in complex political emergencies: (1)
development of techniques and networks to respond to circumstances
that differ from traditional relief missions; and (2) appropriate roles and

role limitations for NGOs in international situations dominated by security concerns.

Chapter 9 examines women's rights NGOs at the UN. This chapter gives a brief overview of human rights NGOs in general and then tells the story of NGOs' activism at the UN to promote women's rights. The discussion focuses on UN-sponsored world conferences and the activities of the UN Decade for Women. It also discusses strategies the international women's NGO community has developed to increase its influence at the UN.

Chapter 10 explains NGOs' role in environmental protection. The chapter outlines the growth and characteristics of environmental NGOs and then discusses NGO roles in the process of making and enforcing international environmental policies. This chapter demonstrates how NGOs engage in the roles outlined in Chapter 3.

Chapter 6

NGOs and Foreign Aid

Overview of foreign aid
Donor-NGO cooperation
Issues and problems

Chapter 3 outlined the diversity of NGO activities around the world. Of the many activities they undertake, social and economic development claims a large share of NGOs' time and attention. NGOs have become identified closely with the development process in the nation-states of Africa, Asia, and Latin America. In that capacity they have become involved increasingly in the provision of foreign aid from Northern donor states. In the 1990s they became the preferred vehicle for the provision of official development assistance (ODA), at least at the rhetorical level. This chapter surveys the development of foreign aid since the end of World War II and then describes the place of NGOs in that policy area. It then assesses the twin problems of NGO influence on bilateral donor programs and the degree of NGO independence from official interference. Finally, it considers the question of effectiveness of NGO service delivery in developing countries.

Overview of Postwar Foreign Aid

Foreign aid as practiced today is an innovation that dates from the end of World War II. While states have long provided financial assistance to one another, ODA is qualitatively different from its historical predecessors. ODA involves "the transfer of public resources on concessional terms (with at least a 25 percent grant element), a significant objective of which is to bring about an improvement in economic, political, and social conditions in any foreign country."[1] ODA has tended to be a government-government transfer of grants that carry no expectation of repayment or loans made on terms that are easier than private market rates. It does not include foreign direct investment, trade, export subsidies, or military assistance. Aid is usually transferred bilaterally from a donor government to a recipient government, or multilaterally from donor governments through the World Bank, United Nations development agencies, or the various regional development banks. In addition to some combination of loans and grants, most donor governments have youth voluntary agencies akin to the Peace Corps that provide technical assistance directly to developing country communities (many NGO staff members get their start as volunteers in these corps). ODA remains largely an international financial flow from the developed countries of the OECD to developing countries.

A signal feature of postwar ODA is its systematic and continual provision. Membership in the OECD is a sign that a country belongs to the "rich nations club" of industrial democracies. Membership on the Development Assistance Committee of the OECD requires a country to have a foreign aid program that provides development funds that meet the specifications for ODA stated above. Over time, consultations among bilateral and multilateral donors centered on the OECD have created a set of norms about foreign aid that have enabled increasing aid policy cooperation among OECD donors.[2]

Postwar foreign aid began as reconstruction assistance to Europe in the wake of World War II. By the 1950s, however, the focus shifted to Africa, Asia, and Latin America. Correspondingly, the purpose of aid changed from relief and reconstruction from war to social and economic development for newly independent states. Because these countries' economic levels were substantially below those of the donor countries of Europe and North America, foreign aid through the 1960s focused on agricultural assistance and large-scale projects such as transportation, telecommunications, and hydroelectric power plant construction to develop basic economic infrastructure.

The focus on infrastructure development began to come under scrutiny in the late 1960s. Large-scale projects tended to increase developing-country official debt because they were financed with loans. They also did nothing to alleviate poverty and economic inequality in recipient countries. In fact, infrastructure development tended to benefit economic elites disproportionately. This was due not only to donor preferences but recipient government priorities as well. Thailand is a typical case: government policymakers consistently favored projects in

Bangkok (the national capital) in their development plans, followed by regional urban centers, and donor aid tended to follow suit.[3]

Dissatisfaction in development circles with these consequences led Northern donors in the early 1970s to reorient their aid priorities toward meeting basic human needs of poorer populations in developing countries. Meeting the needs of the "poorest of the poor" entailed reinforcing agricultural extension programs as well as targeting social, educational, and small-scale economic development programs in rural areas and urban slums. This new approach called for planning and implementation very different from that which had been done for large-scale project aid. In particular, it required donors to engage in small-scale projects that were developed in consultation with beneficiaries. In most cases, however, donor offices in the field were located in national capitals, removed from the people the new aid policy was intended to assist. Donors frequently lacked the technical expertise and staff to carry out the kind of decentralized small-scale development work the basic human needs approach envisioned.

In 1973 Congress mandated a "new directions" approach for United States bilateral aid that would focus more directly on the needs of the poorest majority in the Third World. It also mandated that bilateral assistance be implemented by NGOs and other private-sector actors, in the expectation that these organizations could reach the rural poor through means not available to USAID. Other OECD governments voiced similar reasons for expanding their own subsidies to NGOs. CIDA, which began matching grants to Canadian NGOs in 1968, built on an existing system of subsidies to local NPOs by expanding funding to NGOs operating overseas. The new subsidies allowed the Canadian government to avail itself of NGO expertise in countries in which the federal government had no aid presence at all.[4]

The shift in attention to private-sector alternatives to ODA gained further impetus in the 1980s and 1990s. The perceived inability of conventional aid programs to achieve economic growth and solve long-term inequalities in many recipient countries led to "donor fatigue" in many of the OECD countries. Low levels of economic growth in those countries compounded the concern about aid effectiveness. The election of Margaret Thatcher in Britain and Ronald Reagan in the United States heralded a turn to conservative governments across the industrial democracies. Conservative economic policies emphasized the role of the private sector and a return to civil society "voluntarism" as social programs were scaled back. The extent of a country's public commitment to domestic welfare provision is correlated with its commitment to foreign aid,[5] so this conservative concern with privatizing domestic social programs was matched by renewed interest in NGOs as alternatives to traditional government-to-government aid.

The conservative turn in OECD governments was matched at the World Bank and the IMF by a rethinking of the aims and application of foreign aid in general. In the 1980s the two multilaterals took the lead in instigating a shift away from project-based assistance to program lending and policy dialogue. The World Bank approach emphasized assistance for improvement in macroeconomic growth as the solution to persistent poverty and inequality. Assistance was to be given to help developing country governments reorganize their policymaking processes to make them more effective and efficient. These new bilateral and multilateral priorities came to be known as the New Policy Agenda.

Donor fatigue and the New Policy Agenda resulted in flattened OECD aid budgets in the 1980s and 1990s. At the same time, however, aid channeled through NGOs increased at much faster rates than overall ODA budgets. Private and government funds channeled through NGOs increased from US$1 billion in 1970 to just over US$7 billion in 1990. Official funding among developed country NGOs increased from US$200 million to US$2.2 billion during the same period.[6] The 1980s became known in development circles as the "NGO decade."[7]

NGOs appeared to fit the new policy emphases. Many had been in the field for years, some predating the establishment of official aid programs, either as church-based charities or as secular or religious relief organizations. American NGOs had developed on their own at the time the postwar foreign aid program was forming. In the 1950s they refocused their geographic emphasis from Europe to the decolonizing regions of Asia and Africa,[8] at just the time that donor governments were doing the same with their foreign aid programs. Relief organizations had developed even earlier in response to two world wars. As early as the 1920s, for example, Herbert Hoover's American Relief Administration had relied upon the American Friends Service Committee to provide food aid for famine relief in the Soviet Union.[9] NGOs thus had long assistance pedigrees of their own. They knew the communities in which basic human-needs development was supposed to take place much better than aid officials. They could often claim to know local conditions better than central government officials.

NGOs had developed repertoires of small-scale technology transfer and social, educational, and welfare provision. Usually, their stated objective was to reach the poorest of the poor. They valued empowerment and participation by beneficiaries in their own development activities. Missionary work had gone hand in hand with primary education since the late nineteenth century, and many NGOs, secular and religious, continued to value its impact on development. Because they worked at the local level, NGOs were in a position to understand the links between social service provision and community economic development. Typically, their projects were small, so they were already carrying out unofficial basic human-needs development work.

Furthermore, as private organizations NGOs could operate flexibly. They were not constrained by the cumbersome planning, procurement, evaluation, and reporting procedures that official aid agencies typically use. NGOs were capable of identifying projects, purchasing equipment, and carrying out development work much more efficiently than aid bureaucracies and their recipient government counterparts. As private organizations they could also change project specifications and purposes quickly in the face of obstacles or changes in community circumstances.

Finally, NGOs viewed themselves as independent of the political aspects of donor governments' aid policies. Relief organizations valued their neutrality as a prerequisite for effective humanitarian assistance in wartime. Because they were nongovernmental, they could be dissociated from ideological considerations of the Cold War. Governments valued NGO independence because it provided channels for ODA where government-to-government cooperation was not possible. Policy dialogue and structural adjustment programs financed by the World Bank resulted in rising income inequality and the withdrawal of social services as developing-country governments attempted to make the difficult transition to open-market economies with less intrusive government. NGO projects could help alleviate the community-level consequences of the New Policy Agenda.

In the 1990s donors added democracy assistance to their foreign aid repertoires. In the 1980s military governments across the developing world turned power over to civilians. The late 1980s and early 1990s witnessed the collapse of communist governments in Eastern Europe and the Soviet Union. These two trends pushed the problem of how to create democracies to the fore of OECD countries' foreign policies. The problem was especially acute in the wake of the collapse of the Soviet

Union because Russia and the other successor states had practically no history of democratic government. Foreign aid policies tried to address this by supporting the creation of democratic institutions and civil society in these so-called transition states. NGOs appeared especially suited to address these concerns, as they have long advocated grassroots development independent of the state.

NGOs possess the skills to organize private, voluntary associations and to teach those skills to people in societies where such associations have historically been treated with suspicion and, often, persecution. As such, they have come to play a vital role in helping to establish the basic components of parliamentary democracy: political parties capable of participating in competitive elections, interest groups, independent media, and independent labor unions. Russia, for example, "has been host since the early 1990s to a virtual army of nongovernmental organizations . . . from the United States, Britain, Germany, and elsewhere in Europe."[10] In the last ten years donors have channeled funds to NGOs to support these efforts.

Why NGOs and Donors Cooperate

Cooperation between donors and NGOs has potential benefits for each. Private donations from individuals and foundations and a variety of economic activities (publication subscriptions, for example) are two standard income sources for NGOs, but they fluctuate with economic conditions. In the United States, NGO funding from philanthropic organizations began a long decline in the 1970s, just at the time that governments were expressing interest in increasing their subsidies to development NGOs.[11] The possibility of stable funding from public sources has provided a major inducement for NGOs to cooperate with governments. ODA also provides NGOs with resources to scale up their operations by increasing the size and duration of projects or by replicating projects in more places. This has been the case for SNGOs and NNGOs, and the possibility of external official funding has induced the former actively to seek it out.[12]

Aid agencies have benefited in a number of ways as well. For the smaller OECD aid donors, channeling aid through NGOs allows them to expand the scope of their aid operations, especially in countries and sectors where their official aid presence is thin or nonexistent. Second, because NGOs are less constrained by bureaucratic organization, they can deliver services more efficiently than their public counterparts. Third,

---

Box 6–1. Key Concept: NGO Definitions Again

The problem of how to define an NGO is not just an academic one. As donors look to NGOs to carry out official aid programs, they inevitably face the issue of which organizations can be trusted to carry out the public good. In the mid-1990s the European Commission (which oversees the EU's aid program) asked NGOs to define clearly what qualifies as an NGO and what does not. Clearer definitions, the commission reasoned, would promote better cooperation between NGOs and aid agencies as well as streamline aid administration and budgets.

The NGO community was reluctant. Clear definitions, it feared, would restrict the range of organizations that might qualify for aid funding. It might also undermine NGO independence. In 1997 the NGO-EU Liaison Committee, the umbrella organization for NGO interactions with the European Commission, formulated an NGO charter that outlines key features of an NGO without providing a strict definition.*

---

* Ian Smillie and Henry Helmich, *Stakeholders: Government-NGO Partnership for International Development* (London: Earthscan, 1999).

---

public subsidies for small-scale NGO projects provide donors with a mechanism to implement a basic human-needs approach to development, even if the rest of their ODA program is not designed to do so. Fourth, directly subsidizing voluntary-sector projects allows donors to avoid relying on inefficient or incompetent developing-country bureaucracies to reach local levels.[13]

Table 6–1. NGO Grants as a Proportion of All Financial Flows to Aid Recipient Countries, 2003, in US$ million (% of total)

ODA	Other Official Flows	Private Flows	NGO Grants	Total
69,029 (64)	−1,127 (na)	30,481 (28)	10,162 (9.4)	108,545 (100)

Source: World Bank, *2005 World Development Indicators* (Washington, DC: World Bank, 2005), 346.
Note: ODA percentages equal ODA - Other Official Flows. In other words, the table adjusts the contribution of foreign aid by subtracting debt from government funding outside ODA per se.

NNGOs themselves provide financial assistance to their developing-country counterparts. Table 6–1 gives a sense of NGOs' place in international finance to developing countries. The NGO grants category reflects financial resources other than those provided by OECD government subsidies, a figure that represents what amounts to private foreign aid. In 2003, NNGOs also provided an additional US$4.4 billion in grants to higher-income developing countries that do not qualify for official development assistance, about 2 percent of total financial flows to that group.[14] While the total amount of private NGO funding for development is a small portion of total financial flows to Asia, Africa, Latin America, and Eastern Europe, this increment represents an enhancement of official foreign aid levels.

NGOs do more than supplement declining ODA budgets. Interaction with NGOs also provides aid agencies with outside perspectives on development issues. Joseph Wheeler, former chairman of the OECD Development Assistance Committee, acknowledged the educational effect of NGOs on official programs:

> The voluntary sector has frequently articulated new policy insights reflecting changes that have been taking place in our societies. Ask an aid administrator why he or she has increased the emphasis on environmental concerns—or women in development, or population. Ask where the pressure comes from for more emphasis on reaching the poor, or on health and education. The answer is that these are concerns of our populations expressed through our political processes and usually pointed up by what we call our non-governmental organizations.[15]

Aid agencies, then, can learn about development approaches that challenge them to reconsider the character and structure of their own programs.

Modes of NGO-Donor Interaction

Vernon Ruttan suggests three modes of interaction between foreign aid donor agencies and NGOs.[16] In one mode NGOs operate as donors' clients. In this capacity NGOs carry out development projects on behalf of donors, using donor funds. NGO work is largely project based, and relations between donor and voluntary organization are those of contractor and subcontractor. It is safe to say that donor governments see this mode of interaction as the most convenient. A widespread alternative to this is co-financing, in which official funds supplement private funds to support NGO projects. Comparative evidence from OECD countries reveals that co-financing is the most common kind of donor-NGO interaction.[17]

In a second mode NGOs operate as donors' constituents. Official aid agencies benefit from NGO support for foreign aid. Official funding for NGO development work has created a constituency that can be called upon to support aid programs in an era of donor fatigue and competition for scarce public resources. Public education efforts pointing out the continued relevance of foreign aid, and lobbying during budgetary processes, are NGO repertoires valued by bilateral and multilateral agencies alike.[18] In fact, some European and Canadian public subsidies have been earmarked specifically to support voluntary-sector public education on behalf of foreign aid and development. For NGOs, the benefits of this lobbying effort have accrued in the form of continued subsidies.

NGOs' constituency role, however, also involves costs to donors. NGOs as constituents are interested in the substance of donor aid policy, not simply its implementation. NGO monitoring of the World Bank–led Narmada Dam project, described in Chapter 5, is an example. Advocacy and monitoring roles often lead NGOs to seek changes in donor policies. To a greater or lesser extent, depending on the country or international organization, donors have accommodated this advisory role. In Japan and many European countries, however, NGO advisory roles and capabilities remain weak.

Generally speaking, NGOs seek to influence donor policies at two levels. The first is at the project level, in which NGOs attempt to halt or change the conditions of a particular project. The Narmada Dam project involved NGOs in this capacity. In this case NGOs lobbied not only the World Bank but other bilateral donors that had agreed to support specific aspects of the overall project. Indian and Japanese NGOs teamed up to lobby the government of Japan to discontinue supporting loan aid to the project. As a result, Japan's Overseas Economic Cooperation Fund announced it would withdraw funding from its component of the overall dam development program.[19]

The second level of influence involves overall donor policy. Chapter 5 showed that NGOs have been critical of World Bank program lending because it overlooks the broader social consequences of macroeconomic reforms. NGOs have engaged the World Bank on precisely those issues. In turn, the bank has invited selected NGOs to participate in project and program reviews. To a certain extent, bilateral donors also promote NGO dialogue on aid policy. NGO representatives sit on the boards of directors of the Danish International Development Agency and the Swedish International Development Agency. USAID maintains an advisory board that includes NGO representatives (see Box 6–2).

The two levels of interaction are related. Often an NGO will start by accepting donor funding to carry out a specific project. This leads to an internal debate within the NGO about donor policies and development priorities, which in turn induces the NGO to engage the donor in a broader discussion about the development assumptions that underlie the project. World Vision International's relationship with the World Bank is typical. The NGO was interested in expanding its development work in Uganda. In 1990 it participated in the World Bank's Programme for the Alleviation of Poverty and the Social Costs of Adjustment in that country. The experience led to a top-level debate within World Vision

---

Box 6–2. The Advisory Committee on Voluntary Foreign Aid (ACVFA)

NGO policy advice to donor agencies does not always involve conflict. ACVFA is a good example of longstanding policy discussion between government and voluntary development organizations. It was established by presidential decree at the end of World War II and today is part of USAID. ACVFA has twenty-four members drawn from academia, the business sector, and NGOs. ACVFA is charged with advising USAID on current issues of development and donor-NGO cooperation. Meetings are held periodically, and reports are made available to the public. For example, ACVFA met in February 2002 to discuss issues of reconstruction and relief aid for Afghanistan. USAID also views the committee as a means of increasing public awareness about foreign aid.[*]

[*] For more information about ACVFA, see the USAID website.

International about the wisdom and effects of the World Bank's structural adjustment lending and whether the NGO should continue its participation. The debate resulted in an internal policy designed to guide future relations with the World Bank and to use in discussions with the bank about its lending policies. World Vision has also worked to reform specific aspects of the bank's policies that affect NGOs, including issues of procurement and project implementation.[20]

Accommodating NGO input involves tradeoffs for donors. On the one hand, such policy advice provides perspectives not readily aired in house. One study has found that NGO input on World Bank policies is especially effective when activists find allies within the bank who share their views.[21] This arguably makes multilateral donors more sensitive to policy impacts. On the other hand, it can be argued that including NGOs and other non-state actors in multilateral bank policymaking dilutes those institutions' primary objective of supporting macroeconomic growth and development. The result is "mission creep," in which the World Bank takes on additional tasks that are beyond its capacity to administer effectively.[22] Agreement to consult with some NGOs, moreover, has not prevented continual and vociferous criticism of bank policies by other NGOs.

In a third mode of influence, donors and NGOs have organizations and objectives that differ from one another. A key difference between NGOs and aid donors involves the notion of agency: each has different principals to which it is accountable. Chapter 7 explores this problem in some detail. Suffice it to say here that NGOs see themselves as accountable to their members, their contributors, and the people who benefit from their development work. Any of these may be concerned with one issue or region. Of course, NGOs are also accountable to donors when they receive aid funding, but aid agencies are but one actor to which NGOs feel responsible. Aid agencies are accountable to their government's legislatures and to the citizens represented by them. Aid, moreover, is a foreign policy tool. It is frequently used to achieve a multitude of purposes, meaning more possible principals to which an agency is responsible.

Issues in NGO-Donor Cooperation

Despite the promise and obvious benefits of NGO-donor interaction, long-term issues continue to complicate the relationship. Of these, three stand out: the consequences for NGOs of dependence on donor funding, the related problem of NGO influence on donor programs, and concerns about the effectiveness of NGO development projects themselves.

Dependence on Donor Funding

Seen from the NGO perspective, dependence is the most problematic of the issues that potentially beset the relationship between aid donors and NGOs. The latter value their independence, some to the point that any kind of constructive interaction with government becomes difficult. NGO dependence on aid donors takes a number of forms.

Dependence on donor funding most readily comes to mind. A number of significant US NGOs have become heavily reliant on public funding. USAID and other official funding amounts to 40 percent to 60 percent of the annual incomes of CARE, CRS, Save the Children, and World Vision.[23] CARE is the largest NGO in the world, so this dependence is not insignificant. Compared to the United States, European and Canadian NGOs have encountered less difficulty with the dependency problem because overall they tend to rely on government subsidies less.[24] Nevertheless, NGOs that rely on government subsidies for all or most of their income are not rare and can be found in almost any country.

Government subsidies present NGOs with a number of dilemmas. Subsidies typically carry requirements that NGOs account for the funding provided. Reporting and evaluation reduce flexibility. Scaling up to take advantage of donor funding means developing a bureaucracy. Moreover, donor funding comes with conditions attached. These include not only political conditions (discussed below) but requirements about reporting, competitive bidding for contracts, and application for official funding. NGOs, especially SNGOs, find these requirements cumbersome.[25] Slow disbursement of official funds is especially troubling for voluntary organizations acting in the field; delays can vitally affect project implementation.[26]

Dependence on donor funding raises concerns about NGO independence from government control. This is particularly the case in the United States for two reasons. First, compared to most other OECD donors, US government foreign policy during the Cold War was greatly informed by anticommunist concerns. That led to restrictions on countries in which American NGOs could operate if they received USAID funds. NGOs

---

Box 6–3. Dilemmas of Public Funding

To accept government funds or to refuse them and maintain independence—this is a dilemma that confronts the NGO community. NGOs are not of one mind about the issue. Grameen Bank founder Muhammad Yunus, for example, is ambivalent about accepting donor funding to support Grameen Bank operations. For Yunus, policy conditions attached to donor funding and the inefficiencies of donor organization are serious constraints on Grameen's independence and operating style.

CANHELP Thailand's founder, Harry Wray, is less concerned about the issue. Since 1997 his organization has received grants from the Japan Ministry of Posts and Telecommunications' Volunteer Savings Scheme (postal savings subscribers earmark a portion of their interest payments for the scheme, the proceeds from which are provided to NGOs working overseas). CANHELP Thailand's 2001 grant of just over two million yen (about US$200,000) was among the largest grants made that year. In a 1998 interview Wray praised the program and lamented that the ministry's decision to lower postal savings interest rates would limit the pool of funds available for worthy projects. For a small, all-volunteer NGO like his, government funding is a welcome source of financial stability.

---

were continually concerned about not becoming too closely associated with official foreign policy.[27]

Many voluntary organizations realize that carrying out donor projects entails accepting the political and social agendas that go with them. American NGOs have found that cooperation with US government agencies means resisting pressure to modify their programs. At USAID's behest, NGOs have supported repressive policies in nondemocratic countries. In the mid-1970s, for example, CRS participated in a USAID food program in Chile that used PL 480 (Public Law 480, passed in 1954, also called the Food for Peace Program) food aid as partial payment for labor in a government-sponsored employment scheme. The program exploited workers by substituting US food aid for minimum-wage payments and by employing day laborers with no job security or benefits in place of full-time public employees. "In the perspective of government critics in Chile, [the program] has not been a service to the poor, but one more repressive instrument of the regime being used against them."[28] For this reason many NGOs do not accept public funding at all, preferring to rely on private resources even at the expense of foregoing opportunities.

The current Iraq war provides a contemporary illustration of the problem. NGOs geared up to provide relief for what was expected to be sizable refugee flows into neighboring countries (which largely failed to occur) and then to assist in the reconstruction of postwar Iraq. NGOs faced dilemmas both during the war and in its aftermath. Many NGOs opposed the war itself. Oxfam UK, for example, announced that it would not accept aid funds for Iraq from the British government. It preferred to rely on private donations as a way to distance itself from a government policy it opposed. Japan Platform, the largest of that country's relief NGOs, was forced to withdraw its staff from refugee camps in Jordan in the early summer when Japanese foreign ministry aid dried up.

US NGOs faced a different dilemma once the war had ended. In the summer of 2003 the US military found itself facing low-level military resistance from Iraqi opponents and declining support for the war effort. USAID announced that it wanted NGOs to seek official approval before meeting with media organizations. It also wanted NGOs that received official aid to publicize the fact that they did in order to demonstrate a link between the NGOs and American foreign policy in Iraq. USAID threatened to withdraw funding from NGOs that refused to do so. Some NGOs agreed to comply. Mercy Corps and Save the Children asked USAID to renegotiate their contracts to eliminate the conditions. Nevertheless, in an announcement in early July that it was launching a Community Action Program to aid communities in southern Iraq, Mercy Corps was careful to state that its US$14 million project was being funded by USAID.[29]

Accepting foreign aid funding also means accepting donors' sectoral and geographic priorities. The United States provides a good example of the former. PL 480 aid—foreign assistance in the form of surplus food produced in the United States—has now become a stock item in that country's disaster and humanitarian assistance program. By extension, it has become an important component of NGO subsidies. CARE and other large NGOs have become the conduits for PL 480 surplus-food distribution. In the East African crises of the 1980s and early 1990s, critics argued that food aid was being distributed even in areas where food shortages did not exist.[30] More broadly, Smith argues that the availability of food aid to US NGOs in the early postwar period induced them to retain a relief orientation long after Canadian and European NGOs had developed long-term development perspectives.[31] In short, the type of subsidy available to NGOs has an effect on the kind of work they are likely to carry out simply because the availability of public subsidies is a hard inducement to turn down.

Nigeria provides an example of the consequences of geographic bias in ODA programs. Amina Mama suggests that the absence of democratic government there has made it unattractive to Northern donors. She notes, "Despite its enormous economic potential and rich human resources, Nigeria has not been a popular target for international donors who support non-governmental activity elsewhere in Africa."[32] Consequently, NGOs there have limited financial resources and do not play a major role in national development.

Dependence on donor funding confronts NGOs with other dilemmas. Repeated interaction between donor agencies and NGOs tends to change the latter's organizational character. NGOs that start out as flexible, low-cost, voluntary organizations working at the grassroots level and committed to the development of the communities they serve become over time more like the agencies that fund them. Head offices find themselves devoted to fund raising and donor relations; their measure of performance becomes the ability to raise money and account for it, and they increasingly are divorced from consideration of the welfare of target groups.[33] As NGOs accommodate themselves to the conditions of donor funding, moreover, they take on not only the organizational color of official aid agencies but the official aid mentality as well.[34] If anything, the flow of personnel between aid agencies and development NGOs (many NGO staff begin their development careers as volunteers in the Peace Corps and similar agencies elsewhere) tends to reinforce this common perspective. While common views can substantially enhance donor-NGO cooperation, that cooperation is often conducted on donor terms.

Official funding also creates competition among NGOs. The promise of stable funding has pitted NNGOs against one another as they strive for the promise of stable external funding. Subsidies also foster competition as NGOs attempt to reconfigure their development profiles to qualify for donor funding at the expense of previous work. Furthermore, donors have increasingly bypassed NNGOs to provide aid directly to SNGOs.[35] Of course, many NNGOs themselves have withdrawn from direct implementation of projects in the Third World. They have come to understand that doing so allows SNGOs to rely on local

talent and resources and helps ensure that projects will continue to provide communities with benefits long after NNGO support is withdrawn.
Others, however, fear that direct donor-SNGO contact will cut them
out of the aid process and the public funding on which they depend.[36]

Finally, government subsidies are problematic because dependence is
asymmetrical; NGOs are a lot more dependent on donor funding than
donors are on them. Table 6–2 gives a sampling of ODA subsidies to
NGOs in eleven of the top OECD countries over the last two decades.

Note first that the United States is an outlier among the OECD members. Its level of support for NGOs is nowhere matched among the other
donors. Japan and France, two of the top five bilateral aid donors for the
last thirty years, provide very small NGO subsidies compared to their
overall aid budgets. When we consider that Japan's aid budget was the
largest among the OECD countries during the 1990s, about 50 percent
higher than the United States' until 2001, the lack of NGO presence in
Japan's program is striking. Overall, the major OECD donors support
their NGOs at rates closer on average to the Japanese than the US level
of commitment. The 1997 and 2000 data also suggest that European
donors have achieved 1980s levels of US commitment only recently.

A comparison of the United States and Japan (the two top bilateral
aid donors) reveals the differing government approaches to NGOs that
lie behind the numbers. The US government has developed a
longstanding aid relationship with NGOs. This is consistent with a long
history of community voluntarism and the limited size of the federal
government when compared to other industrial democracies. It also reflects the early development of NGOs. The foreign aid program had
contact with voluntary organizations in the 1950s. As early as 1961 Senator Hubert Humphrey successfully added wording to the annual Foreign Assistance Act that called on USAID to work with private-sector
organizations, including NGOs. The "new directions" legislation discussed above reinforced that policy. In 1981 the Congress mandated
that at least 13.5 percent of the government budget for specified aid
activities be allocated to NGOs. In recent years funds channeled though
NGOs have accounted for as much as 30 percent or more of total bilateral aid.

Compared to other developed countries, and even some developing
countries, on the other hand, Japanese NGOs appear few in number. A
1990 foreign ministry study estimated their numbers at approximately
three hundred, although that figure is clearly too low. The 1994 JANIC

Table 6–2. NGOs and Foreign Aid Budgets: NGO Subsidies as a Proportion of Selected OECD Aid Budgets, 1983–1986, 1997, 2000

Country*	NGO/ODA, 1983–1986	NGO/ODA, 1997	NGO/ODA, 2000
Japan	1.9	2.4	1.7
United States	11.1	37.0	43.4
France	0.3	na	na
Germany**	6.5	16.3	6.4
United Kingdom	1.3	9.2	14.1
Netherlands	7.0	na	8.8
Italy	1.9	3.2	1.5
Canada	10.8	8.6	8.1
Sweden	4.6	1.6	4.3
Switzerland	19.4	6.6	na
Belgium	6.6	5.2	10.3
Average	6.5	10	10.9

Source: UNDP, *Human Development Report, 1993* (Oxford: Oxford Univ. Press, 1993), 89; Gaimusho, *Waga Kuni no Seifu Kaihatsu Enjo* (Tokyo: Keizai Kyoryoku Suishinkyoku, 1999), 208; idem (2000), 46.

* Country ranking is by total aid budget, 2000.

** West Germany in 1986.

directory lists 186. Moreover, Japanese NGOs are relative latecomers to the scene. Few indigenous NGOs are more than twenty years old. The largest NGOs tend to be of three types: branches of INGOs, nonprofit foundations *(zaidan hojin)* with institutional ties to the government, and religious organizations.

The Japanese government did not begin to notice NGOs officially until the late 1980s. The Ministry of Foreign Affairs and the Ministry of Posts and Telecommunications launched separate NGO subsidy schemes in 1989 and 1990, respectively. Their impact remains limited within the overall aid program; the impact of NGOs continues to focus mostly on specific projects. Agenda setting, in which civic groups attempt to alter official policy, appears to be beyond Japanese NGOs' capabilities at this point.[37] The aid bureaucracy sees NGOs in instrumental terms, as conduits for promoting official views of foreign aid rather than partners in development. Recent interactions suggest that typical contacts involve application for subsidies by NGOs; while a few NGOs have recently been included in the planning stages of specific projects, formal interactions appear to consist of voluntary organizations attending meetings arranged by bureaucrats. In short, the institutional links between voluntary and public development agencies are still shallow and largely defined by official needs.

Many of the problems outlined above also apply to interactions among NGOs. SNGOs often find their Northern counterparts to be overly bureaucratic and business oriented in their development project procedures. The largest appear to have internalized the ODA mentality that they previously opposed.[38] Perera found this to be the case with interactions between Sardovaya Sharmadana, one of Sri Lanka's largest NGOs, and NNGOs. Sardovaya Sharmadana's relationship with its northern counterparts is interesting in part because of its complexity; the relationship involves several bilateral aid agencies, four UN agencies, and more than a dozen NGOs. This collection of donors agreed to form a consortium in 1985. Donors liked the idea because it would help them plan and implement financing; Sardovaya Sharmadana personnel supported the proposal because they anticipated that a consortium would help the organization expand its activities.

Perera argues that the new arrangement amplified the differences between a voluntary organization dedicated to community development from the bottom up and developed-country donors that insisted on formal appraisal and reporting procedures from the top down. Donors that had previously been partners in development with Sardovaya Sharmadana became its patrons. Sardovaya headquarters staff spent critical time and resources managing donor reporting requirements and short-term visits from Northern counterparts. Most telling, budgeting became less a donor-SNGO consultation and more of a series of decisions taken by donor headquarters. A unilateral budget reduction by the Dutch NGO NOVIB in 1994 "plunged Sardovaya Sharmadana into a financial crisis."[39] Over time, an SNGO that had articulated its own development vision and capacity was transformed into a subcontractor for NNGOs and ODA agencies.

NGO Influence on Donor Programs

How much impact do NGOs have on donor agencies and aid policies? Journalistic accounts tend to paint a positive picture of NGO influence. Others are not so sure. One article wonders aloud whether NGOs have become no more than "ladles in the global soup kitchen,"[40] instruments to be used to provide short-term assistance instead of independent agents of long-term economic and social development. A study by Brown and Fox of four project-level interactions and four program-level interactions between NGOs and the World Bank found mixed results. Attempts by the NGOs to block objectionable projects tended to succeed. And national governments were usually as committed to going ahead with projects as the World Bank was. A variety of Keck and Sikkink's boomerang strategy applies to the project cases: NGO pressure on the World Bank induced it to withdraw funding from projects that national governments were committed to and which would have gone ahead if NGOs had appealed only to those governments.[41]

At the program level Brown and Fox's findings suggest that rather than accepting NGO consultations in principle, the World Bank reacted to specific advocacy campaigns by inviting NGOs to consult in some capacity. NGO attempts to get basic program information from the World Bank have been hallmarks of these campaigns. By most accounts the IMF is even less willing to divulge information. Similarly, Paul Nelson argues that NGO influence is focused on a few policy areas, which means they have little or no leverage in other areas. NGO influence over multilateral assistance policy, moreover, tends to be concentrated in NNGOs because they have easier access to IGO headquarters. How much SNGOs influence multilateral policy remains problematic, even though such organizations represent coalitions in countries directly affected by assistance policies.[42]

The Effectiveness of NGO Development Projects

Do NGO projects work? That is hard to determine, because NGOs often do not carry out formal evaluations of their work. Even when they do, the reports tend to focus on successes. Independent evaluations are also infrequent, although donor conditions now typically require NGOs to carry out post-project reports. The most widely cited external NGO evaluation (by Judith Tendler for USAID in 1982) is now almost twenty-five years old. Her report found that NGO projects were not as successful as their public images. NGOs were not as good at reaching the poorest sectors of society as they claimed. Nor were they as democratic as thought; decision making was often centralized in the NNGO's headquarters, meaning that recipients had less control over projects than NGO claims suggested. Other assessments since then have identified similar problems.[43] In addition, evaluations note that while NGOs' small size makes them more flexible than donor agencies, the price is limited impact on local communities.

NGO closeness to their communities, combined with limited formal intelligence capabilities, means that they are sometimes unaware of the broader political and social realities that affect the people they try to help. Andrew Natsios, who has directed World Vision and USAID, argues that American NGOs do not understand the political and social contexts in which they carry out development work as well as their European counterparts do.[44] NGO food aid and humanitarian assistance has been criticized for its short-sighted emphasis on immediate relief; NGOs often fail to realize that the aid they provide maintains the status quo that led to conflict in the first place and can be exploited by warring factions intent on controlling local people through famine creation and humanitarian aid distribution.

Summary

NGOs are now a permanent fixture in the international aid system. Their input ranges from project implementation to support of other civil society organizations (CSOs) to advice about official development policies. It is safe to say that they play an indispensable role in the provision of official development assistance. That is likely to remain the case as long as the New Policy Agenda gives priority to private-sector and voluntary-sector development initiative. However, NGOs are not a "magic bullet"; by themselves they cannot conquer the obstacles to third-world development. Nor can they change the course of aid policies by themselves. Access to foreign aid provides opportunities for and constraints on NGO activities. Donor priorities, moreover, are not always consistent with those of NGOs. The community of voluntary development organizations, therefore, remains ambivalent about foreign aid even as its members have become an integral part of it.

Discussion Questions

1. What benefits do NGOs derive from participating in foreign aid? What costs do they incur? Do the benefits outweigh the disadvantages?
2. Should foreign aid remain largely a government-to-government transfer, or should NGOs be more actively involved in foreign aid programs? What disadvantages might governments perceive if they transfer more aid responsibility to NGOs?

Suggested Further Reading

Paula Hoy, *Players and Issues in International Aid* (West Hartford, CT: Kumarian Press, 1998); and Ian Smillie and Henny Helmich, eds., *Stakeholders: Government-NGO Partnerships for International Development* (London: Earthscan, 1999).

Notes

[1] Carol Lancaster, *Transforming Foreign Aid: United States Assistance in the 21st Century* (Washington, DC: Institute for International Economics, 2000), 9.

[2] Robert Wood, *From Marshall Plan to Debt Crisis* (Berkeley and Los Angeles: Univ. of California Press, 1986).

[3] David Potter, *Japan's Foreign Aid to Thailand and the Philippines* (New York: St. Martin's Press, 1996).

⁴ Brian Smith, *More than Altruism: The Politics of Private Foreign Aid* (Princeton, NJ: Princeton Univ. Press, 1990).

⁵ Alain Noel and Jean Philippe Therien, "From Domestic to International Justice: The Welfare State and Foreign Aid," *International Organization* 49, no. 3 (1995): 523–53.

⁶ United Nations Development Program, *Human Development Report, 1993* (New York: Oxford Univ. Press, 1993), 888.

⁷ Terje Tvedt, *Angels of Mercy or Development Diplomats? NGOs and Foreign Aid* (Trenton, NJ: Africa World Press, 1998).

⁸ Landrum Bolling with Craig Smith, *Private Foreign Aid: U.S. Philanthropy for Relief and Development* (Boulder, CO: Westview Press, 1982).

⁹ Cathal Nolan, *Principled Diplomacy: Security and Rights in U.S. Foreign Policy* (Westport, CT: Greenwood Press, 1993).

¹⁰ Sarah Mendelson, "Democracy Assistance and Political Transition in Russia: Between Success and Failure," *International Security* 25, no. 4 (2001): 68.

¹¹ Smith, *More than Altruism.*

¹² Carrie Meyer, "Opportunism and NGOs: Entrepreneurship and Green North-South Transfers," *World Development* 23, no. 8 (1995): 1277–89.

¹³ Smith, *More than Altruism.*

¹⁴ World Bank, *2005 World Development Indicators* (Washington, DC: World Bank, 2005), 346.

¹⁵ Joseph Wheeler, cited in Seamus Cleary, "The World Bank and NGOs," in *"The Conscience of the World": The Influence of Non-governmental Organizations in the U.N. System,* ed. Peter Willetts, 63–97 (London: Hurst and Company, 1996), 68.

¹⁶ Vernon Ruttan, *United States Development Assistance Policy* (Baltimore: Johns Hopkins Univ. Press, 1996).

¹⁷ Ian Smillie and Henny Helmich, *Stakeholders: Government-NGO Partnership for International Development* (London: Earthscan, 1999).

¹⁸ World Bank, *Annual Report* (Washington, DC: International Bank for Reconstruction and Development, 1993); Ruttan, *United States Development Assistance Policy.*

¹⁹ David Potter, "Assessing Japan's Environmental Aid Policy," *Pacific Affairs* 67, no. 2 (1994): 200–215.

²⁰ Steve Commins, "World Vision International and Donors: Too Close for Comfort?" in *NGOs, States and Donors: Too Close for Comfort?* ed. David Hulme and Michael Edwards, 140–55 (London: St. Martin's Press, 1997).

²¹ Jonathan Fox and David Brown, eds., *The Struggle for Accountability: The World Bank, NGOs, and Grassroots Movements* (Cambridge, MA: MIT Press, 1998).

²² Jessica Einhorn, "The World Bank's Mission Creep," *Foreign Affairs* 80, no. 5 (September-October 2001): 22–35.

²³ Shephard Foreman and Abby Stoddard, "International Assistance," in *The State of Nonprofit America,* ed. Lester Salamon (Washington, DC: Brookings Institute, 2002), 251.

²⁴ Smith, *More than Altruism.*

²⁵ Ibid.; Commins, "World Vision International and Donors."

²⁶ Tony Waters, *Bureaucratizing the Good Samaritan* (Boulder, CO: Westview Press, 2001).

²⁷ Smith, *More than Altruism.*

²⁸ Ibid., 147.

²⁹ Mercy Corps, "Mercy Corps Is Launching a Program to Assist Approximately One Million People Living in 50 Communities in Iraq," *InterAction-Media* (July 10, 2003). Available online.

³⁰ Michael Maren, *The Road to Hell: The Ravaging Effects of Foreign Aid and International Charity* (New York: The Free Press, 1997).

³¹ Smith, *More than Altruism.*

³² Amina Mama, "Strengthening Civil Society: Participatory Action Research in a Militarized State," in *Development, NGOs, and Civil Society,* ed. Deborah Eade, 175–89 (London: Oxfam, 2000), 177.

³³ See Commins, "World Vision International and Donors"; Maren, *The Road to Hell.*

³⁴ Smith, *More than Altruism.*

³⁵ Anthony Bebbington and Roger Riddell, "Heavy Hands, Hidden Hands, Holding Hands? Donors, Intermediary NGOs, and Civil Society Organizations," in Hulme and Edwards, *NGOs, States, and Donors,* 107–27.

³⁶ Paula Hoy, *Players and Issues in International Aid* (West Hartford, CT: Kumarian Press, 1998).

³⁷ David M. Potter, "NGOs and Japan's Role in Post Cold War Asia," in *Weaving a New Tapestry: Asia in the Post-Cold War World,* ed. William Head and Edward Clausen, 189–208 (Boulder, CO: Praeger, 1999).

³⁸ Hoy, *Players and Issues in International Aid.*

³⁹ Jehan Perera, "In Unequal Dialogue with Donors: The Experience of the Sarvodaya Shramadana Movement," in Hulme and Edwards, *NGOs, States and Donors,* 156–67.

⁴⁰ Commins, "World Vision International and Donors."

⁴¹ Fox and Brown, *The Struggle for Accountability.*

⁴² Paul Nelson, "Information, Location, and Legitimacy: The Changing Basis of Civil Society Involvement in International Economic Policy," in *Global Citizen Action,* ed. Michael Edwards and John Gaventa, 59–72 (Boulder, CO: Lynne Rienner, 2001).

⁴³ Ruttan, *United States Development Assistance Policy;* Hoy, *Players and Issues in International Aid;* and Cleary, "The World Bank and NGOs."

⁴⁴ Andrew Natsios, *U.S. Foreign Policy and the Four Horsemen of the Apocalypse: Humanitarian Relief in Complex Emergencies* (Boulder, CO: Praeger, 1997).

Chapter 7

NGOs and Transnational Accountability in Bangladesh

NGO accountability
Bangladesh NGOs
Multiple stakeholders
Multiple accountabilities

This chapter may seem out of place in a book about international relations. This is because of the way political scientists look at the topic. *Accountability* is not a widely used term in this field of inquiry. In political science accountability is usually seen as a concern of public administration and domestic government. For state-centered theories of international politics, in particular, the idea seems misplaced; states act on behalf of the national interest or the coalition of powerful domestic groups that claims to represent it. In short, scholars in this field do not take accountability seriously because they tend not to think about it across national boundaries.

We begin with the premise that they should. Development specialists do, with good reason. They understand that seemingly neutral efforts to improve agricultural practices or rural education are political; those activities have real potential to change relationships of power in another society, even if that is not their primary intent. In some cases, of course, changing who has power is precisely the goal of economic and social development.

Thinking in terms of transnational politics forces one to confront the issue of accountability. As we saw in the last chapter, much development activity is financed by aid agencies in the developed countries. Foreign aid and the problems and issues related to development in Africa, Asia, and Latin America are therefore parts of international politics. The work of international donors, development banks, and NNGOs all transcend national boundaries and interests and therefore raise issues that cut across national boundaries. NGO accountability is one such issue that political scientists need to explore. Despite the rarity of the term *accountability* in conventional international relations studies, NGO accountability is becoming a transnational problem. It has become an important concept in development studies in recent years as scholars and practitioners struggle to identify in whose behalf economic and social development is supposed to happen.

It is therefore important to explore the different dimensions of NGO accountability. By exploring this issue in the context of Bangladesh, we hope to give readers some glimpse of what may be happening in other developing countries. The discussion first takes up the question of NGO accountability. Then, it examines Bangladesh as a case study, using several major Bangladeshi NGOs. This discussion addresses the problems of multiple stakeholders and accountability. We finish with a survey on how NGOs in the field see the issue.

NGO Accountability

Most scholars use the term *accountability* to mean responsibility for an organization's actions. Barbara Romzek and M. Dubnick, for example, state that public-sector accountability "involves the means by which public agencies and their workers manage the diverse expectations generated within and outside the organization."[1] Applying this definition to the NGO sector makes one aware that organizations at some point are responsible to a variety of *stakeholders*, including members, executive boards, government, and people and agencies affected by the organization's actions. We believe this definition provides a comprehensive and practical approach to understand NGO accountability.

Assuming that NGOs should take accountability seriously, to whom are they accountable? Adil Najam includes three objects of NGO accountability: patrons, clients, and the NGO itself.[2] Patrons include donors such as foundations, aid agencies, and the government. Clients include direct beneficiaries, the government, and the community at large. The NGO as an organization includes its stated mission, staff, members, and allied NGOs.

The meteoric growth of NGOs in the North and the South has brought NGO accountability to the forefront of critical issues. Concerns about whether NGOs are accountable abound in the relevant literature. NGO-patron accountability tends to be overwhelmingly couched in terms of financial and policy control, which leaves out the question of NGOs' responsibility to their clients. Yet, accountability to clients should be a major emphasis since most NGOs' missions emphasize serving the community in various ways. However, most communities lack mechanisms for holding NGOs accountable, especially poor communities. Furthermore, despite claims that nongovernmental development builds civil society by providing citizens with opportunities for participation, in most cases such participation has been nothing more than communicating the NGOs' goals and activities to the community. Delegation, an effective component of participation in which citizens are asked to decide how projects or programs are to be carried out, is not common.[3]

Concerns are raised about NGOs' internal accountability too, which includes responsibility to their mission, staff, partners, and the broader NGO community. Several scholars suggest that NGOs are often willing to change their own goals about participation and community development in order to fulfill the product demanded by donors.[4] Mechanisms to ensure responsibilities to partners, staff, and other NGOs remain weak.

NGOs have multiple stakeholders, which means they are responsible to different actors; the fact that some of these stakeholders are transnational actors complicates the picture. As an example, in many countries government occupies the status of a patron through its support of the NGO sector in the form of tax benefits, licensing, accreditation, and other advantages. In this relationship the goals that NGOs pursue (often shaped by external and international donors) and the legitimacy of those goals become important components of the accountability issue.

Foreign aid and NGO assistance involve transferring financial and technical knowledge across national boundaries. As Brian Smith explains:

> There is a clear hierarchy in the transnational nonprofit aid network: NPOs in the North Atlantic countries raise private and public funds for development projects overseas. National and regional NPOs in developing countries receive these funds from abroad and disperse them on a project-by-project basis. Finally, local NPOs in these same societies run the actual projects at the grassroots level among the poor.[5]

The recipients of this assistance are typically far removed from the sources of the aid. Moreover, NGO aid (and ODA that is distributed through them) usually bypasses government agencies in favor of direct support of citizen development efforts. Not only can this undermine state authority, but it also creates a situation in which the sources to which recipients are accountable are outside of the country where the development is supposed to take place. Many scholars identify NGO accountability as a major source of this sector's vulnerability.

Bangladesh as a Case Study

We focus on Bangladesh for four reasons. First, Bangladesh is a developing country with some of the world's largest indigenous development NGOs. These include internationally acclaimed domestic NGOs, such as Grameen Bank and BRAC, whose success stories are widely studied. Case studies frequently appear as examples of development success. Indeed, the Grameen Bank and other NGOs, rather than the state, produce the programs that are widely praised as models to be replicated.[6] The UN's report "Human Development in South Asia" argues that a vibrant civil society is Bangladesh's greatest asset and refers to the activities of specific NGOs such as BRAC, Proshika, Rangpur Dinajpur Rural Services, and the Grameen Bank as its key constituents.[7]

Second, the growth of NGOs in Bangladesh is phenomenal, reflecting a trend in the developing countries. According to a 2006 World Bank report, there are approximately 45,000 NGOs registered with the Ministry of Social Welfare. As of 2004, the NGO Affairs Bureau had registered 1,882 NGOs as potential recipients of foreign funds.[8] The NGO Affairs Bureau is the government monitoring agency. The majority of these are either small clubs or cultural groups, but around two thousand NGOs are reported to be involved directly in development activities. Over 90 percent of villages had at least one NGO in 2000.[9] The sheer number of NGOs in Bangladesh makes it a good site to explore the issue of accountability.

Third, NGOs in Bangladesh are almost totally dependent on foreign financing. As discussed in Chapter 2, foreign funding has spurred the meteoric growth of SNGOs, and Bangladesh is no exception. The 2006 World Bank report estimates that aid to NGOs in Bangladesh increased from an annual average of US$233 million in the period from 1990 to 1995 to an average of US$343 million in the period from 1996 to 2005.[10]

All of the indigenous NGOs introduced later in this chapter have a number of aid agencies and NNGOs as financial patrons. Heavy reliance on foreign funds, a common feature among SNGOs, raises several critical issues, the most important of which is accountability. As Syed M. Hashemi argues:

> High level of donor funding has had two major consequences. First, NGOs have become donor dependent, not merely in terms of funding that is essential to their existence but also

---

Box 7–1. Overview of Bangladesh

Population: 144,319,628 estimated (2005)
Per capita GDP (Purchasing Power Parity): $2,100 estimated (2005)
Area: 57,295 sq. miles
Capital: Dhaka
Type of Political System: parliamentary
Type of State: unitary
Type of Party System: multi-party

Located in South Asia, Bangladesh is a very small country, comparable in size to the state of Wisconsin. Formerly a part of Pakistan (called East Pakistan), Bangladesh was established in 1971 after a nine-month liberation struggle. Although religiously, ethnically, and linguistically homogenous, there are wide economic disparities. About 45 percent of its population exists below the poverty line. Approximately 80 percent of its population lives in the rural areas and are dependent, in one way or another, on agriculture. Since its birth, the government of Bangladesh has been heavily dependent on international aid.

Bangladesh has experienced repeated political instability. It has had, in turn, parliamentary, presidential, and military governments. In 1991 the country went back to a parliamentary system of democracy. Since 1991 it has been headed by women prime ministers; Begum Khaleda Zia is the current incumbent. The constitution of Bangladesh provides for formal political equality of men and women.

Statistical data from *The World Factbook*, CIA, July 2005.

in terms of seeking donor assistance to legitimize their activities. Second, upward accountability to donors has skewed NGO activities toward donor-driven agendas for development rather than indigenous priorities.[11]

Fourth, NGOs in Bangladesh are increasingly acting as political entities. According to Mohammed Mohabbat Khan, "Some of the big NGOs have taken sides in recent years either in favour or against major political parties and have tried to influence voter choices in local and national elections, which among other things led to the recent split in the Association of Development Agencies (ADAB), co-ordinating body of NGOs in Bangladesh."[12] This political dimension of NGO activities adds an intriguing facet to the issue of accountability. In short, it raises the questions of whose political agenda NGOs are promoting and whether those agendas conflict with the government of Bangladesh's agenda.

Bangladeshi NGOs

Bangladeshi NGOs grew rapidly throughout the 1980s, supported mainly by donor funds. Occasional periods of martial law did not hamper the growth of this sector. Although there has been a proliferation of local NGOs, the World Bank report cited earlier indicates that the ten largest Bangladeshi NGOs consume nearly 70 percent of all funds in that sector. Grameen Bank, BRAC, and Proshika are now comparable in size and influence to government departments. Grameen Bank has been discussed elsewhere, so here we introduce other major indigenous NGOs.

Bangladesh Rural Advancement Committee

BRAC was established in 1972. It is one of the pioneer organizations to motivate the rural poor to form groups for integrated rural development. BRAC works with people who face extreme poverty, illiteracy, disease, and other handicaps, and strives to bring about positive changes in the quality of their lives. It has two specific goals: alleviating poverty and empowering the poor. BRAC has four core programs in the areas of rural development, education, health, and capacity building. The Rural Development Program carries out activities to bring about social and economic development for rural women and to develop their capacity. The core of BRAC's Rural Development Program is its microcredit program, which gives small loans to poor people, mostly women, with very

---

Box 7–2. NGOs and the Creation of Bangladesh

Bangladesh has a long tradition of private welfare and development work rooted in religious and cultural institutions. Private voluntary work was undertaken by the upper economic class of the community, who organized schools and mosques, and relief activities for the victims of natural disasters. Civil society has a long history of political activism in Bangladesh during the twentieth century—first, as a site of resistance to the British colonial rulers, and second, in the period after India's partition, as a site of resistance to the political subordination experienced by the people of East Pakistan. Organized civil society in the form of student groups and citizen organizations formed coalitions and won a major victory in 1952 with the official recognition of Bangla as a state language.

NGOs emerged as a distinctive type of civic organization during the liberation struggle for independence in 1971. During the liberation war, efforts were made by many young people to render medical and other humanitarian services in the refugee camps across the border in India and "underground" within the country in order to alleviate the suffering of war victims. The massive international relief efforts and foreign aid that immediately came after the liberation war led to the creation of several NGOs. In the postwar reconstruction period these organizations, with the help of foreign aid and prominent NNGOs (such as CARE, Oxfam, and Save the Children) directed their efforts toward complementing the government's efforts to provide relief and rehabilitation. Foreign assistance enabled many of these agencies to sustain their organizational entities for several years after the war. Gradually, some of these NGOs changed their focus from charity to welfare and development and evolved into today's development NGOs.

---

low interest rates. Breaking the barriers of a traditional society, BRAC has trained women to use motorcycles, to operate restaurants, and to do carpentry along with other nontraditional roles.

The Non Formal Primary Education Program provides education to poor children. The Health and Population Division implements and supports different health-related programs at the community and national levels. In order to make these programs effective, the Training Division carries out programs to increase the capacity of the program participants and BRAC staff.

Proshika

Proshika was founded in 1976 by a group of social workers. Its core programs revolve around conscientization of the people. Proshika's mission is to conduct an extensive, intensive, and participatory sustainable development process through empowering the poor. Proshika's programs include building people's organizations among the poor, employment and income-generating programs, a universal education program, and disaster-management programs. Building people's organizations is the backbone of Proshika's poverty-alleviation strategy. It encourages poor people to form groups of twenty to twenty-five members; once the group reaches a certain degree of maturity, Proshika provides it with support services to improve the members' socioeconomic condition. Proshika's universal education program includes adult literacy, enrollment of children of poor households in formal schools, non-formal primary education for dropouts and non-enrolled children in the eight to eleven age groups, and post-literacy centers for the newly literate to reinforce and sustain their literacy skills. The core elements of its employment and income-generating programs include building groups' savings, provision of credit, technical assistance, and marketing assistance. Proshika also has a formal process of disaster management to assist the helpless during disaster situations.

Association for Social Advancement

Established in 1979 by a group of university-educated young people, ASA's mission is to contribute to the establishment of a just society in Bangladesh through empowering powerless people. Originally, it focused on forming "people's organization" and provided legal aid to fight social injustice. In 1984 ASA shifted its focus to the family, recognizing the critical role women must play in development. In the late 1980s ASA began to incorporate management skills for income-generating projects and stressed the importance of savings in development education efforts. At this point credit delivery to rural poor women became a major focus. ASA currently has over 750,000 women borrowers, and its loan recovery rate is above 99 percent. Major ASA programs include an income-generating credit program, development education, health and nutrition programs, social empowerment, and a partnership program providing loans to small NGOs.

Nijera Kori

Nijera Kori ("we do it ourselves") is considered a radical NGO. Its main mission is to raise the consciousness of landless men and women and assist them in finding their own solutions to their problems. Its activities include the formation and development of autonomous democratic and self-reliant organizations; training in human and skills development; collective action and mobilization on social issues, including female suppression, the misappropriation of resources, and taking leases of *khas* (government) land; and legal aid. Instead of giving credit, the common strategy for most NGOs, Nijera Kori prefers to give moral and social support to individuals. In fact, it considers credit programs anti-developmental. Nijera Kori's support to poor people in launching strong opposition and protest against shrimp production in the southwest of Bangladesh is one example of its work. Bangladesh is one of the major

---

**Box 7–3. NGOs in Focus:
Nijera Kori's Transnational Relations**

Nijera Kori's relationships with external donors and networks illustrate how SNGOs are linked globally. The organization currently has partnerships with five Northern donor agencies and NGOs. DFID, Britain's aid agency, is the only ODA donor now supporting the organization, but it has partnerships with ICCO, the Evangelischer Entwicklungsdienst, and the Swallows, faith-based NGOs in the Netherlands, Germany, and Sweden, respectively. It also has a partnership with Inter Pares, a Canadian NGO. These organizations provide a combination of financial support and cooperation with campaigns of mutual interest.

Nijera Kori's external relationships, however, are not confined to those that supply it with assistance. It also belongs to three transnational coalitions: the Industrial Shrimp Action Network, the Environmental Justice Foundation, and the Food First Information and Action Network. The last is headquartered in Germany and has member organizations in sixty countries. Nijera Kori cooperates in these networks to campaign on issues it confronts at home.

Source: The nijerakori.org website.

producers of the world's farmed shrimp, which is considered a luxury product destined for Western markets. Growth in shrimp farming has been accompanied by local elite's grabbing poor peoples' lands and taking control of water resources. Nijera Kori is actively working with the landless poor people to raise their consciousness about the effects of such shrimp production and have joined them in raising protests. Members and staff of Nijera Kori frequently have been victims of violence due to their involvement in shrimp production protests.

ADAB

The Association for Development Agencies in Bangladesh (ADAB) acts as the coordinating body for NGOs in Bangladesh. Since its establishment in 1974, it has grown into a membership organization for more than 750 development NGOs. Membership in ADAB is voluntary. As an umbrella of the NGOs, ADAB coordinates activities of its members and provides technical and advocacy support to small NGOs. Most important, it facilitates contacts among the NGO community, the government, the business sector, and civil society at large. ADAB has also developed a code of ethics for its members. During the 2001 national election several members of ADAB criticized the agency for taking a partisan role in the election. The dispute ultimately led to a split in the agency; several members withdrew from ADAB and formed a new NGO (Federation of NGOs in Bangladesh).

Bangladeshi NGOs are increasingly considered political entities. NGOs that attempt to organize the poor to articulate their demands, fight for their rights, and struggle to change the structural basis of their subordination clearly are engaging in political activities (the work of Nijera Kori is an example). Activities like raising women's consciousness and empowerment (the work of BRAC is an example) are considered by some conservative groups as threats to the existing societal structure. Some NGOs have overtly engaged in political activities too (Gono Shahajjo Shangstha's work outlined in Box 7–4 is a good example). Others, including Grameen Bank, have urged members to participate in elections, even when the NGO leadership does not take a formal position in favor of specific parties or candidates.

Political activities generate criticism of NGOs for two reasons. First, overt political action is seen as violating NGO neutrality, widely perceived to be what makes NGOs different from patronage-driven political parties. Second, politicization raises the issue of the proper role of

---

Box 7–4. NGOs in Focus: Gono Shahajjo Shangstha (GSS) Challenges the Status Quo

GSS's goals were to raise the consciousness of the poor and to assist them in forming their own class-based organization. In early 1992 GSS took a bold step and put up slates of candidates from the poorest class for local elections in five unions in the district of Nilphamari. In one union GSS members actually won the election for the chairman as well as a majority of the ordinary seats for its members. The dominant elite group, which had not before paid attention to GSS's members running for election, launched a reign of terror, burning GSS schools and houses and beating members. The government sided with the local elite group, accused GSS of forming underground revolutionary parties, and arrested some GSS members. GSS was later forced to move away from its confrontational strategy.

---

externally funded organizations in domestic politics. If most NGOs in Bangladesh receive funds and other support from Northern donors and NNGOs, does this lead to undue political influence by foreign organizations? While neither Northern donors nor NNGOs fund electoral activity directly, they do support legal-aid organizations and a host of development and consciousness-raising activities that challenge the political and social status quo.

The politicization of the NGOs is partly fueled by the sustained criticism of Islamic fundamentalists, who do not approve of the widespread secular influence of NGOs at the grassroots, their networking and coalition-building efforts, and their pro-women stance. Islamic fundamentalists have created their own NGOs with funding from the Muslim donor countries to counter such secularizing effects. In turn, the Islamic NGOs' role and legitimacy also becomes suspect due to their donor sources, precipitating the further politicization of the issue of accountability. The course that development NGOs took to protect themselves from the Islamic fundamentalists was to develop strategic alliances with anti-Islamic political forces in the country. "In associating themselves with the pro-liberation forces in the press, in cultural organs, in business, in government, the NGOs again found themselves taking a political position."[13]

Multiple Stakeholders and the Problem of Accountability

As Najam's framework points out, NGOs have multiple stakeholders. That is to say, they are responsible to different development actors. The fact that some of those stakeholders are transnational actors complicates the picture. Figure 7–1 sketches the major development players in Bangladesh and their relationships.

Figure 7–1. The NGO Chain

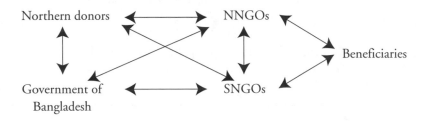

Northern Donors

The Northern donors (the OECD governments, the World Bank, and the UN development agencies) are the primary funders of NGO activities in Bangladesh. There are nearly two dozen such donors now active in the country. The United States, the United Kingdom, the EU, Canada, and Japan are the largest foreign aid donors. These aid agencies provide funds to NGOs directly and through the relevant agencies of the government of Bangladesh, which then disburse funds to SNGOs.

Donors tend to specialize in certain kinds of aid, reflecting their development priorities and technical expertise. Thus, among the possible range of development projects for which a recipient government or SNGOs might seek support, not all will be attractive to donors. As bureaucracies, donor agencies tend to carry out projects according to their established ways of doing things. Among these standard operating procedures are personnel dispatches for set periods of time, a tendency to favor specific projects over more open-ended program aid, and specific procedures for reporting results. NGOs that want to receive funding from the aid agencies are under pressure to make their projects conform to donor goals and procedures. NGOs in Bangladesh work under these constraints. As Hashemi explains:

> The emphasis on credit-based poverty alleviation strategies in Bangladesh may have originated with the experience of the Grameen Bank, but moves among other NGOs to replicate this strategy stem from the easy availability of donor support. In fact, the emphasis on nonformal education, immunization, and diarrhea disease control is due to donor pressure. Conversely, the dropping of adult literacy from NGO agendas is due to lack of donor interest in such programs. Now that donor interest has turned to HIV and AIDS, it is only a matter of time before large members of NGOs begin to integrate HIV and AIDS into their activities. This does not mean that donors are funding programs that are irrelevant or ineffective, but donor dependence creates a situation in which NGOs end up reprioritizing their own agendas.[14]

Another common reality in Bangladesh is that while many NGOs would prefer to implement long-term, open-ended development projects that take local citizens' opinions and experience seriously, donor funding requirements may force them to propose a specific project in one sector, for a limited period of time, with an aid team dispatched from Dhaka (the capital city of Bangladesh) or Tokyo or Ottawa determining whether the project has succeeded or not.

Patronage invites relationships of inequality. This is not inevitable, of course, yet there have been instances in which donors assumed attitudes of superiority in relation to their Bangladeshi counterparts. David Bornstein recounts a particularly galling interview between a Grameen Bank staff member and an Asian Development Bank (ADB) official. The ADB official entered the Grameen staff member's office, put his feet up on the desk, and announced that his institution wanted to lend money to the Grameen Bank. The staff member retorted that Grameen had not asked the ADB for its help.[15]

NNGOs

NNGOs form the second external link in the transnational chain. They operate in Bangladesh in two primary ways: First, they directly carry out projects in target communities. Second, they promote the development of Bangladeshi NGOs. They do this either by financing local NGOs or by strengthening their administration. For example, Dutch NGOs have helped their Bangladeshi counterparts by training senior staff, providing consultancy services, and supporting their counterparts' participation in international conferences.[16]

Oxfam, Save the Children, and CARE are major NNGOs represented in Bangladesh.

Oxfam's first work in Bangladesh dates back to 1954, even before independence. As of 2002 half a dozen Oxfam branches reported carrying out some kind of relief or development project in Bangladesh. Oxfam America represents one extreme, carrying out short-term relief in case of typhoon or flood. AusAid, Oxfam's Australian branch, focuses on carrying out long-term development projects. Reflecting transnational concerns that too much direct NNGO involvement in projects hinders local capacity for development, AusAid concentrates on providing financial support to Bangladeshi NGOs, which then carry out their own projects.

Save the Children is dedicated to making lasting, positive changes in the lives of disadvantaged children. The organization was founded in 1932 as part of a worldwide Save the Children movement. Since Save the Children started to work in Bangladesh in 1972, the organization's program has gone through several changes of emphasis, from an early community-based rural development focus, to an emphasis on improving the socioeconomic status of women, to the present focus on children. Save the Children's child-centeredness goes hand in hand with continuing support for women's empowerment programs, because the well-being of children and of women are inextricably linked.

CARE is another major NGO that carries out projects directly in Bangladesh. CARE dates its first presence in Bangladesh to 1955, a time when it was still part of Pakistan. Over time CARE also turned its attention from relief to longer-term development, although it still provides emergency assistance during Bangladesh's frequent cyclones and floods. CARE International, the parent group for the twelve country chapters in Europe, North America, and Japan, provides about US$35 million each year to projects in Bangladesh. Currently, CARE International carries out projects directly in Bangladesh, emphasizing preventive health care and education, and agricultural and rural development, with CARE-USA and CARE International–UK serving as lead members in the country.

A major difference between NNGOs and SNGOs involves the scope of development efforts. Ian Smillie points out that SNGO activities tend to be programmatic, since development activities are hard to divide into separate projects. For example, poverty alleviation in an area

---

Box 7–5. Case Study: Two CARE Programs in Bangladesh

HIV/AIDS Program
One of CARE's current programs in Bangladesh focuses on HIV/AIDS prevention and education in high-risk groups. Transport workers (who are highly mobile), sex workers, and intravenous drug users are high-risk target groups with which the organization works. CARE has established a behavior change program that provides education and access to condoms, and promotes the use of condom distribution outlets. It also promotes treatment of STDs in brothels. CARE's projects support and train clinic providers. CARE also runs mobile clinics at truck stops and has supported the creation of a self-help alliance of people living with HIV. The alliance provides peer counseling to HIV-positive individuals and fights for their rights.

CAGES (Cage Aquaculture for Greater Economic Security)
CAGES's goal is to provide economic security for eleven thousand poor households by increasing family income through increased fish production. Most project participants are women. They are taught a technique known as cage cultivation. Fish are raised in cages in lakes, reservoirs, and rivers to increase fish stocks. CARE also works with different NGOs that have active aquaculture programs, staff, credit programs, and access to lakes and rivers where new aquaculture projects might be set up in the future. CARE has a center near Dhaka that, in addition to providing useful information on cage culture, trains NGO staff, who, in turn, train their own staff.

---

may involve literacy, primary health care, microcredit, and employment-generation projects, all of which local NGOs see as going hand in hand. NNGOs, however, have tended to take on the perspective of the aid agencies, which tend to view development in terms of discrete projects. Despite the rhetoric of programmatic development, NNGOs tend to assess their cooperation with SNGOs in project terms, just as aid agencies do.[17] They prefer projects because they make planning, implementation, and assessment easier, especially if NNGO staff members do not reside in the country in which the projects are being carried out. However, this limits the spillover benefits from one kind of development activity to another and stifles the ability of SNGOs in the field to identify new problems and adjust their activities to fit changing circumstances.

Bangladesh Government Agencies

Chapter 2 made it clear that any NGO active in the international arena by definition still operates within the borders of a specific sovereign state at any particular time. The government of Bangladesh interacts with the NGO sector through the NGO Affairs Bureau (NGOAB). Any NGO that receives foreign funding must be registered with the NGOAB. In addition, most NGOs are registered as voluntary agencies within the Department of Social Welfare; significant numbers are also registered with the Registrar of Societies or with other agencies.

The NGOAB was created in 1990 to monitor NGOs' activities and their sources of funding. Since all NGOs receiving foreign funds must be registered with the NGOAB, the bureau acts as a gatekeeper; without appropriate registration, local NGOs will not receive external funding. NGOAB registers NGOs, and processes and approves their projects and the disbursement of project funds; approves appointment and tenure of service of expatriate officials and consultants; reviews reports and statements submitted by the NGOs; monitors, inspects, and evaluates NGOs' programs and budgets; and maintains liaison with NGOs and donor agencies.

In Bangladesh, government-NGO cooperation was common in relief distribution, family planning, non-formal education, and microcredit. However, since 1992 the relationship has changed to a less cooperative one. In late July 1992 the NGOAB sent a secret report to the prime minister, accusing NGOs of corruption and anti-state activities. The report charged several NGOs with securing foreign funding without government approval and maintaining illegal bank accounts, among other activities. In August the NGOAB issued an order canceling ADAB and two other NGOs' licenses to operate. The order, however, was canceled by the prime minister's secretariat the same day, following strong intervention by donors.[18] In January 2003 the head of ADAB was arrested on charges of corruption. The government also blocked foreign funding to projects carried out by Proshika and four other NGOs. In 2004 the government introduced a bill that would regulate NGOs receiving foreign assistance.[19] The result has been the development of an uneasy relationship, as these incidents raise questions about the control donors have, through the NGOs, over the government of Bangladesh. Dependence on transnational funding sources thus raises a very difficult issue for national sovereignty.

Currently a complex relationship has evolved between the government of Bangladesh and the NGO sector. The government of Bangladesh often emphasizes NGOs as partners in development, and the NGOs and the government have undertaken several collaborative projects. However, there is no integrated plan to involve the NGOs in the development process. NGOs work in local areas almost completely in isolation, without any interactions with the government functionaries.[20]

Moreover, there is an element of competition in the relationship between the two. The top Bangladeshi NGOs are as large as some government departments, and Bangladeshi NGOs have drawn talented people from government because NGO salaries and prestige are higher than those in civil service. The stream of resources down the NGO chain does nothing to alter this. There is both envy and lack of trust among the bureaucracy because of the resources (both economic and political) that some of the powerful NGOs enjoy. In addition, government officials, obviously, do not wholeheartedly embrace the fact that donors have more trust and confidence in the NGOs.

As we saw in Part I, IGOs like the World Bank are primarily responsible to their member governments. In operational terms that means that the World Bank's lending agencies provide funds, for the most part, directly to national governments. Government agencies then disburse the money to NGOs. This is consistent, of course, with NGOAB's mission to coordinate donor funding to NGOs. A 1996 World Bank study found, however, that Bangladeshi NGOs were dissatisfied with this procedure. They had expected that World Bank funding would go directly to them.[21]

Problems of Multiple Accountability

Najam's framework is useful here because it includes an important aspect of transnational NGO accountability: accountability to multiple stakeholders. Extending his analysis to cover the range of links in the NGO chain affords an even broader understanding of multiple accountability and the problems associated with it.

Table 7–1 presents the various stakeholders to which each set of development actors in Bangladesh is formally responsible. The list is complicated; not only are many actors accountable to one another, but some are individually accountable to stakeholders to whom the others are not.

Table 7–1. Accountable to Whom?

Northern Donors	Government of Bangladesh
Citizens	Citizens
Legislature/executive	Northern donors
Consultants/contractors	Legislature/executive
NNGOs	**SNGOS**
Contributors	Government
Northern donors	Northern donors
SNGO counterparts	NNGO counterparts
Target groups	Target groups
Selves (staff, etc.)	Selves (staff, etc.)

Northern donors, of course, must answer to their own constituencies. First among them are taxpayers, who by definition are not citizens of Bangladesh. More narrowly, the Northern aid agencies are answerable to their governments' legislatures and executives. Then there are the various groups that are part of the aid machinery: consultants and contractors. Aid is not free even when it comes in the form of grants because it is usually tied to the purchase of goods and services provided by donor-country companies.

The NNGOs are also responsible to constituencies outside of Bangladesh. The big charities like Save the Children and CARE depend on Northern governments and private contributions to fund their projects. For example, of the thirteen projects that CARE International–UK carried out in Bangladesh in 2002, twelve were supported by the Department for International Development (DFID), Britain's foreign aid agency. Fund raising is a major NNGO concern, and critics aver that both Save the Children and CARE have ended up subverting their development goals abroad in order to maintain the "business" end of their operations.[22] In addition, as David Lewis and Babar Sobhan point out, a poor "fit" may sometime exist between the views of Northern supporters of NGOs and more radical NGO initiatives in Bangladesh.[23] For example, Diakona (a Swedish NGO), in its recent efforts to develop a more activist approach in Bangladesh, has run the risk of becoming isolated from its traditional church-based support in Sweden. Whenever there is a mismatch between the aims and assumptions of the constituency and the actual work carried out, the organization's ability to communicate experience with its constituency at home will be undermined.[24]

Not only are there a number of donor agencies and NNGOs that cooperate with indigenous NGOs, but some NGOs have projects with multiple partners making the issue of accountability more complex. For example, BRAC's Non Formal Primary Education Program in 2000 included grants from three OECD donor agencies, three NGOs, and unspecified "others" (presumably local organizations). In 1999 the same program had included grants from UNICEF, the German aid agency KFW, and an unidentified government agency. Multiple accountabilities also might lead to waste through duplicated efforts or lack of monitoring if each overseeing authority assumes the others are taking a close look at the agency concerned.[25]

In Bangladesh formal mechanisms exist for NGO accountability to the government and the foreign donors:

Government
- registration and permission for receiving and spending donors' money from the NGOAB,
- project approval from the NGOAB,
- submission of yearly audit reports and implementation reports to the NGOAB, and
- inspection and monitoring of project activities by the NGOAB.

Nonetheless, it is widely acknowledged that the NGOAB lacks the resources to ensure that the processes are followed. As an example, the 2006 World Bank report points out that the NGOAB lacks the trained staff needed to monitor and evaluate systematically the large volume of NGO activities.

Foreign aid donors
- regular submission of audit and implementation reports, and
- donors' inspection and evaluation of NGO activities through their own representatives.

What about Bangladeshi NGOs' accountability to their target groups or beneficiaries? Several scholars point to the lack or inadequacy of mechanisms for this downward accountability. For example, Hashemi argues that "beneficiaries are seldom allowed to make decisions on programs or budgets or even to participate in monitoring and evaluation."[26]

Perspectives from the Field

If NGOs have multiple stakeholders, to whom should they be most responsible? One of the authors of this text undertook field research in 1998, conducting in-depth interviews with several NGO executives and the director of the NGO Affairs Bureau.[27] The objective of the study was to gauge the above informants' perceptions on the various dimensions of NGO accountability in Bangladesh. Interestingly, a study on NGO accountability in Bangladesh conducted by Mohammad Mohabbat Khan in 2003 reported similar findings.[28]

One of the findings of the 1998 study suggested that clients compete with other stakeholders for NGO attention. During the interview, an informant from Save the Children argued: "Our first accountability should be to our community—people with whom we work. We use *community* instead of *beneficiaries*. Accountability here would include whose ideas are to be implemented and how representative they are of the broader society." Interestingly, Bangladeshi NGOs and NGOAB's informants tended to emphasize "accountability to the public." Even more significant, different informants gave different reasons for including the "public." For example, the informant from the NGOAB explained that the "NGOs are accountable to the target population because unless its [the target population] standard of living improves or turns to a positive direction, donors may withdraw their financial support." In sharp contrast the informant from Proshika emphasized that since "NGOs are public institutions . . . every citizen has a right to know what we are doing and has a right to criticize our activities." A BRAC respondent stated that "public accountability will make us work effectively. We take fees from our beneficiaries so that they will feel that they have a right to criticize and complain about our services. This in turn will make us more effective."

All the informants in that study agreed that clients and the public, however defined, were not the only actors to which they were responsible. Proshika and BRAC's staff responded that they were accountable to the government, donors, and their executive boards. In addition, participants from BRAC, ADAB, and Proshika also mentioned their own staff as another body to which they feel accountable.

In other words, donors and Bangladeshi NGOs' own organizations must be taken into account when thinking about accountability. The latter includes responsibility to one's mission, staff, partners, and the broader NGO community. Internal mission responsibility, however, can be compromised by accountability to external donors. As mentioned earlier, several scholars suggest that NGOs are often willing to change their own goals about the process (for example, participation or community development) in order to provide the product demanded by donors.[29] Mechanisms to ensure responsibilities to partners, staff, and other NGOs—if considered at all—also remain weak.

Multiple stakeholders inevitably pose a problem for NGO accountability: accountability for what? One gets a glimpse of this in interview responses from the 1998 study. The NGOAB informant contended that NGOs were accountable for the money they spent on their different programs: "Since they get foreign donations for working for the people, they are accountable for this money." In contrast to this emphasis on fiscal accountability, NGO administrators used a much broader framework in their discussion on this matter. They spoke of the importance of transparency, participation, and social responsibility. For example, the informant from Proshika believed that in addition to goal achievement, NGOs were accountable in terms of "being transparent." BRAC's informant defined accountability as "ensuring people's participation along with achieving the goals of this agency." The informant from ADAB saw accountability in a much broader sense. He argued that "NGOs should have a social responsibility, too. The same applies to the other sectors too. Each should address how it is contributing to the broader society, namely, in alleviating poverty, in improving our environment, in educating our citizens, and in other areas. . . . We think about our own sector's interest without paying any attention to how we affect the other sectors' goals. NGOs are trying to play an advocacy role in this respect."

The 1998 study thus found major differences among the NGOs and their oversight bodies on the conceptualization of the scope of NGO accountability. Their definitions range from a narrow, administrative view to a very broad one (for example, social accountability). One is reminded of a statement made by E. Ahsan and S. N. Muslim, who argue that "it is important to note that in a country like Bangladesh where democratic norms, values, and institutions have yet to be firmly established, the term 'accountability' has different meanings and connotations to different groups of people. In Bangladesh, even the accountability of civil servants and elected representatives at all levels is in a 'diluted, diffused, and fuzzy' state."[30]

In regard to the processes of maintaining accountability, all the informants in the 1998 study mentioned that their board of directors held regular meetings. BRAC and Proshika were also members of ADAB, which has its own code of ethics to which member NGOs must adhere. However, compliance with the code is a voluntary matter. Although the processes appear to be rigorous and systematic, the informant from the NGOAB aired his frustration that a shortage of staff and lack of field offices impede effective monitoring and evaluation of NGOs.

Besides these common mechanisms, several informants mentioned other processes for ensuring accountability. The informant from Proshika explained: "Every six months we sit together and review the quantity and quality of our work. We have like our Proshika parliament. These meetings are attended by representatives from our field offices. Through this process we try to follow a bottom-up approach." Informants from BRAC, Proshika, and Save the Children also emphasized that they encourage their beneficiaries to give feedback on the services delivered.

Donors, government agencies, and, increasingly, large NNGOs prefer formal methods of accountability. For one thing, they are objective. One can say how much money was allocated to a project, how much was spent doing what, how many people received a particular service, and so on. For another, such reports can be shown to donors and stakeholders at home. Formal measures of accountability can also be carried out by the short-term dispatch of inspectors, a common practice of Northern donors and larger NNGOs.

If NGOs, donors, and government officials have different perceptions of what it is that NGOs are supposed to account for, how do we know whether they are responding to the various constituencies with which they interact? If we look at the interview responses above, we can discern two dimensions of accountability: formal and moral. The formal dimension of accountability focuses on the execution of contracts, the delivery of promised services, proper utilization of funds, and the timely reporting of activities. The moral dimension focuses on transcendental values like the advancement of human rights or empowering clients to participate effectively in NGO policies and/or procedures.

Empowerment and consciousness raising of local communities are common themes that run through nearly all public statements made by NGOs and Northern donors operating in Bangladesh. An informant from Save the Children also saw accountability in terms of "how we are using the money and for what. . . . Who defines our goals and how legitimate are those goals?" Yet, how does one measure the success of NGOs in promoting such values? For example, a Dutch government study of fifteen of that country's NGOs noted that empowering women in rural areas was a major focus of their development efforts in Bangladesh. Poverty alleviation, health education, and microcredit projects all tended to be justified in terms of their ability to improve rural women's lives. The report found that stated goals were often unmet, but that women's status tended to improve indirectly because of the NGO projects.[31] Should stakeholders conclude that these projects are successes or failures?

Summary

As seen above, the NGO chain stretches from northern capitals to Dhaka to rural villages. Chains, of course, strengthen elements by joining them. However, chains also bind. The interaction among the elements creates expectations of mutual obligation. These expectations can be summarized in the phrase *who owes what to whom?* The NGO sector's heavy dependence on foreign donors and its increasing engagement in political activities (overt and covert), along with the threat it poses to the status quo, are crucial factors that make accountability a very real and controversial issue here. Thus, funding from Northern donors and NGOs is not the only problem. In the 1990s the New Policy Agenda championed by the international donor agencies (favoring market liberalization and democratic governance) created an environment in which the dominant model for NGOs has become some variant of the credit and income-generation approach. The agenda also supported the addition of a third type of strategy for NGOs—that of policy advocacy—and hence a wider role for such CSOs. Indeed, all the indigenous NGOs introduced act as advisors to the World Bank's Structural Adjustment Participatory Review Initiative. Thus, NGOs in Bangladesh find that a policy agenda created elsewhere gives legitimacy to, but also limits, the kind of development work they do.

Bangladeshi NGOs are also often criticized for their lavishness and high administrative costs. Hashemi explains: "If one compares the major NGOs in Bangladesh with their counterparts in India, striking differences emerge in the level of resources that are available to them. Compared with their Bangladeshi counterparts, Indian NGOs seem more modest, down-to-earth, and resource scarce. This is symptomatic of the general abundance of foreign funds in Bangladesh."[32] The concern here is that since NGOs are heavily dependent on foreign resources, a lack of adequate accountability can make them corrupt and autocratic and may result in pursuance of a few powerful NGO leaders' personal goals at the cost of broader developmental goals.

In the 1998 study, informants from BRAC, Proshika, and Save the Children emphasized that they encouraged their beneficiaries to give feedback on the services delivered. However, such informal and ad hoc processes lack the rigor of the formal kind of accountability government and Northern donors require. Neither local NGOs or NNGOs operating in Bangladesh are particularly good about carrying out formal evaluations of their work, including local participation.[33] In the 1998 study a Proshika official pointed to a lack of beneficiaries' participation in most of these NGOs: "Whatever participation there is, it is only rhetorical participation."

We can safely infer that what we see happening in Bangladesh is a reflection of the general picture for SNGOs. SNGOs, as pointed out in the previous chapters, are overwhelmingly dependent on foreign funds. This raises some crucial questions on NGO accountability. First, to whom can we realistically expect foreign-donor-dependent NGOs to be accountable? Second, even among those few NGOs that give some importance to the notion of accountability to beneficiaries, and that have some processes in place geared to that, how does one actually assess the quality and adequacy of those processes? Third, considering the political role that NGOs engage in, the importance of NGO accountability to the general public cannot be overlooked. However, is it realistic to expect that? What would be the processes and the mechanisms for such accountability? Finally, what mechanisms actually exist for the accountability of NNGOs to their constituents, and how effective are they?

Discussion Questions

1. What is the NGO chain? Are some links more important than others?
2. What is accountability? Why is it a transnational problem?
3. Compare the profiles and goals of the major NNGOs and SNGOs introduced in the chapter. How well do they match? Can you identify possible points of difference or conflict?

Suggestions for Further Reading

For more information on the Grameen Bank, see Muhammad Yunus, *Banker to the Poor: Micro-lending and the Battle against World Poverty* (New York: Public Affairs, 1999). For information on interactions between SNGOs and NNGOs in Africa, see Ann Hudock, *NGOs and Civil Society* (London: Polity Press, 1999). For a general discussion of SNGOs and development, see Julie Fisher, *Nongovernments: NGOs and the Political Development of the Third World* (West Hartford, CT.: Kumarian Press, 1998).

Notes

[1] Barbara Romzek and M. Dubnick, "Accountability in the Public Sector: Lessons from the Challenger Tragedy," in *Current Issues in Public Administration*, ed. F. Lane, 158–76 (New York: St. Martin's Press, 1994), 160.

[2] Adil Najam, "NGO Accountability: A Conceptual Framework," *Development Policy Review* 14 (1996): 339–53.

[3] Michael Edwards and David Hulme, *Beyond the Magic Bullet: NGO Performance and Accountability in the Post–Cold War World* (West Hartford, CT: Kumarian Press, 1996); and John Clark, *Democratizing Development: The Role of Volunteer Organizations* (London: Earthscan, 1991).

[4] See Judith Tendler, *Turning Private Voluntary Organizations into Development Agencies: Questions for Evaluation.* USAID Program Evaluation Discussion Paper no. 12 (Washington, DC: USAID, 1982).

[5] Brian Smith, "Nonprofit Organizations in International Development: Agents of Empowerment or Preservers of Stability," in *Private Action and the Public Good*, ed. W. Powell and E. Clemens, 217–27 (New Haven, CT: Yale Univ. Press, 1998), 217–18.

[6] Sarah C. White, "NGOs, Civil Society, and the State in Bangladesh: The Politics of Representing the Poor," *Development and Change* 30, no. 2 (1999): 307–26.

[7] "The Other Government in Bangladesh," *The Economist* (July 25, 1998), 30.

[8] World Bank, *Economics and Governance of Nongovernmental Organizations in Bangladesh.* Development Series Paper no. 11 (Bangladesh: World Bank Office, Dhaka, 2006).

[9] Anna Fruttero and Varun Gauri, "The Strategic Choices of NGOs: Location Decisions in Rural Bangladesh," *Journal of Development Studies* 42, no. 5 (2005): 759–87.

[10] World Bank, *Economics and Governance of Nongovernmental Organizations in Bangladesh.*

[11] Syed M. Hashemi, "NGO Accountability in Bangladesh: Beneficiaries, Donors, and the State," in Edwards and Hulme, *Beyond the Magic Bullet,* 129.

[12] Mohammed Mohabbat Khan, "Accountability of NGOs in Bangladesh: A Critical Overview," *Public Management Review* 5, no. 2 (2003): 267–78.

[13] Richard Holloway, *Supporting Citizens' Initiatives: Bangladesh's NGOs and Society* (Bangladesh: Univ. Press, 1998), 156.

[14] Hashemi, "NGO Accountability in Bangladesh," 130.

[15] David Bornstein, *The Price of a Dream: The Story of the Grameen Bank* (Chicago: Univ. of Chicago Press, 1996).

[16] IOB Policy and Operations Evaluation Department, Ministry of Foreign Affairs, "Evaluation of Netherlands-Funded NGOs in Bangladesh" (The Hague: Netherlands Ministry of Foreign Affairs, 1996).

[17] Ian Smillie, "At Sea in a Sieve? Trends and Issues in the Relationship between Northern NGOs and Northern Government," in *Stakeholders: Government-NGO Partnership for International Development,* ed. Ian Smillie and Henny Helmich (London: Earthscan, 1999), 29–30.

[18] Hashemi, "NGO Accountability in Bangladesh."

[19] Indo-Asian News Service, "Clampdown on NGOs Could Cripple Bangladesh Development," *Yahoo India News* (February 14, 2004). Available at in.news.yahoo.com/040214/43/2bhoh.html

[20] See Salahuddin Aminuzzaman, "NGOs and the Grassroot Base Local Government in Bangladesh: A Study of Their Institutional Interactions," in *NGOs under Challenge: Dynamics and Drawbacks in Development,* ed. F. Hossain and S. Myllyla, 84–104 (Helsinki: Ministry for Foreign Affairs of Finland, Department for International Development Cooperation, 1998).

[21] Toshiko Hino, *NGO-World Bank Partnerships: A Tale of Two Projects,* Human Capital Development Working Papers 67 (Washington, DC: World Bank, June 1996).

[22] See Eugene Linden, *The Alms Race: The Impact of American Voluntary Aid Abroad* (New York: Random House, 1976); and Michael Maren, *The Road to Hell: The Ravaging Effects of Foreign Aid and International Charity* (New York: The Free Press, 1997), 6.

[23] David Lewis and Babar Sobhan, "Routes of Funding, Roots of Trust? Northern NGOs, Southern NGOs, Donors, and the Rise of Direct Funding," *Development in Practice* 9, no. 1–2 (1999): 117–29.

[24] Ibid., 126.

[25] Edwards and Hulme, *Beyond the Magic Bullet.*

[26] Hashemi, "NGO Accountability in Bangladesh," 129.

[27] Shamima Ahmed, "The Issue of NGO Accountability in Bangladesh: Perspectives and Perceptions of NGO Leaders," *Asian Thought and Society* 25, no. 75 (2000): 255–66. Hereafter, 1998 study.

[28] Khan, "Accountability of NGOs in Bangladesh."

[29] See Tendler, *Turning Private Voluntary Organizations into Development Agencies.*

[30] E. Ahsan and S. N. Muslim, "Accountability in the Bangladesh Civil Service" (report presented at the ASEAN-SAARC Conference on Administrative and Financial Accountability, Dhaka, Bangladesh, January 16–20, 1994), 139.

[31] IOB Policy and Operations Evaluation Department, Ministry of Foreign Affairs, "Evaluation of Netherlands-Funded NGOs in Bangladesh."

[32] Hashemi, "NGO Accountability in Bangladesh."

[33] IOB Policy and Operations Evaluation Department, Ministry of Foreign Affairs, "Evaluation of Netherlands-Funded NGOs in Bangladesh."

Chapter 8

NGOs and
International Security

International security is perhaps the litmus test of NGO influence in international politics. As the sine qua non of traditional "high politics" security, it represents the bedrock of statecraft in the world. It is an arena in which the stakes of sovereignty are highest and in which states most jealously guard their prerogatives as the architects of international order. Unlike foreign aid or other economic development endeavors, states have been reluctant to acknowledge meaningful NGO activity in the security realm beyond the provision of relief. Despite government ambivalence, however, NGOs speak to states across a range of security issues. The awarding of the Nobel Peace Prize to the ICBL in 1997 and Medecins Sans Frontieres in 1999 highlights the roles NGOs play in international security.

The ICBL was not the first NGO to receive a Nobel Prize (see Table 8–1). The ICRC has received three. The American Friends Service Committee and the Friends Service Committee (the Quakers) received one in 1947. The timing of these awards was not accidental. Each award was made in recognition of the organization's efforts to alleviate the effects of war.

This is an important point. NGOs have a long history of involvement with armed conflict. The Red Cross was the product of Henri Dunant's experience at the Battle of Solferino (1859), during the wars of Italian national unification. CARE, Oxfam, and Medecins Sans Frontieres were established in response to war. Whether they meet specific definitions of an NGO or not, the social movements across the industrial democracies that made up the anti-Vietnam War movement were highly visible and played an important role in persuading the US government to end its military engagement in Vietnam. Social movements in Western Europe vigorously opposed deployment of US medium-range nuclear missiles in the region in the 1980s. Voluntary organizations of professionals, such as International Physicians for the Prevention of Nuclear War, Physicians for Social Responsibility, and Women's Action for Nuclear Disarmament, fought for years against the development of nuclear weapons and certain strategic weapons systems during the Cold War.

This chapter considers NGO-state interactions in two new areas of international security: the global campaign to ban landmines, and humanitarian intervention in complex political emergencies. These cases represent the two faces of NGOs in international security. The first might be called the pacifist face. NGOs lobby governments to limit or eliminate certain kinds of weapons systems and their use. The Nuclear Freeze

Table 8–1. NGOs Awarded the Nobel Prize for Peace

Organization/Person	Year of Award
Henri Dunant	1901
Institute of International Law	1904
Permanent International Peace Bureau	1910
International Committee of the Red Cross	1917
International Committee of the Red Cross	1944
Friends Service Committee (UK)	1947
American Friends Service Committee	1947
International Committee of the Red Cross	1963
Amnesty International	1977
International Physicians for the Prevention of Nuclear War	1985
International Campaign to Ban Landmines/ Jody Williams	1997
Medecins Sans Frontieres	1999
Grameen Bank/ Muhammad Yunus	2006

movement in the United States and the movements to stop US plans to deploy medium-range nuclear missiles in Western Europe, both in the 1980s, are examples. The second face might be called the relief face. This also has a long history among NGOs, as noted in Chapter 3. Here, NGOs try to alleviate the effects of conflict on individuals and communities. The medical relief work of Medicins Sans Frontieres among war refugees is an example. The two are not mutually exclusive, of course.

The global landmine campaign represents a recent attempt by civil society actors to change the security policies of states at the international level. The ICBL represents a single campaign, although it has encouraged NGOs to try to limit production and use of other kinds of conventional weapons. It is an outstanding example of NGO forays into traditional high politics issues and illustrates well the potential for transnational NGO coalitions to change state definitions of what are appropriate tools of war. The case of complex political emergencies represents an ongoing interaction between NGOs and security actors. Here, NGOs' repertoires have expanded from their traditional focuses on technical assistance and social and economic development to security and peacebuilding. In the case of complex political emergencies, moreover, NGO interactions with states and IGOs are more diverse than in the landmine campaign.

Traditional and Nontraditional Security in International Relations

Security as understood in international relations for most of the post–World War II era has been seen as beyond the scope of non-state actors. As high politics, security has long been regarded as the proper preserve of states. During the Cold War, especially, the study of security was conducted largely in realist terms, even when scholars themselves were not realists. The great concerns of traditional security studies were maintenance of the attributes of the modern nation-state: sovereignty and territorial integrity. The field of enquiry was seen in terms of military power and capability, with nuclear weapons and their political permutations standing at the apex of the hierarchy of power (and therefore study). Security, moreover, was an issue for resolution between states.[1]

The end of the Cold War and the collapse of the Soviet Union undermined the traditional security perspective. The collapse of the Soviet Union was accompanied by reduced concern about the possibility of nuclear war among the superpowers but a renewed concern with the effects of conventional war. The shift in scholarly attention, moreover, allowed other issues that had existed all along to come to prominence. The so-called nontraditional approach has come to frame national security not only in terms of conventional military threat from other states but in terms of broader threats like transnational crime, light arms proliferation, refugee flows resulting from civil disorders, environmental degradation, and gender and economic inequality.[2]

Human security further disengages the concept of security from its Cold War foundations. The UN first used the concept in its 1993 *Human Development Report*. That document argued for a change in the definition of security "from an exclusive stress on national security to a much greater stress on people's security, from security through armaments to security through development, from territorial security to food, employment and environmental security."[3] While the report recognized the continued relevance of traditional security concerns, it argued that military solutions by themselves are inadequate to guarantee societal security.

Both the nontraditional and human security approaches provide non-state actors, including NGOs, legitimate entry into the international debate. Growing concerns about transnational organized crime, terrorism, and involuntary migration (refugees) are particularly relevant because non-state actors are primary players. Post–Cold War conflicts, moreover, do not lend themselves to resolution by conventional applications of military force, as events as disparate as the African famines of the 1980s and 1990s, the disintegration of Yugoslavia, and terrorist attacks on the World Trade Center and the Pentagon attest. Economic inequality, human rights, and environmental degradation comprise problems NGOs addressed even before the end of the Cold War, so framing them in terms of nontraditional security only increases such organizations' visibility. Human security most radically favors the involvement of non-state actors by shifting the entire focus of "security" away from states to individuals and civil society.

A related post–Cold War trend has been the increasing willingness of UN and other state collectivities to intervene in weak states' domestic affairs on humanitarian grounds. Humanitarian intervention has had a history as unilateral action in behalf of a country's citizens who are in danger or suffering persecution overseas. In a society of sovereign states, however, it has not been a popular practice, especially among the governments of Africa, Asia, and Latin America, at whose expense it is likeliest to be carried out.[4]

Attitudes have changed, however, in the post–Cold War era, and states have been more willing to countenance humanitarian interventions in Northern Iraq, Somalia, Bosnia, Rwanda, Haiti, and Liberia. International efforts have included creating safe havens and humanitarian corridors and supplying humanitarian assistance to refugees and displaced populations.[5] Rather than the unilateral interventions more common for most of the nineteenth and twentieth centuries, these were all multilateral interventions under UN mandates. This makes military intervention more palatable to many governments. Frances Abiew writes: "These actions have ushered in a more vigorous approach to UN conflict management efforts, be it in situations of massive violations of human rights resulting from state collapse or civil wars."[6] NGOs participated in all of these humanitarian interventions.

Despite the encouraging signs in the 1990s, however, the security community has been slow to embrace the presence of NGOs. William Durch's edited survey of UN peacekeeping through the early 1990s never mentions them, reflecting the Cold War era predisposition to view peacekeeping in terms of the UN in relations to nation-states.[7] Jody Williams, who was instrumental in the establishment of the ICBL, noted that in the initial stages governments were not enthusiastic about participation by citizens' groups in a traditionally military field of expertise.[8] One account of UN peacekeeping operations in Cambodia from 1991 to 1993 mentioned NGOs only in passing, despite the fact that NGOs played critical operational and political roles in peacekeeping efforts there.[9]

The International Campaign to Ban Landmines

The ICBL represents one of the most innovative recent endeavors by NGOs in the area of international security. The Convention on the Prohibition of the Use, Production, Transfer and Stockpiling of Anti-Personnel Landmines and on Their Destruction (sometimes called the Ottawa Convention), which entered into force in March 1999, was the result of a "fast-track" diplomatic process that lasted only fourteen months—a dramatically short amount of time in conventional diplomatic terms. Many observers attribute the speed and effectiveness of these negotiations, referred to as the Ottawa Process, in large part to the activities of a broad range of NGOs led by the ICBL.[10] The negotiations for the Ottawa Convention, moreover, are interesting because NGOs involved themselves directly in the initiation of an arms-control disarmament treaty, typically an area reserved for major powers and one in which non-state actors have been significant by their absence. NGOs in the landmines case, moreover, are credited with helping to set a new international security norm.[11]

Anti-personnel landmines did not receive much international attention until the ICBL put them on the disarmament agenda. They had long been considered conventional and strictly defensive weapons. Their proliferation, however, has had a number of consequences for noncombatants. First, they are widely used not only in international armed conflicts but increasingly in civil wars. As a result, the campaign supporters argued, "there are tens of millions of AP [anti-personnel] mines" spread across some seventy countries.[12] These small, inexpensive devices last for years after the cessation of conflict, moreover, and their placement is often forgotten. As a result, thousands of civilians are killed or injured by them every year.[13]

Efforts to ban landmines outright can be traced back to the 1970s, when the ICRC began pressing governments to take action on landmines. The ICRC's efforts did not garner significant results, however, and the issue remained dormant until the early 1990s and the formation of the ICBL. The ICRC was nevertheless able to keep the issue alive until the initial 1993 meetings when the possibility of crafting a treaty to ban landmines was explored. As part of this effort the ICRC developed a public advertising campaign and disseminated both specialist and non-specialist literature that framed the issue of landmines in humanitarian terms.[14]

The establishment of the ICBL is a good example of the entrepreneurial explanation of NGO formation introduced in Chapter 2. Leadership is critical to the formation of voluntary organizations. In the case of the ICBL, the leadership was collective, resulting in the establishment of an NGO network. In 1991 six NGOs took up the landmine issue in earnest. They were Handicap International, Human Rights Watch, Medico International, the Mines Advisory Group, Physicians for Human Rights, and the Vietnam Veterans of America Foundation. All had worked separately on issues related to landmines. A series of discussions among them led to the formation of the ICBL the following year, with a steering committee composed of representatives of the six established in

1993. Jody Williams, who served as the steering committee's coordinator throughout the campaign, credits a 1991 meeting she attended at the Vietnam Veterans of America Foundation headquarters as the very beginning of the campaign.[15] Had particular people and organizations not come together at a particular time, and had they not decided to act together, there would have been no locus around which the more than a thousand NGOs that participated in the campaign could have organized and shared information. The landmine issue might well have remained on the margins of public awareness and security policy debate.

Throughout the campaign the ICBL and its member NGOs employed both traditional and newer advocacy techniques. Two of them, public education and framing, were especially prominent. One of the most widely recognized strengths of NGOs is the generation and dissemination of information. The NGOs also were able to build influence effectively through their organizing skills, which they used to hold workshops for activists and training sessions for those going to inspect and report on landmines. NGOs then disseminated information and statistics about the effects of landmines on people and societies. This in itself was an innovation because there had been practically no research done anywhere on landmine numbers and effects. While at least one scholar considers NGO estimates of landmine quantities in war-torn countries like Afghanistan and Cambodia to have been overstated, the figures nonetheless were widely reported in the media.[16] NGOs unleashed the full panoply of tools geared toward information dispersion: radio, TV, documentary films at international conferences, and appeals in the elite print media like the *Washington Post, The New York Times,* and *The Economist.* Landmine victims' voices were particularly instrumental in pushing the agenda ahead, providing an emotional appeal not often seen in interstate deliberations about arms control. The Landmine Survivors Network, established in 1995, actively publicized both to the public and to governments the trauma its members had undergone. Network members also gained admission to official negotiating sessions, bringing the reality of victims' plights directly to arms-control negotiators for the first time.[17] The campaign also harnessed the energies of famous people such as Nelson Mandela, then president of South Africa. Princess Diana's highly publicized tours of mine-ridden areas were coordinated by member NGOs.[18]

NGO public education efforts were critical in framing the landmine issue in nontraditional terms. By addressing landmines as a human rights issue, and by targeting landmines as a killer of civilians, NGOs framed the issue of their use in humanitarian and human rights terms rather than in terms of conventional weaponry. This allowed for a redefinition that placed them outside the boundaries of acceptability normally associated with such types of weapon. Consequently, the campaign changed the moral climate of debate, which put states opposed to the ban on the defensive. The new frame also provided a rationale for civil society participation in an arena usually monopolized by states. The ICBL carefully avoided engaging the issue on the grounds of military utility because to do so would refocus debate in a framework from which states could make strong arguments.[19] They also tried to keep landmines separate from other arms-control issues. German NGOs, for example, wanted to include a ban on tanks, but were vetoed by other organizations in the network who believed to do so would derail the entire campaign.[20]

Finally, isolating the landmine issue through the fast-track Ottawa Process enabled the ban's supporters to avoid the normal international forums in which arms-control and disarmament issues are debated (notably the UN Council on Disarmament and the Convention on Conventional Weapons). Because these venues rely on consensus decision making, negotiations take years to complete, even if they do not fail.[21] Framing in this case sustained the momentum to bring the issue to successful conclusion as a treaty.

The ICBL's transnational scope makes it a significant case for thinking about NGO involvement in security issues. As a transnational network it contrasts with the usual picture of single NGOs, for example, opposing states on security issues, or of national level social movements, like the anti-missile movements in Europe in the 1980s. Like the Narmada Dam network, which organized in opposition to World Bank policies (see Chapter 5), the ICBL included organizations from North and South. In 1993 the ICBL assumed leadership of the anti-landmine campaign under a closely knit steering committee of NGOs. The ICBL served as an umbrella organization composed of NGOs from a number of different countries. The loosely structured group's early approach was simply to encourage each respective NGO to pursue its own particular strategy appropriate to banning landmines. By 1996 six hundred NGOs from over forty countries had signed on to the campaign, the beginning of a coalition in which over twelve hundred NGOs from over sixty countries would participate.[22]

NGOs, of course, did not act alone; they worked in concert with key states, Canada being among the most important. Jody Williams, ICBL co-founder and critic of US landmine policy, openly acknowledged the importance of states to the ban process. It is governments that ultimately sign treaties that create international law.[23] Consistent with the findings in Chapter 3, interactions varied. NGOs sometimes took confrontational positions, at other times cooperative positions. In some cases NGO interactions with their governments were thin and ineffective.[24] Deciding how to deal with individual states, especially those that opposed the ban, elicited a great deal of discussion within the campaign. Whether to confront the US government publicly over its opposition to a total ban or to work quietly with it to change its position proved to be so controversial that it split the ICBL leadership in 1998.

A key feature of the relationship was the cooperation each party afforded the other. Senator Patrick Leahy, himself a key participant, stated that "never before have representatives of civil society collaborated with governments so closely, and so effectively, to produce a treaty to outlaw a weapon."[25] Indeed, NGOs were able to work closely and effectively with a core group of supportive states that provided forums in which NGOs could interact with official delegations. Most of these core states were small or medium sized: Denmark, Norway, Austria, Belgium, the Netherlands. In each of these countries, and in Canada, NGOs were

---

Box 8–1. The Ottawa Convention: Key Points

Article 1
General obligations:
1. Each State Party to the treaty undertakes never under any circumstances:

 a) To use anti-personnel mines;

 b) To develop, produce, otherwise acquire, stockpile, retain or transfer to anyone, directly or indirectly, anti-personnel mines;

 c) To assist, encourage, or induce, in any way, anyone to engage in any activity prohibited to a State Party under this Convention;

2. Each State Party undertakes to destroy or ensure the destruction of all anti-personnel mines in accordance with the provisions of this Convention.

Article 19
Reservations
The Articles of this Convention shall not be subject to reservations.

able to push the national government to take a position favorable to the treaty yet largely consistent with the state's existing political and social posture. Moreover, some were willing to provide NGO activists with access to official decision making rarely afforded to non-state actors in the security realm. Canada served as the model case, including selected Canadian NGO representatives in its official delegations to interstate negotiations. This close government-NGO interaction prompted Lloyd Axworthy, the head of the official delegation, to argue that this marked a new kind of "unconventional diplomacy" in which non-state actors were an integral part of the regular negotiation process.[26]

The Ottawa Process culminated in the adoption of the convention by ninety-one states in Oslo on September 8, 1997. Three months later, at the beginning of December, 122 states signed the treaty in Ottawa. On March 1, 1999, the convention entered into force, with 137 signatories and 65 ratifications. As of April 26, 2006, 154 states had "signed or acceded" to the treaty and 151 were ratifications or accessions,[27] making it the most comprehensive landmine convention ever.

What does an NGO network do once it has accomplished its mission? There are three possibilities. First, it can disband. Second, it can drift into irrelevance. Third, it can redefine its mission. The ICBL remains significant to international security politics because it has taken the third option. Every year since 1999 it has published a Landmine Monitor Report documenting treaty accession or ratification; mine disposal efforts; continued landmine production and trade; and assistance for victims. The global network of local NGOs established during the Ottawa Process allows it to maintain researchers in ninety countries. Further, the collaborative relationship seen in the Ottawa Process became the model for cooperation between governments and NGOs in the effort to expand the powers of the International Criminal Court to try government leaders for war crimes.[28] It has encouraged other networks, moreover, to organize campaigns that target other conventional weapons. ICBL joined the ICRC in condemning the use of cluster bombs, for example. Global campaigns to reduce the use of light weapons and child soldiers in civil conflicts have drawn their inspiration and organizational models from the ICBL.

Issues

Two major issues remain despite the success of the ICBL campaign. The first involves the problem of noncompliance. The transformation of the

ICBL into Landmine Monitor suggests that the hard work of maintaining pressure on signatory states to abide by the terms and spirit of the landmine convention continues to be necessary. On some fronts the campaign has been successful. Although the pace of treaty accession has slowed, governments continue to sign on. The annual reports, for example, collectively document the destruction of over seventy-five million stockpiled landmines since the treaty was signed. Landmine use has decreased, and even those governments that have not signed have, in notable instances (such as the United States), ceased to produce mines. Mathew J. O. Scott points out that signing the treaty acted as a terminal point for many states and the international press. As attention has shifted to other issues, budgets for landmine clearance and victim rehabilitation have not been forthcoming at levels envisioned by key campaign members.[29]

The treaty remains flawed, moreover, because it does not include key states. The United States, China, Russia, and India remain opposed to the treaty. There has been limited acceptance by Middle Eastern countries.[30] The states that remain outside of the treaty at the time of this writing possess something on the order of 200 million mines, more than the entire number reported as destroyed since the treaty took effect. The United States remains opposed to a comprehensive ban, arguing on one hand that technological change could render mines safer and on the other that its defense strategy on the Korean peninsula depends on landmine deployment. Non-state organizations that are not party to international treaties, of course, remain outside the convention's jurisdiction. These include militias in failed states and governments not recognized by the international community (the Taliban in Afghanistan until 2001, for example). This means that international law banning anti-personnel landmines does not bind military organizations that could be expected to use them.

Complex Political Emergencies

Scholars of international relations widely agree that localized wars in the developing world (which now includes significant portions of the post-communist world) have become a key component of political violence in the last decade. Of twenty-eight violent conflicts in the world in 1998, twenty-six were civil conflicts in which violence tended to concentrate within one country. "These conflicts tended to be prolonged, drew in other countries, became highly destructive of life and property, and frequently generated large flows of refugees and internally displaced people."[31] These refugees typically arrive in camps without resources and therefore require large expenditures for food and shelter on the parts of host governments and the international community. Andrew Natsios observes that complex political emergencies are "more lethal, destructive and insidious than any other form of conflict because the entire society is so completely traumatized."[32] Mary Kaldor argues that these wars differ fundamentally from modern wars of the nineteenth and twentieth centuries.[33] Often referred to as complex humanitarian emergencies, we use the term *complex political emergency* here to highlight key features of these events.

There are different explanations of why these conflicts have emerged. One interpretation emphasizes longstanding tribal, ethnic, or religious cleavages that give rise to communal violence.[34] Another argues that the end of the Cold War removed the unifying symbols and antagonisms that had propped up fragile national governments in Asia, Africa, and southeastern Europe. The result was failed states that could not manage conflicts in civil society.[35]

Complex political emergencies tend to have the following characteristics. First, whatever their long-term origins, civil conflicts in the short term revolve around ethnic, tribal, and religious animosities. Widespread atrocities often accompany these conflicts, to the point that some cases take on the public image of genocide. Civilians are frequently the deliberate targets of violence. Indeed, the new wars take their toll on civilians in far higher ratios than traditional wars. Bosnia and Rwanda are examples of this cycle of violence. Second, the national government disintegrates to the point that public services disappear, and political control passes to regional warlords and provincial governors. Third, mass population movements occur as displaced persons (usually civilians, mostly women and children) try to escape conflict and to find food. The establishment of refugee camps creates a series of public health emergencies, including malnutrition and contagious disease. Fourth, economic destruction in the form of hyperinflation, destruction of the currency, and collapse of markets occurs. Fifth, "these first four characteristics, sometimes exacerbated by drought, contribute to a general decline in food security." Localized malnutrition can "degenerate into widespread starvation."[36] Indeed, the onset of famine is typically a political act in that it results either from deliberate state policy or from state disintegration.[37]

Lack of state authority complicates attempts to resolve complex political emergencies or even to alleviate their consequences in the short term. Kaldor argues that a feature of new wars is the total collapse of the formal economy, a consequence of state failure. The result is both a severe contraction of economic activity and increasingly ambiguous relationships among economic, criminal, and military activities.[38] In a manner similar to that which Maren describes in Somalia in the 1980s and early 1990s,[39] humanitarian aid becomes a resource to be used to pursue political or military ends. In the Bosnian war of 1992–95 the warring parties depended on outside sources, including other governments, remittances from emigrants, black-market activities, expropriation of expelled people's property, and humanitarian assistance. "The local militia were funded by municipalities who received the 'taxes' from humanitarian assistance collected on their territory and also continued to tax citizens . . . and enterprises on their territory."[40] As with Somalia in the previous decade, NGOs helped provide the relief funds that were siphoned off to further war efforts. In sum, there are no clear lines between relief, food aid, and the war economy.

Actors in Complex Political Emergencies

Compared to the landmines treaty negotiations, complex political emergencies are distinctive because of the wide range of actors involved. Kaldor contends that the process of globalization affects the character of these new wars. They are now global events, with actors not drawn simply from the disintegrating societies and surrounding areas but from around the world. Worldwide communications technologies enhance the international awareness of these events and help provoke the humanitarian responses to them. Humanitarian aid agencies and NGOs are part of this global response. Thus, we may divide the actors in complex political emergencies into two categories: the international community and the local community.[41]

The international community is comprised of a broad array of actors. Chief among the IGOs present are the UN agencies, in particular the UNHCR, UNICEF, WHO, and the Food and Agriculture Organization. The Organization for Security and Cooperation in Europe, the African Union, and Organization of American States have played roles in emergencies in their respective regions.

The military comprises a second set of international actors that consist of UN peacekeeping forces, NATO forces (in the case of former

Yugoslavia), and other multinational and national military (such as the United States Marine Corps in Somalia in 1993). Multinational peace-keeping forces play critical roles in maintaining order and ensuring humanitarian supply efforts, both of great concern to NGOs on the ground. In recent years they have also undertaken relief and development projects of their own, under the rubric of civil-military affairs, as a way to win support from local populations (see Table 8–2). In this capacity they potentially act as NGOs' competitors. NGO representatives also point out that civil-military affairs blur the distinction between peacekeeping and relief. In this situation NGO workers can become potential targets of violence because local militias fail to see the difference between the two kinds of organization.

Table 8–2. Civil-Military Affairs Activities by UN Peacekeeping Forces in East Timor

Country of Peacekeeping Force	Type of activity
Portugal	Medical assistance, film society award
Australia	Medical assistance, sports education, road construction
South Korea	Medical assistance, sports education, scholarships, clothing distribution, technical assistance
Thailand	Medical assistance, agriculture assistance, sports education, computer education
Japan	Road construction, heavy machinery driving training, soccer facilities construction
Singapore	School construction

Source: *Asahi Shinbun* (May 7, 2003), 6.

Northern aid donors are significant financial actors in complex political emergencies. They provide nearly all of the disaster relief funding and two—the United States Office of Disaster Assistance and the European Community Humanitarian Organization (ECHO)—provide about half of those resources.[42] While donor agencies typically provide funding through UN agencies, NGOs, or sometimes the civil arms of their peacekeeping forces, occasionally they will participate directly in an emergency. Speaking from their experience as former NGO employees, Waters and Maren separately contend that donors are the real principals in humanitarian interventions because they provide the funding for relief work and because NGOs cannot afford to alienate them.[43]

Hundreds of NGOs can be involved in specific relief events. However, there is a core of about three dozen—CRS, CARE, Oxfam, Medecins Sans Frontieres, Lutheran World Federation, and Save the Children, to name a few—that receive the majority of donor food aid and other assistance. They also provide a continuous and dominant presence across all major disaster relief efforts. Various NGOs are active in complex political emergencies. Some play advocacy roles in Northern countries. Others operate for short periods in specific emergencies. Still others maintain a long-term presence in the field.

The international media play an ambivalent role in humanitarian emergencies. On the one hand, they are crucial to the international dissemination of news about civil conflicts and their humanitarian consequences. NGOs have come to depend on the media to increase public awareness about complex political emergencies and relief efforts. The media are also indispensable for NGO attempts to raise funds. Some observers point out that the media and NGOs are mutually dependent; that is, the NGOs provide newsworthy items for journalists, and the media provide the NGOs with outlets for their appeals. On the other hand, media attention is inconsistent. Some emergencies are saturated with coverage. Other disasters—Rwanda in 1994 and Western Sudan in 2004, for example—do not get the timely coverage NGOs wish they had. Even when the news media provide timely coverage, media attention tends to shift as new crises arise. Recently, the 2003 war in Iraq displaced coverage of Afghanistan. Renewed violence and resulting distress in Liberia in the early summer of 2003 produced a short-lived burst of media attention on that country's long-term civil war. Only when violence in Afghanistan erupted anew in mid-2003 did media attention shift, temporarily, back to Kabul.

The local community comprises an equally diverse array of actors. Chief among them are national governments, either those left intact (as in Cambodia, Rwanda, and Sudan) or neighboring host governments in the case of refugees. Warring parties in civil conflicts, including warlords and their militias (often supplemented by mercenaries), make up the remainder of civil authority in the absence of national governments. Warlords and their militias pose special problems for peacekeeping and humanitarian missions. Such groups commandeer humanitarian aid shipments, kidnap peacekeepers, and harass local populations as part of their conflict strategy. Thus, they not only interrupt the humanitarian efforts NGOs undertake, but they also worsen the security environment in which NGOs operate and contribute to the problems NGOs attempt to address.

In addition, there are local civilians not directly involved in the conflict. In some cases refugee camps are established close to existing communities. The major international actors typically set up their operations in inhabited areas even where there are no refugee camps. Many of these civilians find the influx of international aid a source of livelihood.

Refugees form a significant element of the local community. They are commonly the target of international relief, but they are also participants in the events that lead up the humanitarian interventions as well. Waters notes the tendency by the international agencies and NGOs to view refugees as empty vessels to be cared for by tried-and-true assistance measures, but he also argues that as citizens of failed polities, they have loyalties to the various parties in conflict, and some are not innocent of atrocities that led to refugee flight in the first place. In the Rwandan case, for example, NGOs knew that members of the Hutu militias that had carried out mass murder against Tutsis lived among the refugees in the camps in neighboring Zaire and Burundi. How NGOs could provide fair access to humanitarian relief without supporting people directly responsible for the refugee crisis in the first place provoked a debate that still continues.[44]

Finally, local NGOs exist. Often overshadowed by the better-publicized INGOs mentioned above, and sometimes turned away by the IGOs that intervene to help, local NGOs possess valuable knowledge about populations and available resources. Because they are local, they remain after the international agencies have departed. This said, the availability of international funds often leads, as it does with foreign aid in general, to what one observer calls "briefcase NGOs" that form to receive aid and then disappear.[45]

The relationship between the international community and local communities is complicated. Kaldor notes that complex political emergencies

> epitomize a new kind of global/local divide between those
> members of a global class who can speak English, have access
> to faxes, e-mail, and satellite television, who use dollars or

deutschmarks, and who can travel freely, and those who are excluded from global processes, who live off what they can sell or barter or what they receive in humanitarian aid, whose movement is restricted by roadblocks, visas and the cost of travel, and who are prey to sieges, forced famines, landmines, etc.[46]

Thus, while the two communities are interdependent, the gap between NGOs and the international agencies, on the one hand, and their target populations and counterparts, on the other, is not always bridged. Miscommunication and failure to communicate at all are not uncommon.

NGO Roles in Complex Political Emergencies

NGOs command public attention by their quick emergency responses and urgent public appeals for donations, but they now do a great deal more than simply supply emergency relief. Broadly, NGO have five roles in complex political emergencies. The first category comprises relief and refugee assistance roles. This is their most public role because these activities are linked to appeals through the media for private donations. While this category is sometimes seen as no more than "do gooding," it takes on a special significance given the informal division of labor within the international humanitarian assistance community. In particular, neither the UNHCR nor the Office for Coordination of Humanitarian Assistance, the two lead UN agencies, is operational. In other words, they do not carry out relief operations; they coordinate UN efforts and the flow of funds from donors to NGOs and other organizations that do. Currently, about 20 percent of the UNHCR operating budget goes to NGOs.

Relief and refugee assistance efforts are complicated affairs both in number of tasks and number of actors. Refugee relief typically involves shelter provision, food and supply distribution, and disease prevention and treatment. As displaced populations and refugees settle into camps, some of which remain populated for years, problems of long-term development challenge the priority of the traditional components of relief.[47] NGOs have taken on coordination and consultation roles in their relationships with the UNHCR, donor agencies, and military commands. Sometimes, one of the larger NGOs coordinates operations among the NGOs present. In the case of the current civil war in Darfur, western Sudan, the UNHCR office in Khartoum coordinates the activities of some forty or so INGOs and the International Organization for Migration, which actually administer the displaced persons centers in the region. NGOs therefore carry out the significant work of actually implementing the relief operations organized by the UN and funded by Northern donor governments.

The major NGOs have developed a great deal of efficiency in their standard disaster repertoires. The largest have professionalized their disaster responses. In the Rwandan conflict in 1994, NGOs built three separate camps in Zaire for 750,000 refugees within a few days. One source describes the process as the construction of the infrastructure for a city.[48] Medecins Sans Frontieres has developed a protocol for which diseases it will treat in refugee camps, with acute conditions given priority over chronic ones. In the refugee camps set up in Macedonia in the wake of Bosnian Serbs' expulsion of Muslims from neighboring Kosovo in 1999, NGOs knew upon arrival which organizations would supply tents and blankets, which would supply drinking water facilities, and so on.

This efficiency facilitates NGO-IGO interactions in the field. The UNHCR, donor agencies, and key NGOs like CARE and Medecins Sans Frontieres have developed a division of labor that has become standard to the point that NGOs can set up an operation efficiently anywhere; the UNHCR can begin subcontracting work as soon as it arrives on the scene. The NGO-military division of labor is less well defined. The assumptions and procedures that underpin military and NGO operations are radically different, and the two sides often view each other with suspicion. Consultation has begun to take place in recent interventions, but not with the same level of interaction found between NGOs and UN and other development agencies.

Refugee repatriation and relocation inevitably become NGO concerns. NGOs are frequently critical of official refugee policies, as the sanctuary movement in the United States during the Central American wars of the 1980s demonstrates. As NGOs deal with refugee relief and long-term consequences of refugee flows, they also engage their advocacy and public education roles.[49]

The second role NGOs play is acting as sources of information about local conditions in civil wars or refugee sites. They are often on the scene well before the international peacekeepers, which gives them valuable insights into local conditions. And they often stay well after the UNHCR and peacekeeping forces have left. During the Soviet war in Afghanistan in the 1980s, NGOs were the only Western development presence in the country; NNGOs often entered the country illegally. They have remained in Afghanistan since then. They have served as vital sources of information for the multilateral relief agencies, but at the same time their information role puts them at odds with their military counterparts. In the fall of 2001, for example, Oxfam and other NGOs publicly called upon the United States to halt its retaliatory bombing campaign against Afghanistan in order to allow INGOs to distribute humanitarian aid before the onset of the Afghan winter.

Security comprises a third set of NGO roles. This category is not widely studied because peacekeeping forces typically dominate the security maintenance aspects of complex political emergencies. If the problem is defined in human security terms, of course, much of the standard NGO repertoire of relief and development takes on this character. Landmine disposal, however, is one field in which NGOs are involved in hard security. The UN subcontracted de-mining operations to a group of NNGOs in Cambodia during its operations there in 1991–93, and to local NGOs in Afghanistan.[50]

Peacebuilding represents a fourth role. UN humanitarian intervention has moved increasingly from strict peacekeeping (monitoring ceasefires and separating warring parties) to peace enforcement (active intervention against one or another party in a civil war) and peacebuilding. Peacebuilding entails measures to foster the conditions for return to a peaceful, vigorous (presumably democratic) civil society. The military typically is unequipped to deal with this role, and the UN relief agencies do not stay in the field long enough, so it has fallen mainly on NGOs to implement these activities. Post-conflict election monitoring and conflict resolution, including acting as intermediaries in conflicts, are typical activities. NGOs are particularly well placed to act as intermediaries and to promote dialogue across communal lines because of their neutral stance to refugee and disaster assistance.

Fostering the formation of CSOs in conflict-torn societies is another peacebuilding role. Not simply a process of establishing or communicating with local NGOs, this entails helping to establish organizations as diverse as citizens groups, sports clubs, and neighborhood associations. NGO concerns with sustainable development, once crises pass, sensitize many of them to the need to promote indigenous NGOs that can carry on peace and human rights work after the INGOs have departed.[51]

Statistical research suggests the significance of these roles. Scholars have examined the factors that promote and inhibit peacebuilding after

---

Box 8–2. Peacebuilding in Bosnia

Traditional peacekeeping involves military and other measures to end conflict and to prevent parties from restarting it. Peacebuilding involves long-term, non-military efforts to resolve the root problems that led to conflict in the first place. The International Human Rights Law Group's efforts to reestablish the rule of law in post-conflict Bosnia-Herzegovina provide an example of peacebuilding.

The International Human Rights Law Group established an access-to-justice program in Bosnia in 1997, two years after the Dayton Accords formally ended military conflict there. At the time, ethnic discrimination was carried out as a matter of official policy and unofficial government action. The group worked with local activists to identify discriminatory policies and practices. Educational policy was targeted, and the group and its local counterparts worked to raise public support for equal schooling for all ethnic groups in the country. It also fostered legal training and worked with Bosnian parties to regularize judicial practices (such as determining whether defendants on trial have the right to translation of court proceedings in their ethnic language). As an important component of the reconstruction of civil society in the country, the group's fostering of communication among representatives of different ethnic nationalities has provided a way to explore common ground on judicial and social issues.

Source: Adapted from Mark Bromley, "The International Human Rights Law Group: Human Rights and Access to Justice in Post Conflict Environments," in *NGOs and Human Rights Promise and Performance,* ed. Claude Welch, 141–50 (Philadelphia: Univ. of Pennsylvania Press, 2001).

---

civil wars. Michael Doyle and Nicholas Sambanis found that net current transfers per capita (including food and other forms of aid) and multidimensional peacekeeping operations that include "extensive civilian functions, economic reconstruction, institutional reform, and election oversight" enhanced the success of international attempts to end civil conflicts.[52] Their conclusions read like a laundry list of NGO roles in complex political emergencies. In theory, then, NGO presence can enhance peacekeeping.

Fifth, it can be argued that NGOs have a role in attempting to undermine warfare itself. Nicholas Berry argues that the ICRC and similar NGOs continue to contest the nature of warfare. Like most observers, Berry defines the Red Cross's primary mission as neutral relief in wars and other disasters. But he argues that other "unspoken missions" have emerged from its professed neutral political stance. The ICRC and other NGOs undermine civil wars by inducing governments and the UN to provide assistance to victims and to intervene; publicizing the effects of civil wars and thereby limiting instances of brutality and abuse; protecting and sustaining the populations of warring parties while promoting diplomatic settlement over total victory by one side; mobilizing the international community to comply with international humanitarian law; and acting as a neutral intermediary between warring parties.[53] The unofficial goal here is clearly more than simply humanitarian relief.

Issues

Three issues remain controversial regarding the nature of NGO operations in complex political emergencies. One is the problem of humanitarian goals in such settings. A second involves the tension between NGO ideals of neutrality and independence as expressed in the NGO Code of Conduct in Disaster Relief (see Box 8–3) and the operational realities that attend NGO relations with donors and other authoritative actors. The third concerns the unintended consequences of international humanitarian intervention in failed state settings.

Waters argues that vague goals are a chronic problem in humanitarian interventions. His claim is couched in terms of administration and is based on his observation that humanitarian responses to complex political emergencies are increasingly bureaucratic affairs. A key problem then becomes how to define the goal of humanitarian relief in measurable terms that can lead to determinations of success and failure. Such determinations cannot be made, he contends, because the product of relief efforts is ambiguous and typically couched in moral terms. For example, how does one measure alleviation of suffering? What does it mean to say that an organization "saves" refugees? Worse, success or failure is typically measured in terms of indirect and suspect measures such as media attention or donor-government satisfaction rather than whether beneficiary needs were addressed adequately. Moreover, the tools to ensure predictability, efficiency, and control simply do not exist, given the crisis environments in which NGOs operate.[54]

NGOs' self-defined roles further the ambiguity of their goals. Their peacekeeping counterparts in the military typically enter with rules of engagement and clearly defined exit strategies that emphasize short-term engagement. NGOs typically enter with strategies that allow for contingencies, which means their presence is open ended. NGOs often stay in the field when IGOs' and peacekeeping forces' standard operating procedures compel them to leave. Consequently, NGO staff sometimes run higher security risks than their UN and military counterparts. At least eleven Red Cross workers were killed in eastern Africa in 1996; in December of that year six medical staff were murdered in their hospital in Chechnya.[55] International staff members were pulled out of Afghanistan following threats of reprisal by President George Bush against the Taliban government after the bombing of the World Trade Center and the Pentagon in September 2001. Local staff remained, however, some of whom became victims of American-led bombing in October. The rash of bombings of international agency facilities in Iraq during 2003 led the major NGOs to withdraw their international staff from the country. Local staff remained.

Neutrality is a cherished NGO value with a long history. It occupies a central place in the NGO Code of Conduct in Disaster Relief (see Box 8–3), and its foundations go back to the founding of the Red Cross in the 1860s. In its traditional ICRC definition, neutrality operationally means gaining the consent of warring parties to intervene in conflicts in behalf of civilians and wounded combatants. In principle, the ICRC will not participate in humanitarian interventions until this condition is met. Newer organizations like Medecins Sans Frontieres criticize this conception of neutrality as state centered and unnecessarily restrictive. The alternative definition stresses provision of succor to all victims of conflict regardless of status, an understanding based more squarely in the ideals of the Universal Declaration of Human Rights and similar humanitarian documents. This, of course, leaves NGOs free to define for themselves when and how to provide relief in complex political emergencies. When Medecins Sans Frontieres and other NGOs cross closed borders to aid internally displaced populations, they clearly exercise this alternative definition.

The NGO definition of neutrality carries its own dangers, physical and moral. Medecins Sans Frontieres was expelled from Ethiopia for its aggressive stance on this issue. More broadly, humanitarian assistance

Box 8–3. The NGO Code of Conduct in Disaster Relief

The NGO Code of Conduct in Disaster Relief was developed by eight major NGOs in 1994. It lays out the NGO community's position in natural and human-made disasters. The code is one of several existing or proposed guidelines that have been formulated to steer voluntary-sector activities in a variety of fields. The code summarized here suggests that the key players have begun to develop a deliberate professionalism in the course of more than a decade of responding to civil and natural disasters. While the code is not binding on NGOs or any other parties to emergencies, it serves as a benchmark for considering roles and performance.

1. The humanitarian imperative comes first.
2. Aid is to be given regardless of race, religion, nationality or other distinction, and is calculated on the basis of need.
3. Aid will not be used to further a particular religion or political viewpoint.
4. NGOs should not act as instruments of government foreign policy.
5. NGOs respect culture and custom.
6. NGOs attempt to build disaster response on local capacity.
7. Program beneficiaries should be involved in program provision.
8. Relief aid should try to reduce future vulnerability to disaster.
9. NGOs are accountable both to donors and to target populations.
10. NGOs recognize disaster victims as human beings, not as hopeless objects.

Annexes to the code call upon governments and IGOs to recognize NGO independence, neutrality, and humanitarian relief roles and further request that host governments expedite NGO access to disaster victims and promote the timely flow of relief goods and information.

For the full text of the code, see Deborah Eade and Suzanne Williams, *The OXFAM Handbook of Development and Relief* (Oxford: Oxfam UK and Ireland, 1995), 801–8; the code is also available at the icrc.org website.

necessarily benefits some parts of society (refugees, particular ethnic or clan identities, and so on) at the expense of others (other ethnic or clan identities, host populations, militias); assistance is not neutral. Recent events in Iraq illustrate this point vividly. Attacks against American and allied military forces, the UN headquarters in Baghdad, and near the Red Cross headquarters in the same city make it clear that opponents of the American-led occupation view the international community, non-governmental or otherwise, as the common enemy.

A related issue of neutrality involves NGO relations with donor governments and IGOs. According to the NGO Code of Conduct, NGOs should not act as instruments of government foreign policy (Principle 4) and NGOs are accountable both to donors and target populations (Principle 9). These two principles may be in conflict. NGOs jealously guard the privileges of monitoring and criticizing donor government and UN policies. They also insist on independence of action if they deem it necessary.[56] Yet, NGO neutrality and independence of action are compromised by dependence on donor funding. While individual levels of government support for NGOs vary, both by organization and by country, donor funding is especially critical in complex political emergencies because famine and refugee relief are expensive and time sensitive. Former practitioners acknowledge that donor governments are the ultimate principals to which NGOs are accountable. Funding flows can quickly change depending on donor policy priorities. In the Rwandan crisis of 1994–96, USAID and ECHO began to withdraw funding for refugee camps in Zaire and Tanzania in 1995, expecting that refugee repatriation to Rwanda would make them superfluous. The result was that NGO contracts with the UNHCR went unpaid. More important, NGOs had to accept repatriation policies, some of them forced by host government coercion, even though the humanitarian community in the field had no evidence that Rwandans would be safe if they returned home.[57]

Natsios points out that NGOs' activities often reinforce donor policies whether they intend to or not. When NGOs, donors, and peace-keeping forces engage in their various roles in humanitarian interventions, NGOs cannot help but support broader political policies.[58]

Finally, NGO assistance may actually prolong or complicate complex political emergencies. As Kaldor notes, food aid is part of the war economy that sustains parties in civil conflicts. Maren graphically demonstrates the seizure of food aid by Somali militias. He argues further that food aid served the interests of the Somali government under General Aideed because it attracted nomads to camps where they came under government control.[59] In Afghanistan in the 1980s and 1990s NGOs providing relief in the interior found it necessary to work through local military commanders. The price of safety and cooperation was a significant portion of the development assistance, so NGOs ended up supporting one set of military groups over others whether they intended to or not.[60]

Slave liberation is another problematic case. Prolonged civil war and accompanying famine led to the reintroduction of slavery in Sudan. In the mid-1990s a number of church-based NNGOs undertook slave redemption, buying back enslaved people. While the NGOs argued that they were acting to rid Sudan of an evil, critics pointed out that buying slaves from slave traders had the same perverse effects that food aid does in the war economy: it created incentives to engage in slave raiding and enriched the traders who brokered deals between raiders and buyers in different parts of the country. Investigative journalism revealed cases of fraud, moreover, in which village members colluded to provide an ersatz stock of local slaves for redeemers to buy back.[61] The fly-in and fly-out method of redemption used by NGOs based in Europe and North America undoubtedly facilitated deception.

Summary

Both cases considered in this chapter—the ICBL and humanitarian intervention in complex political emergencies—represent positive NGO activities in international security. By positive we mean simply that each represents more than a reaction by non-state actors to state-defined "realities" of that policy arena. NGOs now make up a vital component of humanitarian intervention in complex political emergencies. They are important international actors whose specialized functions cannot easily or efficiently be duplicated by intergovernmental or military agencies. In this capacity they act as significant actors in the maintenance of international security. NGOs in the landmine campaign aspired to more than system maintenance. Rather, they actively tried to force state action by reshaping understandings of security. Neither function is readily recognized by the traditional security approach.

It is important not to overdraw the new character of international security and concomitantly to point out the innovative nature of NGO interactions with states in that environment. Civil society attempts to limit the development and deployment of nuclear weapons in Europe, Japan, and North America have a pedigree as old as nuclear weapons themselves. The antinuclear movements in North America and Western Europe were, of course, the foundations of significant social movements. Humanitarian relief during two world wars, moreover, served as the catalyst for many of the major NGOs that now operate in complex political emergencies.

The history of the ICRC illustrates the attempts by civil society to curb the effects of warfare. Rules about appropriate behavior in warfare have evolved over time. Humanitarian treatment of civilians and wounded during wartime are codified in the Geneva Convention, which, Martha Finnemore argues, was not the product of sovereign states but of citizen organizations that later came to make up the ICRC. These groups "drafted and sold" the principles of the convention to governments.[62] In effect (and in constructivist terms), NGOs changed the nature of international warfare by advocating principles that limited certain aspects of interstate violence. Thus, there is precedent for the kind of network the ICBL organized in the 1990s. The ICBL clearly acted in the tradition of the Red Cross. In both cases NGOs engaged in advocacy and public education with the intent of creating international norms. That is, they aimed at changing expectations about how states ought and ought not act. By framing issues in new ways, they affected international behavior. We may say that both have succeeded, although it is too early to tell whether the ICBL's efforts will have the kind of long-term impact the ICRC's activities have.

NGO roles in complex political emergencies are at once more varied and more prosaic. While advocacy and public education are important roles (especially because they are linked to emergency funding from private donations and foreign aid budgets), the traditional relief and development roles also inform NGO actions. Unlike the ICBL, NGO participation in complex political emergencies represents a continual presence in one aspect of international security. NGOs have been involved in providing assistance in complex political emergencies in East Africa since the 1980s and in former Yugoslavia since the early 1990s. They tend to cause less direct conflict with states than the ICBL did because long-term interactions between donors and NGOs have allowed each to understand the strengths and weaknesses of the other and to adjust to them. Moreover, while the ICBL aimed at creating new norms of security, NGOs in complex political emergencies have tended to play roles that try to maintain stability in the regions surrounding military conflict.

Discussion Questions

1. Why have NGOs been able to exercise a higher profile in international security issues in the last decade?
2. How successful was the ICBL? By what criteria?
3. What roles do NGOs play in civil conflicts? Should NGOs, as some critics argue, not get involved in relief aid during complex political emergencies?

Suggested Further Reading

For an inside account of the ICBL, see Maxwell Cameron, Robert Lawson, and Brian Tomlin, *To Walk without Fear: The Global Campaign to Ban Landmines* (Toronto: Oxford Univ. Press, 1998); also see the icbl.org website. For accounts of the problems humanitarian agencies face when working in complex political emergencies, see Mary B. Anderson, *Do No Harm: How Aid Can Support Peace—or War* (Boulder, CO: Lynne Rienner, 1999); and Fiona Terry, *Condemned to Repeat? The Paradox of Humanitarian Action* (Ithaca, NY: Cornell Univ. Press, 2002).

Notes

[1] For an elegant presentation of the basic assumptions of security, see Hans Morgenthau, *Politics among Nations,* 5th ed. (New York: Knopf, 1972), 404.

[2] See Michael Klare and Yogesh Chandrani, eds., *World Security: Challenges for a New Century,* 3rd ed. (New York: St. Martin's Press, 1998).

[3] UNDP, *Human Development Report* (New York: UN, 1993), 2.

[4] Michael Akehurst, "Humanitarian Intervention," in *Intervention in World Politics,* ed. Hedley Bull, 95–118 (Oxford: Clarendon Press, 1984).

[5] Refugees are defined by the UN as persons who have crossed an international border; displaced persons are those who have been uprooted by civil conflict but remain within the borders of their home countries. NGO personnel frequently express frustration with UN peacekeeping rules that prevent humanitarian organizations from assisting displaced persons in the same manner as refugees.

[6] Frances Abiew, *The Evolution of the Doctrine and Practice of Humanitarian Intervention* (The Hague: Kluwer Law International, 1999), 139.

[7] William Durch, ed., *The Evolution of UN Peacekeeping* (Basingstoke: MacMillan, 1993).

[8] Jody Williams, "World Citizens and International Cooperation" (public address before the Campus Forum in Nagoya, Chukyo Univ., Nagoya, Japan, November 20, 1998).

[9] Trevor Findlay, *Cambodia: The Legacy of UNTAC*, SIPRI Research Report no. 9 (Oxford: Oxford Univ. Press, 1995).

[10] Maxwell Cameron, Robert Lawson, and Brian Tomlin, eds., *To Walk without Fear: The Global Campaign to Ban Landmines* (Toronto: Oxford Univ. Press, 1998).

[11] Richard Price, "Reversing the Gun Sights: Transnational Civil Society Targets Landmines," *International Organization* 52, no. 3 (1998): 613–44.

[12] Jody Williams and Stephen Goose, "The International Campaign to Ban Landmines," in Cameron, Lawson, and Tomlin, *To Walk without Fear*, 21.

[13] Cameron, Lawson, and Tomlin, *To Walk without Fear*, 2.

[14] Stuart Maslen, "The Role of the International Committee of the Red Cross," in Cameron, Lawson, and Tomlin, *To Walk without Fear*, 80–98.

[15] "Jody Williams: The Woman Who Waged War on Landmines," CNN—The 1997 Nobel Prizes. Available online.

[16] Kenneth Rutherford, "The Evolving Arms Control Agenda: Implications of the Role of NGOs in Banning Antipersonnel Landmines," *World Politics* 53, no. 1 (2000): 74–114.

[17] Jerry White and Ken Rutherford, "The Role of the Landmine Survivors Network," in Cameron, Lawson, and Tomlin, *To Walk without Fear*, 99–117.

[18] Rutherford, "The Evolving Arms Control Agenda."

[19] Price, "Reversing the Gun Sights"; Rutherford, "The Evolving Arms Control Agenda."

[20] David Long and Laird Hindle, "Europe and the Ottawa Process," in Cameron, Lawson, and Tomlin, *To Walk without Fear*, 248–68.

[21] Rutherford, "The Evolving Arms Control Agenda."

[22] Williams and Goose, "The International Campaign to Ban Landmines."

[23] Williams, "World Citizens and International Cooperation."

[24] See Motoko Metaka, "Building Partnerships toward a Common Goal: Experiences from the International Campaign to Ban Landmines," in *The Third Force: The Rise of Transnational Civil Society*, ed. Ann M. Florini, 143–76 (Tokyo: Japan Center for International Exchange; Washington, DC: Carnegie Endowment for International Peace, 2001).

[25] Patrick Leahy, quoted in Craig Warkentin, "A New Politics of Multilaterism? NGOs, the WWW, and the Dynamics of Contemporary International Organization" (paper presented at the 41st Annual Convention of the International Studies Association, Los Angeles, March 2000).

[26] Price, "Reversing the Gun Sights"; Williams, "World Citizens and International Cooperation."

[27] To monitor the progress of accession and ratification, see the icbl.org website.

[28] Barbara Bedont, "Negotiating for an International Criminal Court: The Like Minded and the Non-governmental," *Peace Magazine* (September-October 1998), 21–24.

[29] Mathew J. O. Scott, "Danger—Landmines! NGO-Government Collaboration in the Ottawa Process," in *Global Citizen Action,* ed. Michael Edwards and John Gaventa, 121–34 (Boulder, CO: Lynne Rienner, 2001).

[30] Rutherford, "The Evolving Arms Control Agenda."

[31] Carol Lancaster, *Transforming Foreign Aid: United States Assistance in the 21st Century* (Washington, DC: Institute for International Economics, 2000), 59.

[32] Andrew Natsios, *U.S. Foreign Policy and the Four Horsemen of the Apocalypse: Humanitarian Relief in Complex Emergencies* (Boulder, CO: Praeger, 1997), 6.

[33] Mary Kaldor, *New and Old Wars* (Cambridge: Polity Press, 1999).

[34] See Natsios, *U.S. Foreign Policy and the Four Horsemen of the Apocalypse.*

[35] See Gerald Helman and Steven S. Ratner, "Saving Failed States," *Foreign Policy* 89 (Winter 1992–1993): 3–20. For a useful survey of perspectives on the origins of complex political emergencies, see Tony Waters, *Bureaucratizing the Good Samaritan* (Boulder, CO: Westview Press, 2001).

[36] Natsios, *U.S. Foreign Policy and the Four Horsemen of the Apocalypse,* 7.

[37] Alex de Waal, *Famine Crimes: Politics and the Disaster Relief Industry in Africa* (Bloomington: Indiana Univ. Press, 1998).

[38] Kaldor, *New and Old Wars.*

[39] Michael Maren, *The Road to Hell: The Ravaging Effects of Foreign Aid and International Charity* (New York: The Free Press, 1997).

[40] Kaldor, *New and Old Wars,* 49–50.

[41] The following discussion draws from Pamela Aall, Daniel T. Miltenberger, and Thomas G. Weiss, *Guide to IGOs, NGOs, and the Military in Peace and Relief Operations* (Washington, DC: United States Institute of Peace, 2000); Kaldor, *New and Old Wars*; and Waters, *Bureaucratizing the Good Samaritan.*

[42] Aall, Miltenberger, and Weiss, *Guide to IGOs, NGOs, and the Military in Peace and Relief Operations,* 13.

[43] Waters, *Bureaucratizing the Good Samaritan*; Maren, *The Road to Hell.*

[44] See Fiona Terry, *Condemned to Repeat? The Paradox of Humanitarian Action* (Ithaca, NY: Cornell Univ. Press, 2002).

[45] Jonathan Goodhand with Peter Chamberlain, "Dancing with the Prince: NGOs' Survival Strategies in the Afghan Conflict," in *Development, NGOs, and Civil Society,* ed. Jenny Pearce, 91–108 (Oxford: Oxfam GB, 2000).

[46] Kaldor, *New and Old Wars,* 4.

[47] Peter Sollis, "The Development-Relief Continuum: Some Notes on Rethinking Assistance for Civilian Victims of Conflict," *Journal of International Affairs* 47, no. 2 (1994): 451–71.

[48] Aall, Miltenberg, and Weiss, *Guide to IGOs, NGOs, and the Military in Peace and Relief Operations.*

[49] See Elizabeth Ferris, "The Churches, Refugees, and Politics," in *Refugees and International Relations,* ed. Gil Loescher and Laila Monahan, 159–78 (Oxford: Clarendon Press, 1990).

[50] Findlay, *Cambodia;* Goodhand and Chamberlain, "Dancing with the Prince."

[51] Mark Bromley, "The International Human Rights Law Group: Human Rights and Access to Justice in Postconflict Environments," in *NGOs and Human Rights: Promise and Performance,* ed. Claude Welch, 141–50 (Philadelphia: Univ. of Pennsylvania Press, 2001).

[52] Michael Doyle and Nicholas Sambanis, "International Peacebuilding: A Theoretical and Quantitative Analysis," *American Political Science Review* 94, no, 4 (2001): 791.

[53] Nicholas Berry, *War and the Red Cross: The Unspoken Mission* (New York: St. Martin's Press, 1997).

[54] Waters, *Bureaucratizing the Good Samaritan.*

[55] Aall, Miltenberger, and Weiss, *Guide to IGOs, NGOs, and the Military in Peace and Relief Operations.*

[56] Not surprisingly, this causes tension between NGOs and their UN and military counterparts in the field.

[57] Waters, *Bureaucratizing the Good Samaritan.*

[58] Natsios, *U.S. Foreign Policy and the Four Horsemen of the Apocalypse.*

[59] Maren, *The Road to Hell.*

[60] Goodhand and Chamberlain, "Dancing with the Prince."

[61] Richard Miniter, "The False Promise of Slave Redemption," *Atlantic Monthly* 284, no. 1 (1999): 63–70.

[62] Martha Finnemore, "Rules of War and Wars of Rules: The International Red Cross and the Restraint of State Violence," in *Constructing World Culture,* ed. John Boli and George Thomas (Stanford, CA: Stanford Univ. Press, 1999), 150.

Chapter 9

NGOs and Human Rights: Women's Rights at the UN

Human rights NGOs
Women's NGOs and the UN
NGO strategies
Outcomes

On September 30, 2004, Human Rights Watch (HRW) released a report entitled "Struggling to Survive: Barriers to Justice for Rape Victims in Rwanda." The report documented the persistent weaknesses in the Rwandan legal system that hampered the investigation and prosecution of sexual violence. On October 13 HRW criticized the UN Security Council's resolution on Sudan for its failure to provide protection for endangered civilians of the country and to impose sanctions on the Sudanese government. In May 2004 Oxfam published a briefing paper entitled, "Protecting Civilians: A Cornerstone of Middle East Peace." Oxfam urged the international community to find an external mechanism to protect civilians in the Occupied Palestinian Territories. The above illustrate some of the important work done by human rights NGOs.

This chapter first explains the roles and activities of human rights NGOs in general. Next it focuses on one specific group of human rights NGOs—the women's rights NGOs—and explains their contribution in bringing the women's rights issues to the international policymaking arena. The discussion highlights not only the accomplishments of women in the international policymaking arena but also the barriers that they faced and the strategies that they undertook to overcome those barriers. A major reason for this chapter's focus on the human rights of women is that it illustrates well NGO activism in global policymaking.

Human Rights NGOs:
A General Overview

Human rights NGOs are advocacy organizations whose goals are to monitor and report human rights violations, exert pressure on governments to promote human rights, hold them accountable, and build pressure to create international machinery to end human rights violations. Human rights NGOs have existed for centuries. Even before the UN Charter was adopted, the Anti-Slavery Society had been preoccupied since the eighteenth century with lobbying for the establishment of standards to outlaw slavery—one of the oldest human rights abuses.

The first antislavery society was formed in 1783 in England by a group of Quakers. The Society found a powerful voice for articulating its views in the Parliament—William Wilberforce. He lobbied constantly, until the British government, under Prime Minister Charles James Fox, abolished slavery in 1807. The founding of the Anti-Slavery Society as a formal organization happened in 1839. Several years later it merged with The Aborigines Protection Society. Through intensive lobbying this group persuaded the governments of Austria, France, Britain, Prussia, and Russia to adopt a treaty in 1841 that would recognize the rights of each government to halt ships on the seas of any one of the groups engaging in the slave trade. In 1990 it changed its name again and became the Anti-Slavery International for the Protection of Human Rights.

Currently there are numerous INGOs working to promote a human rights agenda. Some, like AI, HRW, the International League for Human Rights, the Lawyers Committee for Human Rights, and the International Commission of Jurists, are widely known. However, most of the newer and smaller ones working in different parts of the world are unknown (for example, the Arab-American Discrimination Committee, Legal Assistance Center in Namibia, World Organization against Torture).

Human rights NGOs engage in a variety of roles. Setting standards, providing information, lobbying, and providing assistance are their most important activities. All of these culminate in another significant role—participation at the UN level on various aspects of the human rights agenda.

Standard setting: Human rights NGOs have actively participated, lobbied, and exerted pressure on the UN to adopt different human rights convention. For example, several American NGOs persuaded the United States delegation to refer explicitly to human rights in the Charter of the United Nations. Other examples of major international conventions in which human rights NGOs' participation has been highly significant include the Declaration on the Protection of All Persons from Being Subjected to Torture and Other Cruel, Inhumane or Degrading Treatment for Punishment; the Convention on the Rights of the Child; and the Convention on the Prohibition, Stockpiling, Production and Transfer of Anti-Personnel Mines and on Their Destruction. NGOs participate in different ways in the development and adoption of these conventions. They work with sympathetic governments to prepare the drafts and bring them to conferences; they also provide legal and other technical expertise; they mobilize public opinion; and, most important, they lobby at the UN for their adoption.

Providing information: Gathering, verifying, and disseminating information are central goals of human rights NGOs. Information is the major weapon for all advocacy NGOs, including human rights NGOs. They publish reports and disseminate those to relevant parties. They use information to mobilize public opinion. A recent example is the 2005 annual review published by the HRW. The report reviewed human rights practices around the globe; the lead essay focused on the abuse of detainees in Abu Ghraib prison in Iraq.

Lobbying: Lobbying is a common function of human rights NGOs. They lobby for ratification of different treaties and conventions and to bring pressure on governments who are violating various forms of human rights. As an example, the American-Arab Anti-Discrimination Committee, founded by US Senator Jim Abourezk in 1980, includes a Government Affairs Department. Tens of thousands of letters to Congress and the White House have been written through this department.

Providing assistance: Several human rights NGOs provide direct service to poor clients. For example, the Urgent Assistance to Victims program of the World Organization against Torture provides victims of torture medical, legal, and/or social assistance. The Legal Assistance Center in Namibia offers different types of legal assistance to protect constitutional and human rights for individuals who cannot afford legal fees. Other NGOs that primarily engage in relief and development activities have added human rights to their agendas. Oxfam International and Medecins Sans Frontieres are two examples.

Human Rights NGOs at the UN Level:
The Women's Rights Movement

As Chapters 3 and 5 showed, NGOs have formed an effective partnership with the UN. Active pursuit by NGOs has placed crucial issues on the UN policymaking agenda. Human rights NGOs are noteworthy in this aspect too. Reports issued by NGOs about atrocities—torture, disappearances, and political killings—motivated different governments to support the formation of various UN machineries and bodies to address such violations. "In virtually every instance—before the UN decided to appoint Rapporteurs on Guatemala, Bolivia, El Salvador, Poland, Afghanistan, Iran, Cuba, Myanmar, Sweden, Zaire, and following emergency sessions in 1992 and 1993, former Yugoslavia and Rwanda—NGOs stepped forward with documentary evidence of abuses, often detailed in plenary speeches at the Commission on Human Rights."[1]

The work of NGOs in advocating women's rights stands out. There is no doubt that NGOs remain the most committed group in promoting human rights, uncovering human rights abuses worldwide, and monitoring states' commitments in this area. Human rights, however, did not always include women's human rights. In fact, the human rights of women have been taken seriously by states and IGOs only within the last two decades and at the persistent insistence of women's NGOs, despite the fact that the equality of men and women is clearly stated in Article 1 of the UN Charter.

Women's NGOs and the UN: Background

The origin of women's NGOs' participation at the UN lies with its predecessor, the League of Nations. Different NGOs, including women's transnational organizations, had informal consultative interactions with the League. Throughout the history of the League, women's organizations were able to form consultative bodies to lobby on a wide range of issues, including social reform, women's rights, and peace. Although few in number compared to today, women's organizations sent deputations and maintained correspondence with the League. Some of the most widely known of these include the Women's International League for Peace and Freedom, the World Young Women's Christian Association, the International Council of Women, and the International Woman Suffrage Alliance. The League provided an important venue for women's organizations to appeal for universal suffrage and other rights.[2] For example, in 1935, by invitation from the secretary general, women's organizations provided reports and made statements to the League on the unequal status of women in regard to employment practices and laws. It was at the League of Nations that women's organizations developed the parallel conference, a repertoire of collective action now used by NGOs in a range of issue areas.

When the UN was formed in 1945, women representing national and international women's organizations, such as the Inter-American

---

Box 9–1. UN Commission on the Status of Women

The ECOSOC established this commission in 1947, marking the first formally organized women's diplomatic force in the UN arena. The commission is composed of forty-five member governments, with one-third of its members changing annually. The commission meets once a year. Its functions are to "prepare recommendations and reports to the Economic and Social Council on promoting women's rights in political, economic, civil, social and educational fields," and to make recommendations "on urgent problems requiring immediate attention in the fields of women's rights." Most of its appointees tend to rely for political, intellectual, and moral support on the NGOs from which they are drawn.* Over time, this body has turned into a significant arm for women activists and groups and is now recognized by the UN as a source of expertise on women's concerns. The commission has regularly made suggestions on urgent problems in the field of women's rights to the ECOSOC and to other UN organs. Its Division for the Advancement of Women maintains close contact with women's organizations and relies on their information for the preparation of reports and documents. This unit plans policies and programs on women, compiles reports on the monitoring of the implementation of international agreements on women, organizes experts' meetings, and conducts research on important women's issues.

---

*Jane Connors, "NGOs and the Human Rights of Women in the United Nations," in *The Conscience of the World: The Influence of Non-governmental Organisations in the UN System,* ed. Peter Willetts, 147–80 (London: Hurst and Company, 1996).

Commission on Women, founded in the 1920s, helped to create the climate and support needed to include the principle of equality between men and women in the UN Charter and recommended the formation of the UN Commission on the Status of Women (CSW). During the UN's first thirty years the only women's NGOs that had consultative status with the UN were those that were both representative and international.

Gradually the number of women's NGOs has increased, in line with the general trend for NGOs. While the traditional women's NGOs had focused mostly on religion, suffrage, and welfare, those created during and after the 1970s focused on issues like health, reproductive rights, human rights, the environment, and child labor. These new groups of women brought energy and vitality to the traditional women's movement worldwide. The following section describes women NGOs' activism at the UN level, the processes and strategies they used, and the outcome of their efforts.

Activism during the 1970s and 1980s

Starting in the 1970s, women's groups began to lobby seriously and persistently to bring women's issues and agendas into the global policymaking arena. UN-sponsored conferences along with the accompanying workshops, regional meetings, and tribunals facilitated this endeavor.

The earliest NGO initiative at the UN was the call for an International Women's Year. At the insistence of the Women's International Democratic Federation, which had consultative status with the UN, and the recommendation from the CSW, the General Assembly declared 1975 to be the International Women's Year (IWY) and also authorized the First World Conference on Women. The idea was "to devote this year to intensified action: (a) To promote equality between men and women; (b) To ensure full integration of women in the total development effort . . . ; (c) To recognize the importance of women's increasing contribution to the development of friendly relations and cooperation among States and to the strengthening of world peace."[3] UN agencies acknowledged the IWY in special reports, seminars, and ceremonies. Several countries observed IWY and issued proclamations and declarations supporting its spirit. Numerous conferences, seminars, and special events were organized during the year. Women's NGOs formed an IWY Committee to publicize IWY and to sponsor special seminars and conferences.

The significance of the IWY cannot be overemphasized. It had two major effects. First, it brought the women's movement to the global level. Second, it marked the beginning of a new era in the UN in which NGO activism grew on an unprecedented scale.

The First World Conference on Women was held in Mexico City the same year. Over six thousand women participated in the NGO forum in Mexico City, more unofficial participation than any previous UN world conference. Delegations from 133 member states, 113 of them headed by women, took part in the official conference, in which 192 NGO representatives participated. The forum organized ninety-two informal sessions on topics as diverse as law and women's status, population, and planned parenthood.[4]

Eventually, a World Plan of Action was adopted, "the first such document the world had seen to concentrate specifically on problems and concerns of women, covering all possible aspects of their lives from food, health and education to family planning and political participation."[5] The World Plan of Action offered a set of comprehensive guidelines for the advancement of women until 1985 and put forward minimum targets to be met by 1980. These included equal access for women to every level of education and training, the enactment of legislation ensuring political participation of women, increased employment opportunities, and improvements in health services, sanitation, housing, nutrition, and other matters.

An unsettling revelation during the Mexico City Conference was the wide philosophical gulf between activists in the North and South. While feminists in the South emphasized development and social justice, their counterparts in Europe and North America emphasized discrimination and equality. The Mexico City Conference was a critical consciousness-raising event that made women realize that collective action across borders is key to bringing about major change.

In December 1975 the General Assembly approved the recommendations of the Mexico City Conference and declared 1976–85 to be the UN Decade for Women. In a resolution adopted on December 15, 1975, the General Assembly declared that the decade would be devoted to the implementation of the Mexico City initiatives and called on governments, NGOs, IGOs, and UN organizations to engage in a broad array of activities to improve the status of women. The very existence of the Decade for Women served to promote and legitimize the international women's movement. Its activities at the national, regional, and international levels helped to bring women's issues to the forefront of world attention. A UN blue book noted:

> The Decade contributed to a fundamental transformation of the United Nations itself from an Organization in which Governments set policies and agendas to one in which policy and direction were also generated from the grass-roots level and by NGOs. NGOs brought the voices of women suffering from discrimination, poverty and oppression to the attention of the United Nations.[6]

The Second World Conference on Women was organized in Copenhagen in 1980 to mark the midpoint of the decade and to assess to what extent the targets set in the World Plan of Action had been attained. This conference covered a broader range of development issues and perspectives than those covered in Mexico City, including the reassessment of past approaches in development, employment, health, and education for women. Approximately eight thousand people, mostly women, attended the NGO forum. The official conference was attended by delegates from 145 governments; 134 NGOs registered with the official conference. CONGO had established the planning committee for the forum. The committee worked to integrate a broad geographic perspective in the planning and to develop the program, media contacts, and a forum newspaper. As a result, 150 to 175 workshops were held each day at the Copenhagen forum, a level of activity not previously seen.[7]

After intense debates, delegates adopted a Conference Programme of Action and forty-eight resolutions calling for stronger national measures to ensure women's ownership and control of property, as well as improvements in women's rights of inheritance, child custody, and loss of nationality. Significantly, the conference document recognized the contribution of NGOs. Paragraphs 100–104 in the Conference Programme of Action focused on the role of NGOs and recommended mutual cooperation between governments and NGOs. The delegates also recommended that future data collection needed to include gender and age, arguing that this was especially important in assessing the situation of rural women, the unemployed, migrants, the young and elderly, and single mothers.

As with the Mexico City Conference, serious divisions among NGOs were at the core of debates. One author has described the Copenhagen

Conference and the NGO forum as the "most conflictive" of all the conferences of the women's decade.[8] Women's NGOs representing the views of radical, moderate, and third-world feminism split between those that believed that women were being used by male-dominated political and revolutionary movements to further patriarchy and others who asserted that they could not separate their national struggles from their feminist ones. There was also clear realization that the concept of equality was broader than the Western feminists' conception of women's civil and political rights.

The UN Decade for Women closed with the convening of the Nairobi Conference in 1985. This conference had two objectives: (1) to review and appraise the progress achieved and obstacles encountered in attaining the goals and objectives of the UN Decade for Women, and (2) to adopt the "Forward-Looking Strategies for the Advancement of Women to the Year 2000." This document was the result of a long process of preparation and government negotiations with the CSW. Women's organizations contributed to this negotiation through collaboration and lobbying their governments and through observer status at meetings of the commission. A record number of participants attended the official conference and the forum. Over two thousand delegates from 157 countries and several hundred NGO representatives attended the official conference. Over fourteen thousand women from some 150 countries attended the NGO forum.[9]

The final document of the Nairobi Conference, entitled "Forward Looking Strategies for the Advancement of Women," provided a framework as well as prescriptive measures to address the obstacles to the advancement of women. The heart of the document was a series of measures for implementing equality at the national level. There were three basic categories: constitutional and legal steps, equality in social participation, and equality in political participation and decision making. Specific measures were recommended in many key areas, especially employment, health, education, food, agriculture, industry, science and technology, and housing. There were references to NGOs in at least forty-five paragraphs of the document.[10]

Outcome of the UN Decade for Women

The UN Decade for Women produced several significant results. First was the Convention on the Elimination of All Forms of Discrimination against Women, also referred to as the Women's Convention. Its origin can be traced to the Declaration on the Elimination of Discrimination against Women drawn up by the CSW in 1963. Adopted by the General Assembly in 1967, the declaration aimed to "ensure the universal recognition in law and in fact of the principle of equality of men and women." After the declaration, the CSW drafted the Convention on the Elimination of all Forms of Discrimination against Women (CEDAW). The UN General Assembly adopted the convention, which was signed by some fifty countries at the opening ceremony of the 1980 UN Conference on Women in Copenhagen. The convention, once labeled the international bill of rights for women, mandates that states meet minimum standards for achieving equal rights of women. Signatories are required to submit progress reports on the degree to which their domestic laws conform to the international standard. Article 11 of the declaration states that "governments, non-governmental organizations and individuals are urged, therefore, to do all in their power to promote the implementation of the principles contained in this Declaration." The Committee on the Elimination of Discrimination against Women is the body to which the parties to the convention must report. It comprises twenty-three members who are elected for four-year terms by the governments that have ratified the convention. As of March 2005, 180 nations had ratified the convention, making it a significant pillar of international human rights law. The committee meets annually to review the governments' reports on the implementation of the convention.

A second major outcome is that governments and international organizations have begun to take steps to integrate a gender perspective into various policies, programs, and procedures. Before the UN Decade for Women, development policies and programs were considered to be gender neutral, meaning that such policies and activities were assumed to benefit both men and women. More important, they also were based on traditional gender roles. Hence, development policies and programs designed for women mostly involved nutrition, child care, and health and population.

Women researchers and activists began to make women visible as active participants in economic production, in the household, and in other sectors of society. Studies revealed that many development programs actually benefited men only and furthermore often had detrimental effects on women and on the community. By the mid-1970s a new policy geared to "integrate women in development" started to be implemented among different development agencies, including the World Bank. The assumption behind the new policy was that neglect of women could be remedied and their situation improved by including them in development projects and programs. This approach is commonly called women in development (WID). The World Bank, for example, designed programs and projects on small-scale income generating projects (for example, sewing, handicrafts) with the goal that these will provide opportunities to women to participate actively in development efforts. The WID approach was later criticized by women's groups for its failure to include women's perspectives in planning and development policymaking, thus marginalizing women in development efforts. Moreover, the approach did not question the existent male model of development based on economic growth. Nevertheless, the WID approach, developed out of women's activism during the UN Decade for Women, helped promote the idea of women as an untapped resource for economic growth and the rights of women to participate in development planning and policymaking arenas as legitimate actors.

The WID approach led to the gender and development (GAD) approach. The term *gender* here is used to refer to the social construction of roles and to separate this socially constructed difference from the biological differences between men and women. The term *sex* is reserved to refer to the latter distinction. The GAD approach seeks to mainstream women in development, away from the integration approach of WID. Different strategies are used by the GAD approach to make gender a central focus of development programs. These include strengthening women's groups and organizations so that they work as strong pressure groups; gender-role awareness and gender analysis of projects and programs; building a critical mass of women inside development agencies; and lobbying and pressuring development institutions.[11]

Third, the decade resulted in new UN agencies dealing with women's issues and concerns. In 1976 the UN Development Fund for Women (UNIFEM) was established. In 1982 the UN International Research and Training Institute for the Advancement of Women (INSTRAW) was set up. UNIFEM, working in association with UNDP, provides direct financial and technical support to low-income women in developing countries and funds programs geared to bring women into mainstream development decision making. INSTRAW conducts research and training intended to integrate women into development processes and to promote women's participation in politics and public life.

Finally, the experiences during the UN Decade for Women gave women's groups extensive exposure to the UN system. Equally important, it gave them the opportunity to forge relationships and networks with one another. Different network organizations were formed to sustain the process. One notable example is the Development Alternatives with Women for a New Era. This is a network of scholars and activists in the South. Other significant ones are the International Women's Tribune Center, the Women's International Network, and Isis. Through networking and conference participation, women developed skills, built ongoing relationships, and realized the strength of their coalitions.

As Martha Chen explains, women gained insights and lessons from their experiences at these world conferences.[12] They realized, first, that in order to be heard they had to be active and well versed in UN procedures. Second, the best time to influence world conferences is during the preparatory process, and NGOs have to learn to lobby during that phase. And third, the international women's movement needed to build consensus and coalitions to bridge the ideological and material differences among women. Women's groups effectively put these experiences and insights to use in later conference and advocacy activities.

Activism in the 1990s

The 1990s gave women new opportunities to participate in the UN arena. Several major UN conferences were held at which women's NGOs used the experiences gained during the 1970–80s to participate more effectively and in more concerted ways.

In 1989 the UN declared that the Conference on Human Rights would be held in Vienna in 1993, and women's groups and activists began to make preparations. In 1991 the Center for Women's Global Leadership organized a strategic planning meeting of grassroots activists from twenty countries. At that meeting the decision was made to make gender-based violence a women's rights issue. The ultimate goal was to make women's rights an issue of human rights. Women faced huge obstacles on this due to the prevailing distinction between women's rights and human rights inside the UN. The distinction was justified mostly with the argument that women's rights violations, in contrast to human rights violations, occur extensively in the domestic sphere, where the state has no right to interfere, and are perpetrated by private individuals instead of state officials.

NGOs called for a global campaign that included developing strategies, promoting consensus building, holding petition drives, documenting violence against women, and drafting a consensus document on integrating women's rights into human rights. In the process numerous national, regional, and international meetings were held; extensive information was collected; and documents were prepared, exchanged, and revised. In almost all of the regional conferences, women's groups prepared consensus documents and successfully lobbied for the inclusion of gender violence in the general platform of action. The networking efforts of the women's groups received support from mainstream human rights organizations, especially AI and HRW. The preparations for the 1993 conference thus strengthened connections between the international human rights network and the women's network.

A significant mechanism for organizing women's action and informing public opinion on women's human rights was launched in late 1991 by a coalition of women's groups and organizations during the Sixteen Days of Activism against Gender Violence. This was a worldwide petition drive asking the preparatory committee for the World Conference on Human Rights to "comprehensively address women's rights at every level of the Conference proceedings" and demanding that "gender violence" be recognized as a violation of human rights requiring immediate action. The petition's drive to recognize women's rights as human rights eventually gathered more than 300,000 signatures in 123 countries. Over 800 groups joined the petition. The drive continued after the Vienna Conference, and by November 1994 had gathered more than 500,000 signatures and 2,000 cosponsoring groups.[15]

More than three thousand participants representing fifteen hundred NGOs participated in the Vienna Conference. Throughout the conference the NGO Women's Caucus met daily to assess the conference proceedings. One of the most notable events in the forum was the Global Tribunal on Violations of Women's Rights, organized by the Center for Women's Global Leadership and other NGOs. During the tribunal women from twenty-five countries provided testimonies as survivors of different forms of violence—domestic and political. The tribunal was presided over by four international judges, who discussed the human rights principles that were violated and made concrete suggestions to redress such abuses. The Global Tribunal on Violations of Women's Rights made a powerful impact on the international community. The organizers successfully secured time on the official agenda for a report on the tribunal and its recommendations. The determination and active lobbying succeeded. Article 18 of the Vienna Declaration and Programme of Action states:

> The human rights of women and of the girl child are an inalienable, integral indivisible part of universal human rights. The full and equal participation of women in political, civic, economic, social and cultural life, at the national, regional and international levels, and the eradication of all forms of discrimination on grounds of sex are priority objectives of the international community. . . . The human rights of women should form an integral part of the United Nations human rights activities, including the promotion of all human rights instruments relating to women.[14]

The Vienna Conference also called for the appointment of a special rapporteur on violence against women by the UN Human Rights Commission as well as the adoption of the Declaration on the Elimination of Violence against Women. In December 1993 the UN General Assembly adopted the declaration and in February 1995 appointed a special rapporteur on violence against women. The declaration stresses violence that results in physical, sexual, or psychological harm to women occurring in public or private life. Violence includes rape, battery, sexual abuse, torture, trafficking, forced prostitution, kidnapping, sexual harassment, dowry-related violence, female genital mutilation, violence perpetuated or condoned by the state, and other practices.

The UN hosted the Third Conference on Population and Development in Cairo in 1994. In preparation, women's activists from Asia, Africa, Latin America, Europe, and the United States working on women's health (later called the Women's Voices '94 Alliance) met in 1992. This was a meeting of a small group of women associated with women's health organizations. The alliance drafted a report entitled "Women's Declaration on Population Policies" that defined women's ability to control their fertility as a human right and specified seven ethical principles that population policies and programs should honor in order to ensure the centrality of women's well-being.

The document, however, triggered substantial criticism from the Vatican and from segments within the women's health movement. The Vatican viewed it as promoting unlimited rights to abortion. Different women's health organizations criticized the declaration for both procedural and substantive reasons. Procedural reasons arose out of the concern that it was drafted by an exclusive group of women whose perspective did not represent the entire women's movement. The substantive argument was that the focus on population policy would not address problems like poverty and would only reinforce the existing power structures. Such opposition prompted the alliance to rethink and alter its strategy.[15]

The declaration was sent out to different groups; eventually it was reviewed and revised by over one hundred women's organizations across the globe. In the spring of 1994, shortly before the International Conference on Population and Development, women activists organized another important strategy meeting in Rio de Janeiro. In contrast to the London meeting in 1992, the Rio Conference was much more inclusive. More than two hundred participants had been invited to the meeting; the criteria for selection were nationality, culture, age, sexual orientation, income level, and philosophy. Moreover, the meeting in Rio was much more accessible for Southern women. Participants at the Rio Conference agreed on a twenty-one-point statement considerably broader in scope than the Women's Voices '94 Alliance declaration. Contrary to the declaration, which had justified women's reproductive rights and health in terms of human rights, the Rio statement placed them squarely into the development framework. It claimed inequitable models and strategies to be responsible for existing problems with respect to population and called for "alternative development strategies" starting from the concerns and priorities of women. Women activists also used the meeting to rehearse individual and group responsibilities for the Cairo Conference.

The U.S. Network for Cairo '94 coordinated the activities of a broad spectrum of population, environmental, and development organizations in support of the women's agenda.[16] During the conference, in the NGO forum, the Women's Caucus met every morning to review the proceedings. Similar to the previous conferences, women's representative from different NGOs actively lobbied the different government delegates.

The outcome was a clear victory for women's NGOs and for women in general. The Conference Programme of Action document shows a new approach to population and development and places women's health and rights at the center. The conference affirmed that there are four requirements for any program of population and development: gender equality and equity; the empowerment of women; the ability of women to control their own fertility; and the elimination of all violence against women.[17] The conference made three basic recommendations: establish mechanisms for women's equal participation and equitable representation at all levels of the political process and public life; make efforts to promote women's education, employment, and skills development; and eliminate all discriminatory practices, including those in the work place and those affecting access to credit, control of property, and social security.[18]

The Fourth UN Conference on Women was held September 4–15, 1995, in Beijing, China. The NGO forum, with thirty thousand participants, was held August 30 through September 8 in Huairou. Approximately fifty thousand men and women gathered in Beijing. Three thousand NGOs represented by over four thousand individuals participated in the official conference. It was reportedly the largest international meeting convened under UN auspices. At the forum every class from peasant to worker to movie star and every race, ethnicity, religion, nationality, and sexual preference were represented, and for the first time a large number of young people, babies, and men attended.[19]

The Beijing Conference broke new ground for women. It asserted once and for all that women's rights are human rights. The Platform of Action adopted by the 189 governments represented at the conference obligates governments to empower women in twelve critical areas: poverty, education and training, health care, violence against women, armed conflict, inequality in economic structures, power and decision making, institutional mechanisms for the advancement of women, human rights, media, environment, and the rights of the girl-child. Strategies for action are listed for each of the areas. For example, under the critical area of violence against women, the platform lists:

- *Strategic objective D.1.* Take integrated measures to prevent and eliminate violence against women. . . .
- *Strategic objective D.2.* Study the causes and consequences of violence against women and the effectiveness of preventive measures. . . .
- *Strategic objective D.3.* Eliminate the trafficking in women and assist victims of violence due to prostitution and trafficking.

In addition to defining the strategies, the platform spells out the actions and roles to be taken by governments, the international community, NGOs, and the private sector. The role of governments is to implement the platform; the role of the NGOs is to hold them accountable and to assist them in implementation.

In a number of issue areas the platform addressed subjects that had been considered taboo, at least in international conferences. Domestic and sexual abuse, forced pregnancy, sexual orientation, and pornographic materials as a cause of violence against women were taken up for the first time.

Box 9–2. Comments on the Beijing Platform of Action

From the Platform of Action's mission statement:
  The Platform for Action is an agenda for women's empowerment.
  . . . This means that the principle of shared power and responsibility should be established between women and men at home, in the workplace and in the wider national and international communities. Equality between women and men is a matter of human rights and a condition for social justice and is also a necessary and fundamental prerequisite for equality, development and peace.

Gertrude Mongella, secretary general of the conference, speaking at the welcoming ceremony:
  A revolution has begun. There is no going back. There will be no unraveling of commitments; neither today's, nor last year's, and certainly not this decade's commitments. This revolution is too just, too important, and certainly long overdue.*

An Australian law professor at a session on the NGO forum:
  The Platform for Action reads like a women's studies course.**

---

  *Gertrude Mongella,"A Revolution Has Begun," *Women's Studies Quarterly* 24, no. 1–2 (1996); 116.
  **Florence Howe, "Editorial," *Women's Studies Quarterly* 24, no. 1–2 (1996): 12.

Preparations for the Beijing Conference among women's NGOs around the world were unprecedented in scope and breadth. The Conference Platform of Action was the result of a two-year process including meetings at the community, national, and international levels engaging thousands of women in the policymaking process. National committees set up by governments and NGOs reviewed the status of women in their respective countries, analyzed the draft platform, and adopted their own recommendations. The CSW conducted numerous preparatory meetings in which NGOs participated. In addition, five regional meetings discussed recommendations and defined regional plans of action. In both the conference itself and in the recommendations of the platform, the role of NGOs was highlighted, perhaps more strongly than ever before.

NGOs were key players in pushing governments to make specific commitments and in suggesting compromise language for the conference's final documents. The conference's declaration, which is similar to a preamble to the Conference Platform of Action, declares:

> The participation and contribution of all actors of civil society, particularly women's groups and networks and other non-governmental organizations and community-based organizations, with full respect for their autonomy, in cooperation with Governments, are important to the effective implementation and follow-up of the Platform for Action.

Box 9–3. Making Governments Keep Their Promises

NGOs can push governments to make policies, but governments ultimately implement them or do not. A constant challenge for NGOs, then, is to make governments live up to their pledges. During the Beijing Conference, NGOs put up a "commitments" board that recorded what each government promised to do. These commitments ranged from a pledge by Cote d'Ivoire to have 100 percent of girls enrolled in schools by the year 2000 to a promise by India to increase education investment to 6 percent of GDP with a focus on women and girls. "Daily briefings hosted by the NGOs centered around the Scoreboard, with NGOs from different countries rating the performance of various governments."[*]

---

[*]Ellen Dorsey, "The Global Women's Movement: Articulating a New Vision of Global Governance," in *The Politics of Global Governance: International Organizations in an Interdependent World,* ed. Paul F. Diehl (Boulder, CO.: Lynne Rienner, 1997), 347.

NGO Strategies

Women's NGOs have been successful in redefining the global agenda to make it more inclusive of the issues they espouse. What strategies have helped women to accomplish this? A careful reading of this history of the global women's movement shows a variety of strategies at work, at times refined based on women groups' cumulative experiences at the UN.

First, conscious efforts were directed to maintaining regular communication and networking between and among women's NGOs and other NGOs who share women's concerns. Several NGOs were created to facilitate this process. For example, the creation of Isis and the Women's International Network has helped women maintain connections among themselves throughout the year through their reports and newsletters. "More than any other groups, women's organizations use the terms 'network' and 'networking' to describe their interactions. Indeed, many international women's groups are named 'networks.'"[20] Telecommunications and advanced technologies facilitated women's networking, expanding participation and providing a means to argue points of view. For example, in preparation for the Beijing Conference, women used email to communicate logistical problems and to organize panel and travel arrangements. At the NGO forum Apple Computer, Hewlett Packard, and the Women's Networking Support Program of the Association for Progressive Communications staffed a computer center that generated seventeen hundred free email accounts and 100,000 visits to Internet sites, and included the use of email, electronic conferencing, data bases, Internet navigation tools, access to conference documents, and user support.[21]

Women's NGOs have actively built transnational advocacy networks. On several occasions women's networks followed a pattern described by Keck and Sikkink (see Figure 9–1).[22] Keck and Sikkink explain this pattern using the issue of violence against women. A dispersed network of groups from different regions began to create global awareness about this issue. These efforts were intensified and united with the emergence of a "target," in this case the World Conference on Human Rights and later the Beijing Conference. Incidents of violence like rape in Bosnia and dowry burning in India served as condensation symbols of violence against women. The Center for Women's Global Leadership at Rutgers University organized the Global Campaign on Women's Human Rights and served as a catalyst to create global awareness on this issue. Keck and Sikkink argue that women groups have successfully used this strategy to advance their cause.

Second, efforts geared to building consensus among the diverse groups of women were emphasized. Since their meeting at the First World Conference on Women, women's groups have become aware of their religious, cultural, and regional differences. Women realized that they would have to work together to build pressure on the UN. To do that, women's

Figure 9–1. Pattern of Women's
Transnational Advocacy Networks

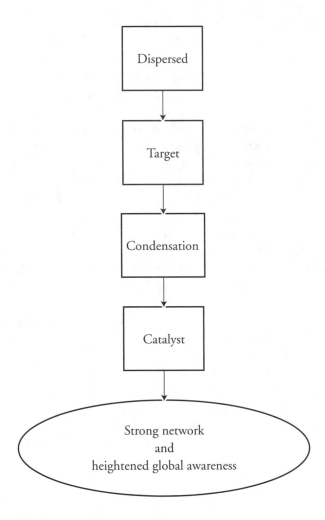

groups have held preparatory meetings in different regions, have formed committees with diverse members, and have debated issues in panels at the NGO forums.

Third, over time women's groups have prepared themselves better for official conferences. They have collected data and prepared reports to be used in official debates. Moreover, with the realization that most of the decisions and documents are prepared at the preparatory meetings of the official conferences, women have increased their presence and participation at this phase. Several of the conferences had preparatory meetings lasting as long as two years. Instead of lobbying government delegates during the official conference, women's NGOs have learned to lobby more during the preparatory phase by submitting their reports, data, and suggestions.

Fourth, NGOs took advantage of the generally positive UN attitude toward non-state actors. Compared to the World Bank and the IMF, the UN has provided NGOs with an important resource in the form of international forums in which NGO participation is a key feature. NGOs were regularly allowed to organize the NGO forums alongside the official conferences. In this environment constant liaison can be maintained between the official delegates and the members of the NGO forum. In most cases the NGO forum was organized very close to the official conference. NGOs kept both sides apprised of events through daily newspapers and other media. Official delegates, especially the NGOs in consultative status, regularly attended these forums.

The last but perhaps the most important strategy that women used was consciously to bring one issue after another before the UN and to maintain constant pressure, demanding that it sponsor conferences on women. Women's groups know very well that they have had to fight, even for very basic rights like voting and property ownership. All these different strategies helped women's groups to create and maintain momentum at different periods.

Outcomes

Specifically, what did women accomplish? There have been some significant achievements: a major convention on women's rights (CEDAW), integration of women's rights as human rights, a permanent UN commission on the status of women (the CSW), adoption of the Declaration on the Elimination of Violence against Women, and appointment of a special rapporteur on violence against women. Gender rights are now part of international law. This, in turn, has pressured national governments to change domestic law to conform to the treaties they have signed. Responding to the UN call, many countries have undertaken legal reforms and removed discriminatory provisions in civil, penal, and personal status law governing marriage, women's property ownership, and political and working rights. For instance, Ethiopia and Morocco have strengthened provisions in their constitutions guaranteeing equality between women and men and the protection of women's human rights. Oman enhanced the political rights of women by granting them the right to vote in 1997. A number of African countries (Senegal, Ghana, Togo, Djibouti, Burkina Faso, and the Central African Republic) have outlawed female circumcision, commonly known as female genital mutilation.

But has women's status significantly improved because of all these conventions, declarations, and platforms? Here the answer is less clear. The final documents of Beijing or of any other UN conference are only policy statements; they are not binding on governments. Moreover, while women's organizations have been successful in advocating the placement of social and political rights into international law, they have been less so in advocating equal economic rights. Report after report has shown continuing widespread violence against women, growing poverty among women, lack of education, poor health, and other issues that women have tried so hard to bring before the UN.

The twenty-third special session of the General Assembly, "Women 2000: Gender Equality, Development and Peace for the Twenty-first Century," took up that problem in June 2000. One of its major goals was to assess progress made on the implementation of the Platform for Action from the Beijing Conference. Findings showed that some progress had been made but much remained to be done. Women still lag far behind men in assuming leadership and decision-making roles, in earnings, in education, and in other significant areas.

Part of the problem lies in the fact that the UN is not the only IGO that influences international economic policies. The World Bank and the IMF are also key actors. Chapter 5 noted that the UN has generally been more hospitable to NGO advocacy than the international financial institutions, which provide few points of access for women's NGOs. Moreover, the debate at the World Bank has not been about equal social and political rights but about economic equality and appropriate policies that make that possible. Women's organizations that advocate fundamentally different gender relations in the economy from those that currently exist have made little headway in convincing the World Bank to alter its policy advice to national governments.[23]

The fact of the matter is that one cannot easily assess the contribution of these NGOs using outcome variables. The gains that are made in the process are equally important. Ellen Dorsey puts it succinctly in her discussion of the effects of the global women's movement:

If the movement's success were to be measured by whether the broad vision that women's organizations are articulating for a new global order is achieved, many will likely claim it is an abject failure. But, if we think in terms of the process forged for articulating a new vision, organizing communities of disparate people to fight for that vision, and the advancement of new norms around which the practices of international institutions, social and economic forces, and government policies are increasingly held accountable—the successes have already been overwhelming.[24]

Conclusion

This chapter described human rights NGOs and specifically focused on the women's rights movement at the UN, where women's NGOs have played an important role in norm creation about human rights. They have helped solidify the expectation that human rights are universal. The UN has proved an effective place for women's NGOs to argue that a core body of human rights is binding regardless of national policies. A major accomplishment has been putting violating states on the defensive, forcing them to explain why their policies do not conform to international law and expectations. Here, women's NGOs are in good company with NGOs that advocate other human rights issues. Norms and international law regarding political rights have expanded because NGOs advocate them and IGOs have provided forums in which to make claims about appropriate ways for states to treat their citizens.

Human rights NGOs are not above reproach. One of the emerging criticisms is that most of the high-profile human rights NGOs basically promote the Western world's idea of human rights. We saw a similar tension with the women's rights NGOs with the difference between Northern and Southern feminist groups. The other major criticism focuses on the reality that most international human rights NGOs have board members from the Northern countries who bring with them a world view that tends to focus on issues of concern in those countries. However, these are criticisms that apply to all types of INGOs.

It is not easy to measure the effectiveness of human rights NGOs, as explained with the women's rights issue. For example, AI is primarily an advocacy organization. How does one calculate the number of prisoners who have not been unjustly imprisoned, tortured, or unfairly tried for political crimes because of AI? It is not easy to quantify the effectiveness of human rights NGOs, which are mostly advocacy organizations like AI. It is important to realize, though, that effectiveness should take into consideration not only accomplishment in relation to human rights NGOs' programmatic objectives but also in terms of their achievement in promoting the idea of international human rights and in building the human rights movement as a whole.

Discussion Questions

1. How has the relationship between the UN and women's NGOs developed over time?
2. What advantages do women's NGOs derive by taking their concerns to the UN?
3. What kinds of problems hinder the advancement of human rights globally?

Suggestions for Further Reading

For the history of the global women's movement, see Ester Boserup, *Women's Role in Economic Development* (London: Earthscan, 1998). Boserup's book was a major catalyst in redefining gender roles in development. The text of the Conference Platform of Action adopted at Beijing is available online.

Notes

[1] Felice D. Gaer, "Reality Check: Human Rights NGOs Confront Governments at the UN," in *NGOs, the UN, and Global Governance,* ed. Thomas G. Weiss and Leon Gordenker (Boulder, CO: Lynne Rienner, 1996), 53.

[2] Nitza Berkovitch, "The Emergence and Transformation of the International Women's Movement," in *Constructing World Culture: International Nongovernmental Organizations since 1875,* ed. John Boli and George Thomas, 100–126 (Stanford, CA: Stanford Univ. Press, 1999).

[3] Excerpts from the General Assembly resolution proclaiming 1975 International Women's Year, A/RES/3010 (XXVII), December 18, 1972.

[4] Hilkka Pietila and Jeanne Vickers, *Making Women Matter: The Role of the United Nations* (London: Zed Books, 1994).

[5] Ibid., 78–79.

[6] UN, *The United Nations and the Advancement of Women, 1945–1996,* Blue Book series 6, rev. ed. (New York: UN Department of Public Information, 1996), 38.

[7] Jane Connors, "NGOs and the Human Rights of Women in the United Nations," in *Conscience of the World: The Influence of the Non-governmental Organizations in the UN System,* ed. Peter Willetts, 147–80 (London: Hurst and Company, 1996).

[8] Jane S. Jaquette, "Losing the Battle/Winning the War: International Politics, Women's Issues, and the 1980 Mid-decade Conference," in *Women, Politics, and the United Nations,* ed. A. Winslow (Westport, CT: Greenwood Press, 1995), 45.

[9] See Carolyn Stephenson, "Women's International Nongovernmental Organizations at the United Nations," in Winslow, *Women, Politics, and the United Nations,* 135–53.

[10] Ibid.

[11] Marilee Karl, *Women and Empowerment: Participation and Decision Making* (London: Zed Books, 1995), 103.

[12] Martha Chen, "Engendering World Conferences: The International Women's Movement and the UN," in *NGOs, the UN, and Global Governance,* ed. Thomas Weiss and Leon Gordenker, 139–55 (Boulder, CO: Lynne Rienner, 1996).

[13] Ibid.

[14] Vienna Declaration and Programme of Action, World Conference on Human Rights, Vienna, U.N. Doc. A/Conf. 157/224, 1993, para. 18.

[15] Jutta Joachim, "Framing Issues and Seizing Opportunities: The UN, NGOs, and Women's Rights," *International Studies Quarterly* 47, no. 2 (2003): 247–74.

[16] Irene Tinker, "Nongovernmental Organizations: An Alternative Power Base for Women?" in *Gender Politics in Global Governance,* ed. Mary K. Meyer and Elisabeth Prugl, 88–104 (Boulder, CO: Rowman and Littlefield, 1999).

[17] UN, *The United Nations and the Advancement of Women 1945–1996.*

[18] Ibid.

[19] Fauzia Ahmed, "Beyond Beijing: Making Room for Feminist Men," *Sojourner: The Women's Forum* 22, no. 2 (1996): 18.

[20] Margaret E. Keck and Kathryn Sikkink, *Activists beyond Borders* (Ithaca, NY: Cornell Univ. Press, 1998), 167.

[21] "Technology Links Forum to the UN and the World," *NGO Forum on Women '95 Bulletin* (December 1995), 10.

[22] Keck and Sikkink, *Activists beyond Borders.*

[23] Robert O'Brien, Ann Marie Goetz, Jan Aart Scholte, and Marc Williams, *Contesting Global Governance: Multinational Economic Institutions and Global Social Movements* (Cambridge, MA: Cambridge Univ. Press, 2000).

[24] Ellen Dorsey, "The Global Women's Movement: Articulating a New Vision of Global Governance," in *The Politics of Global Governance: International Organizations in an Interdependent World,* ed. Paul F. Diehl (Boulder, CO: Lynne Rienner, 1997), 356.

Chapter 10

NGOs and
Global Environmental Activism

Overview of environmental NGOs
NGO roles and strategies
NGOs and international environmental treaties

The problem of environmental destruction and how to remedy it has emerged as a major issue in international politics in the last four decades. As Gareth Porter and Janet W. Brown have argued, "By the early 1990s, it was not an exaggeration to say that the global environment had emerged as the third major issue in world politics, along with international security and global economies."[1] There is growing agreement on the need for international cooperation, although not always about what that cooperation should produce. Global environmental regimes have been negotiated on a wide variety of projects ranging from whale protection to climate change to desertification to sustainable development. States, international institutions, and NGOs have all played a fundamental role in the creation, development, and operation of international environmental regimes.

This chapter explains the role of environmental NGOs in environmental protection. Chapter 3 described the traditional role and the new roles of NGOs. The traditional role was relief, and the new roles include socioeconomic development, advocacy, lobbying, public education, consciousness raising, and monitoring. This chapter shows how environmental NGOs engage in all of these new roles.

We follow the convention in the research on transnational environmental politics by referring to environmental NGOs (ENGOs) throughout this chapter. ENGOs are a subset of the broad spectrum of organizations that make up the transnational NGO community. These are NGOs that directly or indirectly work to protect the environment.

Depending on the issue, they may include NNGOs and SNGOs. Similarly, both INGOs and national NGOs may be found working in this issue area.

The chapter first outlines the growth and characteristics of ENGOs and then notes some of their variations. Second, it considers NGO roles and strategies in promoting environmental causes. Third, it looks at NGO participation in environmental treaty formation and monitoring.

Development and Nature of ENGOs

The proliferation of international ENGOs has occurred largely since the end of World War II. During the nineteenth and early twentieth centuries environmental concerns were viewed primarily as local matters. A variety of local and national ENGOs was formed during this period. In the Western world ENGOs developed around local conservation and nature preservation.[2] Examples of these earliest organizations are the Royal Society for the Protection of Birds (UK), the Sierra Club (US), National Audubon Society (US), and the Wildlife Preservation Society (Australia), all of which are active today. INGOs specifically concerned with the environment started to form only at the beginning of the twentieth century. The earliest of these are the Society for the Preservation of the Wild Fauna of the Empire (1903), the Commission for the International Protection of Nature (1913), and the International Joint Commission (1909).

After World War II this growth accelerated. In 1956 the Commission for the International Protection of Nature was renamed the International Union for the Conservation of Nature (IUCN). It remains a key organization in the promotion of environmental protection. The World Wildlife Fund (WWF) was created in 1961. During the 1960s and 1970s INGOs working on environmental protection grew exponentially; at the same time their scope of operations expanded. Environmental issues moved beyond preservation and conservation to include pollution, nuclear concerns, resource depletion, and waste management. Friends of the Earth International and Greenpeace—two major ENGOs—were established during that period.

In Asia and Africa ENGOs mostly focusing on conservation of animals had existed during the colonial era. In post-colonial times ENGOs in the developing countries (mostly grassroots organizations) broadened their focus to emphasize the relationship between environment and development. Several of the major southern ENGOs were formed during the 1970s and the 1980s. Environment and Development Action in the Third World, the African NGO Coalition, and the Asia Pacific Peoples Environment Network are examples.

Four factors have prompted the emergence of the environmental movement and the growth of ENGOs. First, advancement in scientific knowledge on global environmental issues, especially environmental degradation, its effects, and the role that human activity plays in environmental destruction, brought growing awareness of the issue. Second, the emergence of post-industrial values in the 1960s and 1970s made the public in the developed countries receptive to appeals about environmental concerns. Third, there was a growing realization that many problems affect two or more countries and thus cannot be addressed by individual countries acting alone. Finally, the growth of international organizations has provided space in which transnational issues can be discussed. In this vein David J. Frank and his colleagues argue that the development of the transnational environmental movement parallels the growth in international organizations since the end of World War II.[3]

It is estimated that there are tens of thousands of NGOs working in some capacity to protect the environment. According to the *World Directory of Environmental Organizations Online*, as of August 10, 2006, there were 517 international ENGOs. However, the list includes only NGOs that have substantial membership in different countries. These are only the larger ones, many of which are actually umbrella bodies of countless smaller local and grassroots organizations. It is also difficult to estimate their total number because there are numerous other related NGOs whose main emphasis is on another issue—human rights, women in development, grassroots development—but who nevertheless also have environmental protection as part of their agenda. Because environmental issues are so interrelated with other transnational issues, the boundaries become blurred.

Not only is it difficult to count ENGOs, but it is also misleading to think of them as a unified community. NGOs can have very different understandings of what would promote a healthy environment. In the United States, for example, there are NGOs that are networked with industry-based groups and play an advocacy role for industries and businesses that oppose governmental regulation on certain issues. The Global Climate Coalition represents one such organization.

Box 10–1: NGOs in Focus: Global Climate Coalition (GCC)

The Global Climate Coalition (GCC) aggressively fought in the United States against reducing greenhouse gas emissions. Established in 1989 as an organization of trade associations to coordinate business participation in the international policy debates on global climate change and global warming, its members represented collectively more than six million companies across the economy.

GCC activities included aggressive lobbying at international climate negotiation meetings and raising concern about unemployment, which it claimed would result from emissions regulations. In 1997 the GCC responded to international global warming treaty negotiations in Kyoto, Japan, by launching an advertising campaign in the United States against any agreement aimed at reducing greenhouse gas emissions internationally. According to a *Los Angeles Times* report the GCC spent US$13 million on this anti-Kyoto ad campaign, an amount equivalent to Greenpeace's annual budget. GCC's website stated: "The coalition opposed Senate ratification of the Kyoto Protocol that would assign such stringent targets for lowering greenhouse gas emissions that economic growth in the U.S. would be severely hampered and energy prices for consumers would skyrocket."

The growing scientific and public consensus in the late 1990s regarding global warming made a number of members rethink their affiliation with the GCC. Several prominent companies, such as BP/Amoco, Dow, Dupont, Texaco, and General Motors, abandoned the group. The GCC disbanded in early 2002, explaining that "the industry voice on climate change has served its purpose by contributing to a new national approach to global warming. The Bush administration will soon announce a climate policy that is expected to rely on the development of new technologies to reduce greenhouse emission, a concept strongly supported by the GCC."

Source: globalclimate.org and prwatch.org websites

There are also differences along the North-South divide that parallel those of women's rights NGOs, discussed in the previous chapter. Southern ENGOs tend to be as much concerned with poverty, land use, forest management, and other development issues as with strictly environmental issues. In contrast, NNGOs tend to focus on global warming, biodiversity loss, and conservation of endangered species. SNGO's environmental priorities have been urban air and water pollution, the loss of agricultural land, and toxic chemical contamination. This difference in views was widely felt during the 1992 United Nations Conference on Environment and Development (UNCED), discussed later in this chapter. UNCED demonstrated that environmental NGOs do not always agree on the means for environmental protection. Northern and Southern NGOs, for example, voiced very different views concerning the policies necessary for the preservation of tropical forests.

ENGO goals and organizational structures are highly varied. In regard to goals, Walter Rosenbaum identifies three types of US ENGOs: the mainstream "pragmatic reformists," the deep ecologists, and the radicals.[4] This classification roughly fits environmental organizations in other developed countries as well. The pragmatists consist of the large, mainstream, politically active and publicly visible groups like the Sierra Club. These organizations prefer to work within established political processes in order to influence public policy. The deep ecologists include groups that believe that all forms of life have an equal right to exist; they challenge the underlying institutional structures and social values upon which governments are based and argue the need for fundamental social change as a prerequisite for effective environmental management. Earth First! is one such group. Radicals consist of groups that are frustrated with mainstream environmentalism and believe in the use of direct action to bring about urgently needed political action and social change. Greenpeace is the most notable example of such groups.

ENGOs vary in regard to their internal structure. John McCormick discusses five categorizes of ENGO, depending on how they are organized:

Internationally oriented national organizations and national NGOs are partly or wholly focused on international issues. The former includes the Sierra Club; the latter includes the World Resources Institute. The former is mainly active on the domestic political front but also campaigns on issues such as human rights and the environment. The World Resources Institute focuses on policy research and relies primarily on its technical expertise to influence environmental policy.

Regionally defined membership organizations are those whose interests are restricted to a particular continent or regions, such as African Wildlife Foundation (Kenya) and the European Community (EC).

Federations of international and national organizations are bodies set up to facilitate communication and cooperation among member bodies. Some of them have national offices (examples are Greenpeace and Friends of the Earth) in different countries, but these offices are autonomous and have their own funding and strategic priorities. Friends of the Earth International, based in Amsterdam, is a confederation of fifty-three national, independent affiliates, half of which are in developing countries; Greenpeace has more than 3.3 million members in twenty countries. Federations also take the form of umbrella bodies that bring together different organizations that act either as conduits for contacts between NGOs and an IGO (for example, the Environment Liaison Centre International provides a point of contact between NGOs and

---

Box 10–2: NGOs in Focus:
International Union for the Conservation of Nature (IUCN)

The IUCN was founded in 1948. Its mission is "to influence, encourage and assist societies throughout the world to conserve the integrity and diversity of nature and to ensure that any use of natural resources is equitable and ecologically sustainable." It is a partnership among more than 800 states, 111 government agencies, and thousands of NGOs across the world. The IUCN operates through the following commissions, made up of different networks of experts who offers information, guidance, and policy ideas:

- Commission on Education and Communication
- Commission on Environmental, Economic and Social Policy
- Commission on Environmental Law
- Commission on Ecosystem Management
- Species Survival Commission
- World Commission on Protected Areas

Source: iucn.org website

---

the UN Development Program) or as a channel for contact among NGOs (such as the African NGOs Environment Network).

Intercontinental membership organizations are bodies whose interests go beyond a particular region but do not have global membership. Birdlife International is a network of "partner" organizations of 115 countries that work collectively to gather and share information and to build strong national bodies working to protect birds and natural habitats. It has a global secretariat in Britain and regional offices in Ecuador, Indonesia, and Belgium.

Universal membership organizations are bodies that have a widespread, geographically balanced membership. According to McCormick, the only environmental INGO that really fits this category is IUCN, which brings together both NGOs and government agencies. IUCN is a hybrid organization of governmental organizations and NGOs.[5]

ENGO Roles and Strategies

ENGOs perform a variety of roles in environmental politics. Over time, they have developed a number of strategies to address issues of concern. What follows is a description of the important roles and strategies in which ENGOs engage and those that have made them a significant institution in environmental regimes.

Global Environmental Agenda Setting

ENGOs participate in and influence the global policymaking process in various ways. They actively participate in different UN conferences. The most extensive participation of NGOs in the global policymaking process was at the UNCED, held in Rio de Janeiro, Brazil in 1992. Also called the Earth Summit, it is seen as marking a new era in ENGO involvement in global policymaking. Considering the active involvement of NGOs in the preparation and in the deliberations of the conference, a brief description of the origin and deliberations of the UNCED is warranted here.

The origin of the UNCED process is traced to the World Commission on Environment and Development, better known as the Brundtland

Commission, set up in 1983. The commission produced the 1987 Brundtland report, entitled *Our Common Future*. The report was prepared with input from governments, UN agencies, and NGOs. The report identified the causes of global environmental problems as social and political: unsatisfied needs of the world's poorest population and limitations imposed by the state of technology and social organizations on the environment's ability to meet present and future needs.

The commission is generally given credit for defining the concept of sustainable development, although, in fact, several NGOs played a significant role in defining the concept. The concept first appeared in 1980 in the IUCN's *World Conservation Strategy: Living Resource Conservation for Sustainable Development.* IUCN viewed sustainable development as a means of natural-resource conservation and management mainly at a national level; governments were to manage the resources, their use, and the corresponding risks. ENGOs such as the IUCN were to contribute to development planning, project implementation, and consciousness raising activities. The Brundtland Commission adopted this concept of sustainable development as natural-resource management and transferred it from the national to the global level.

The UNCED was set up as a series of five preparatory meetings in which the Rio Declaration, Agenda 21, environmental financing, and possible institutional arrangements were negotiated. Although these negotiations took place exclusively among representatives of governments, NGOs did have some input in the process. The UNCED forced ENGOs and other NGOs to mobilize their constituencies and organize themselves to provide input to the process.

Two important coalitions came out of that realization. One was the Center for Our Common Future, which created the International Facilitating Committee (IFC) in 1990. The IFC's task was to coordinate NGO activities for the UNCED. It included not only NGOs but also the private sector. It was thus a coalition of various independent sectors that found it difficult to agree on anything except the concept of sustainable development and NGOs' role in it.

Due to the above concern with the IFC, the second coalition—the Environmental Liaison Committee International (ELCI) was formed. Several politically conscious NGOs and Southern grassroots NGOs joined this coalition. The ELCI set up an international steering committee and sponsored regional and national meetings. The main focus of the committee was to identify local solutions to global problems that can contribute to changes in lifestyle and consumption patterns. The committee organized a global NGO conference in Paris and produced an NGO position paper entitled "Roots for Our Future," which contained, among other things, a synthesis of NGO positions and a plan of action that dealt with issues like climate change, biodiversity, forestry, biotechnology, the GATT, lifestyle, and resource transfer. This document became the politically conscious ENGOs' input to the Rio Conference.

The NGO presence at the UNCED summit was in many ways the focal point of transnational environmental activism in the 1990s. NGOs enjoyed not only an unprecedented presence at the UNCED but also influence. A key vehicle for NGO influence was their participation in official delegations. More than two dozen countries had ENGO representatives on their national delegations. As with the ICBL (discussed in Chapter 8), this helped ensure that NGOs' views would be heard in the interstate conference. During the conference the IFC also facilitated NGO participation by organizing the parallel Global Forum, in which approximately twenty thousand people representing sixteen hundred organizations participated. The ELCI led a second parallel conference, known as the International NGO Forum. Of all the NGO events, this one had the most substance.[6]

According to observers, NGOs were not very successful at affecting the outcome of the official conference. However, the UNCED helped strengthen the already existing international ENGOs. It also helped create links among NGOs. For SNGOs, the UNCED provided an opportunity to gain prominence, visibility, and access to power.

The UN General Assembly followed up the Rio Summit by creating the Commission on Sustainable Development to implement Agenda 21. The commission began meeting in 1993, and since then it has devoted much of its attention to reviewing the reports submitted by states on steps they have taken to implement Agenda 21. It has been an effective forum for continuing discussions among governments, international organizations, and NGOs on how to carry out the plan of action on environment and development as set forth in Agenda 21. It has stimulated the creation of sustainable development commissions in at least 117 countries, and nearly 2,000 cities in 64 countries have adopted environmental plans.[7]

Policy Research and Development

NGO agenda setting at international conferences commands public attention, but NGOs also engage in agenda setting in ways that are more prosaic. NGOs can influence policy by providing information about policy options. Global environmental protection is a highly complex domain. NGOs devoted to research and policy research provide valuable information and knowledge bases to interested policy communities. Some NGOs maintain large professional staffs and produce regular extensive, well-researched reports. The World Resource Institute (WRI) publishes reports on the global environment and policy studies; the International Institute for Environment and Development and the International Institute for Sustainable Development of Canada are involved in active policy research. The IUCN has helped draft treaties and has provided a secretariat for several conventions. This helps states gain valuable information while minimizing expenditures. As Sheila Jasanoff points out, "NGOs have recognized that scientific knowledge is potentially one of their strongest allies—and sometimes an obdurate impediment—in the struggle to protect the environment."[8] She explains that on different issues such as whaling, oil spills, ocean dumping of chemical or radioactive wastes,

---

Box 10–3. NGOs in Focus: World Resource Institute (WRI)

Founded in 1982, the WRI is an environmental think tank whose mission "is to move human society to live in ways that protect earth's environment and its capacity to provide for the needs and aspirations of current and future generations."

Currently WRI has four hundred professionals from more than fifty countries and is connected to a network of advisors, collaborators, international fellows, and partner institutions. The network provides information, ideas, and solutions to global environmental problems. WRI's staff works on different projects related to the mission of the organization.

As an example, one of its current projects is CAIT (Climate Analysis and Indicators Tool), an interactive information and analysis tool on global climate change that includes data on different countries' greenhouse gas emissions and other indicators. This will assist policymakers in making informed decisions and also promote informed debates on environmental protection.

Source: wri.org website

and the safety of nuclear power, disputes among environmentalists, industry, and frequently states have centered on different assessments of the probability and magnitude of adverse environmental effects. NGOs may usefully open up the debate by questioning prevailing expert opinion or by expanding the available base with relevant bodies of local knowledge.

Changing Environmental Norms

ENGOs set agendas not only by engaging governments but also by working to change public norms about the environment. Paul Wapner explains that environmentalism can be viewed as a sensibility that values nature and believes that the quality of life on earth depends upon the well-being of the planet's air, water, soil, and so forth. Many cultural practices reveal an anti-ecological orientation; people throughout the world do things that degrade the environment because they operate according to traditions or within "ideological structures that support anti-ecological practices."[9] ENGOs work to make people more environmentally conscious.

For example, as Wapner points out, in East Asia people believe that the bile from bears' gall bladders acts as an antidote to liver cancer and hemorrhoids, as well as having other health benefits. Such a belief system endangers all bears in that region. ENGOs work to protect bears and other wildlife by making people more aware of the environmental consequences of their belief systems.

Stopping the trafficking of endangered species at national borders represents a key way to protect bears and other species. NGOs realize the limitations of such a practice; it is more important to change the cultural practices. The WWF, for instance, has been working with consumers and medical practitioners throughout East Asia to alter the way they understand endangered species and the necessity of using such species for medicinal purposes. Another way, as Wapner explains, is to change people's view of animals; that is, to see them not as objects to be consumed but as creatures to be preserved in the wild. As he points out, for years whales were seen as simply another resource for human consumption (for food and oil). Greenpeace, WWF, the Sea Shepherds Conservation Society, Friends of the Earth, and others have worked for years trying to change this image. Through photographs, films, and audio

Box 10–4. NGOs in Focus:
The Convention on
International Trade in Endangered Species
of Wild Fauna and Flora
(CITES)

The convention's goals are to ensure that international trade in specimens of wild animals and plants does not threaten their survival. Today, it accords varying degrees of protection to more than thirty thousand species of animals and plants.

CITES was drafted as the result of a resolution adopted in 1963 at a meeting of members of the IUCN. It was finally agreed upon at a meeting of representatives of eighty countries in Washington, D.C., in March 1973. CITES is a voluntary international agreement. Although CITES is legally binding on the parties (states that agreed to follow the convention), it does not take the place of national laws. Instead, it provides a framework to the parties with the expectation that each will adopt domestic laws consistent with CITES.

CITES works through implementing certain controls in international trade of specimens. These require that all import, export, and re-export of species covered by the convention be authorized through a licensing system. The species covered by CITES are listed in three appendices ranged according to the emphasis of protection needed.

Appendix I includes species threatened with extinction. The agreement allows very limited trade and then only under exceptional circumstances.

Appendix II includes species not threatened with extinction but whose trading needs tight controlling in order to avoid overutilization.

Appendix III contains species that are protected in at least one country, which has asked for CITES' assistance in controlling the trade.

Source: cites.org website

Box 10–5. NGOs in Focus: World Wildlife Fund

Established in 1961, WWF has become one of the world's largest transnational environmental activist groups. It has a central international office in Gland, Switzerland, and a second central hub in the United States. While the majority of WWF's offices are located in the developed countries, it has a substantial number of offices in the developing and underdeveloped countries. For example, WWF has offices in Cameroon, India, Malaysia, and Turkey. With almost five million supporters distributed throughout five continents, WWF has over twenty-eight national organizations and twenty-four program offices.

WWF's mission is "to stop the degradation of the planet's natural environment and to build a future in which humans live in harmony with nature by:

"Conserving the world's biological diversity
Ensuring that the use of renewable natural resources is sustainable
Promoting the reduction of pollution and wasteful consumption."

Since 1985 WWF has funded over eleven thousand projects in 130 countries. Currently, it is funding two thousand conservation projects and employs approximately four thousand people all around the world.

Source: wwf.org website

---

recordings, they have portrayed whales as a special species with intelligence and unique vocalizations that deserve not only protection but also respect. All of these have led to wide-scale support for acts such as Operation Rescue, wherein a US$5 million effort was waged in 1988 to save three whales trapped in ice in Alaska.

Environmental Policy Formulation and Implementation

ENGOs actively lobby or pressure their own governments or other governments to accept a more advanced position toward an issue by initiating consumers' boycotts and educational campaigns and/or by bringing lawsuits. These are among the most effective means for NGOs to influence international regimes. According to Porter and Brown, NGO negotiations on Antarctic minerals with key government officials are an exemplary one in this respect.[10] From 1982 to 1988, the members of the Antarctic Treaty System negotiated guidelines for mining activities in Antarctica. Nevertheless, the final agreement, the Convention on the Regulation of Antarctic Mineral Resources Activities, never came into force. In 1987, despite momentum toward adoption of this convention, the Antarctic and Southern Oceans Coalition, in which Greenpeace, Friends of the Earth, and WWF were the most active participants, put forward a detailed proposal for an Antarctic World Park that would exclude mineral exploration. Two years later a World Bank proposal was the basis for a new policy rejecting a treaty to govern future mineral exploitation in Antarctica. A coalition of twenty Australian NGOs were instrumental in convincing Australian prime minister Bob Hawke in 1989 to reject the Antarctic mineral treaty that his negotiators had just helped negotiate and to adopt the Antarctic World Park in its place. Effective lobbying by NGOs affiliated with the Antarctic and Southern Oceans Coalition brought support from Italy, Belgium, and other countries to support the Australian position. In 1991 the Protocol on Environmental Protection to the Antarctic Treaty was signed, banning all mining activities including prospecting, exploration, and development in the Antarctic region for fifty years. International ENGOs are credited for this endeavor and outcome.

Monitoring International Policy Formulation

NGOs also monitor the actions of state delegations during negotiations. Decentralized modes of monitoring that rely on interested outside parties to alert principals (states) of agents' (delegations) actions have been termed *fire alarms*.[11] NGO participation is one means by which governments can create fire alarms and allow outside parties to monitor delegates' action and inform governmental principals. In the United States, for example, members of Congress have been kept abreast of administration activities within international forums by NGO oversight. In recent congressional hearings, for example, NGO representatives castigated the US delegation's actions (and inactions) at ongoing negotiations of the climate convention.[12]

Modifying Existing Regimes

Wapner points out that NGOs play a key role in collecting new scientific evidence on the nature and intensity of environmental degradation, publicizing it, and working to upgrade regimes to reflect new environmental realities.[13] As he explains, due to the complexity of environmental issues, international accords are almost always in need of periodic revision. NGOs encourage such revisions and have been responsible, in a few instances, for proposing the content of treaty upgrades. For example, after states established the Montreal Protocol on Substances that Deplete the Ozone Layer, there was a need to revise national commitments due to scientific evidence of an expanding ozone hole over Antarctica and new understanding of the severity of the threat. Friends of the Earth, the Environmental Defense Fund, and other NGOs persuaded state officials to enhance the protocol. Along with NGOs, numerous scientist and policymakers also pressed for revisions. Before the meeting of government officials in London, several leading international environmental groups held press conferences and distributed informational brochures to the press, the public, and the officials. NGOs coordinated much of the effort, and their activities won government support for establishing the 1990 London Amendments to the Protocol, which led eventually to the Copenhagen Agreements that set the terms for a complete ban on ozone-depleting substances. While not single-handedly responsible for the London and Copenhagen revisions, NGOs provided an essential component in the overall political effort.

Eco-development

A number of NGOs have engaged in different sustainable development projects. Wapner discusses how the WWF has engaged in such activities. We use one of his examples explaining the WWF's activities in Zambia to protect wildlife.[14]

Zambia has been trying to protect its wildlife by establishing a number of national parks and forbidding people to live or hunt within park borders. Surrounding these parks are lands known as game management areas. These are semi-protected regions designated for game utilization. Safari hunting, for example, is legal within these zones. This system has not been successful, however, because of illegal poaching. Poaching is a very attractive business. For local poor people, it is one of the easiest ways to make money. A single rhino horn can fetch as much as twenty-four thousand dollars in Asia or Yemen.[15] The Zambian government's efforts to address this problem were not successful.

The WWF realized that the central problem with a preserve system of wildlife conservation is that while it attends to the needs of the animals, it ignores the needs of human beings. With that realization, the WWF has been working to halt the slaughter of wildlife by poachers in Zambia using a totally different strategy. The WWF started to fund and direct a new approach to anti-poaching. The program is called Administrative Design for Game Management Areas. It has two central features. First, it includes local residents in the program. Young local men are hired as village scouts. They receive training in anti-poaching techniques, record keeping (animals killed), and monitoring legal wildlife use. This program thus provides employment to people who would otherwise look to poaching for income. The second major feature of the program is that revenue earned from tourists and safari hunting is reinvested in the local community. This creates an incentive structure for game management area inhabitants to conserve wildlife. Before, this revenue went to the National Finance Ministry. Now, a significant portion of this money is returned to the local community and is spent in different community development projects (building schools and health clinics, and digging wells). This also generates employment. This program has been successful. Since 1990, USAID has also contributed significantly to the project; the money is being administered by the WWF in cooperation with the Zambian National Parks and Wildlife Service, which oversees the program. This program represents one of the WWF's more successful projects for saving wildlife through local participation and economic development.

Influencing Other Transnational Actors

The complexity of global environmental issues means that ENGOs interact with more than just governments. Two other sets of transnational actors, IGOs, and transnational corporations (TNCs), often find themselves either in concert or in conflict with NGOs.

Influencing IGOs

The World Bank, its Global Environment Facility, the International Tropical Timber Organization, and the WTO are some of the major IGOs involved in environmental regimes. NGOs not only maintain close contact with them and observe their activities but also have influenced some of these agencies' policies and structures.

One of the most successful of such NGO efforts was influencing the restructuring of the Global Environment Facility. The Global Environment Facility was established as a three-year pilot project to support several global environmental objectives involving climate change, protecting the ozone layer, biodiversity, and international waters. It began essentially as a unit of the World Bank, with UNDP and UN Environment Programme providing technical and scientific advice. Donor countries wanted to use the Global Environment Facility as the only channel through which they would commit new and additional resources for global environmental protection, but developing countries rejected it. SNGOs opposed the Global Environment Facility as the sole funding mechanism for environmental projects on the ground that it had been set up by a few industrialized countries without consultation with the developing countries themselves. They were also concerned that the World Bank, the environmental record of which had been amply demonstrated in the Narmada Dam case, would run the facility. Their argument was that it would focus only on environmental issues of interest to developed countries at the expense of the developing countries. In the UNCED PrepComs, the Group of 77 proposed a separate fund that would be governed on the basis of "one country, one vote" as an alternative to the Global Environment Facility. They were frustrated to see that most Global Environment Facility projects were actually attached to larger World Bank projects. NGOs also criticized the Global Environment Facility's lack of accountability and its failure to consult with grassroots groups in the recipient countries or to permit NGOs to attend Global Environment Facility meetings as observers.

NGOs, both Northern and Southern, were thus highly critical of the Global Environment Facility as administered by the World Bank during its 1991–93 pilot phase. After a negotiation period of nearly two years, the developing countries won a major victory with some concessions. The two groups of countries agreed to a voting system requiring a 60 percent majority of the members of the governing body (one state, one vote) and 60 percent majority of states making the contributions for a decision. They pushed successfully for a secretariat independent of the World Bank and for project approval by a council of all treaty parties. Criticisms still abound, but the Global Environment Facility has emerged as a useful complement to other sources of financial assistance for environmental projects in developing countries.

The World Bank is the largest lender for environmental projects in the developing world. Environmental assessments were not given serious consideration until 1987; therefore, it was widely criticized for not paying attention to the environmental consequences of its lending policies. Some of its projects have had serious environmental consequences, such as acceleration of deforestation and destruction of natural resources and biodiversity. Bank officials were also not accountable to different stakeholders. Their key goals were the promotion of economic growth and economic development. In the late 1980s, NGOs campaigning for the World Bank reform began to focus on issues of public participation and accountability. It is generally recognized that the environmental movement was pivotal in securing increased links between NGOs and the World Bank.[16] Chapter 5 discussed the NGO campaign with the Narmada Dam Project. In May 1987, Barber Conable, the World Bank's president, admitted that the organization had made some serious errors in its environmental policy and announced organizational reforms, including the creation of an environment department. Since 1987 the bank has expanded its focus on environmentally sustainable development and has striven to incorporate environmental concerns into policymaking. In 1993 the bank also established a three-member, independent inspection panel with power to investigate complaints from any group that can show that it has been harmed by the World Bank's failure to follow its policies or procedures. It is widely acknowledged that ENGOs in cooperation with other NGOs played a pivotal role in bringing about these reforms.

The WTO case is somewhat different. ENGOs turned their attention to trade and environmental issues only in the 1990s. The WTO's goals are to reduce tariffs and other trade barriers and thus to liberalize world trade. Neither the WTO nor its predecessor, the GATT, had provisions for NGO observers. However, in 1996 the secretariat was given prime responsibility for liaison with NGOs and was empowered to engage in an expanded dialogue with NGOs.[17] The secretariat provides briefings on its work programs and receives representation from NGOs. In addition, the secretariat has organized symposiums with representatives from NGOs.

Through their pressure on the NAFTA process and the Uruguay Round, NGOs made "trade and environment" a major international issue for the 1990s. The WTO was criticized for not allowing states to use trade restrictions as a means of enforcing both national and international environmental laws. Many environmentalists also argued that the WTO should employ broader criteria (the goal of sustainable development, for one) to evaluate the multilateral trading system. Supporters of free trade, on the other hand, questioned the assumption that growth through trade liberalization actually harms the environment. Gary Sampson, for example, argues, "The source of environmental damage from liberalization is not trade per se; rather, it is inappropriate production and consumption patterns and the failure to implement environment-management programs to deal with the negative implications of growth."[18] NGOs have been highly responsible for creating this debate. NGOs, through publicizing reports, engaging debates, and initiating demonstrations, have increased public consciousness of the WTO-environment issue.

Influencing TNCs

ENGOs are increasingly targeting corporations, especially multinationals, and focusing on their operations to make them more environmentally friendly. According to Peter Newell, "The increased attention of ENGOs to TNCs may simultaneously reflect a frustration with the pace of inter-state reform and the capture by business interests of the institutions set up to address environmental problems."[19] ENGOs use a variety of strategies in their efforts to influence corporations. Holding corporations accountable to the general public is a central strategy. One of the prominent strategies for corporate accountability consists of establishing voluntary codes of conduct by which corporations agree to abide. The most widely known environmental code was established in 1898 by the Coalition for Environmentally Responsible Economies. Its principles provide concrete criteria against which corporations can strive to improve their environmental record and against which activist groups and citizens can evaluate corporate environmental performance. The code calls on companies, among other things, to minimize pollution, conserve nonrenewable resources through efficient use and planning, and consider demonstrated environmental commitment as a factor in appointing members to their boards. The code has been embraced by at least one Fortune 500 company and a number of other MNCs.[20]

Recently, some ENGOs have begun to collaborate with corporations. The goal is to reward good business practice with financial endorsements or awarding companies a symbol of responsible environmental practice. One of the most famous examples of NGO-TNC cooperation is the project undertaken between the Environmental Defense Fund (EDF) and McDonald's Corporation, often held as a model of NGO-TNC collaboration.[21] Environmentalists were concerned about

McDonald's "clamshell" polystyrene containers for hamburgers. "In August 1990, representatives of McDonald's and the EDF signed an agreement to establish a joint task force to address the company's solid-waste issues. The agreement retained provision for EDF to criticize the company, and if parties disagreed on research findings in the final report on the project, separate statements from EDF and McDonald's could be produced. McDonald's required each EDF task-force member to work in one of its restaurants for at least one day. Public appreciation of this effort was obvious. . . . By January 1991, a Gallup poll found that McDonald's was regarded as the most environmentally responsible food chain."[22]

NGOs can also inform the public about environmentally sound products and encourage consumers to buy them rather than other products. Such a bottom-up approach can induce private firms to restructure their production if and when they realize that the markets for environmentally sound products will grow. In the early 1990s, for instance, Greenpeace made great efforts to persuade consumers to buy CFC (chlorofluorocarbon)-free refrigerators manufactured by the East German firm Foron. This campaign prompted other firms to change their line of production to CFC-free refrigerators and cooling systems.

Another trend has been the growth of organizations solely devoted to surveillance of the activities of corporations. These organizations work to expose activities that degrade the environment and publicize the information to the general public. Corporate Watch (UK) and Multinational Resource Center (US) are two such NGOs. Newell explains another recent trend, which is referred to as "shareholder activism."[23] Environmental and other groups buy a small number of shares in a company and encourage their supporters to do the same as a way of obtaining access to the annual general meeting so that they can influence the company's decision making. Shell Transport and Trading, the UK branch of Shell International, felt the effects of shareholder activism in its April-May 1997 meeting, when a group of shareholders holding just 1 percent of the company criticized the company's environmental and human rights records in Nigeria. "In Nigeria, Shell was accused of running its operations in an unusually ruthless manner, sharing few of the benefits of its economic success with local people, allowing repeated pollution incidents to contaminate river and coastal waters, treating the needs of local people with disdain in matters of siting pipelines and other plants, and flaring off gas in a way that was not only wasteful but also polluting."[24]

The shareholders group called for a resolution to improve the company's record. The resolution, supported by different NGOs, called on Shell to publish before the end of the year a report on its controversial activities in Nigeria. In March 1997, in an attempt to preempt the shareholder motion and to avoid further criticism, Shell revamped its "Statement of General Business Principles" to include human rights and sustainable development and published its first report on worldwide health safety and sustainable developmental activities. In May of the same year Shell hired an environmental expert to provide further guidance.[25]

Monitoring Environmental Treaties

International environmental agreements are usually not well monitored. Nearly every international environmental treaty, like many other treaties, relies on national self-reporting. A study by the United States General Accounting Office found that the percentage of parties actually reporting as required by various major international environmental agreements varied widely, but for many important agreements, such as the London Dumping Convention and CITES, the reporting compliance rate was well under 50 percent.[26] NGOs provide an alternative route for information about state compliance. Through monitoring, NGOs also bring instances of environmental abuses to public attention.

NGOs were rarely acknowledged in multilateral environmental treaties before the 1970s, and rarely granted access. Early international environmental treaties rarely contained provisions for NGOs. For example, the 1933 Convention Relative to the Preservation of Fauna and Flora in Their Natural State says nothing about non-state actors. The major environmental treaties negotiated in the last four decades, however, contain rules for NGO participation, and NGOs have become very active and visible participants in many regime activities. Since the 1970s several environmental treaties contain provisions for NGO participation in varying degrees (see Table 10–1).

The 1972 Convention for the Protection of the World Cultural and Natural Heritage explicitly permits NGOs to assist in treaty implementation. The operational guidelines explicitly request the International Council of Monuments and Sites and the IUCN to assist in monitoring. These NGOs have played significant roles in monitoring and

Table 10–1. Formal NGO Participation
in Six Environmental Treaties

Treaty	Date	NGOs are formal partners
World Heritage Convention	1972	Yes
London Convention of 1972	1972	No
Convention on International Trade in Endangered Species (CITES)	1973	Yes
International Tropical Timber Agreement (ITTA)	1985	No
Montreal Protocol on Substances that Deplete the Ozone Layer	1987	No
UN Framework Convention on Climate Change (Kyoto Protocol)	1992 (1997)	Yes

Source: Edith Brown Weiss, "The Five International Treaties: A Living History," in *Engaging Countries: Strengthening Compliance with International Environmental Accords,* ed. Edith Brown Weiss and Harold Jacobson (Cambridge: MA: MIT Press, 1998), 91; see also United Nations Framework Convention on Climate Change, 1997.

implementation. They evaluate requests to put cultural properties and natural sites on the World Heritage List, review requests from countries for financial and technical assistance, and also monitor selected sites. The World Heritage Committee uses IUCN's reports to determine whether to include a site on the "Danger List" or to initiate other follow-up actions. The 1973 CITES gives relatively more opportunity for NGO participation and has become the model for the language in many recent treaties. The secretariat may seek assistance from "suitable . . . non-governmental international or national agencies and bodies technically qualified in protection, conservation, and management of wild fauna and flora." NGOs have been active participants in CITES meetings;

they can express their opinions directly at the Conference of the Parties and receive copies of all reports compiled by the secretariat. Opinions of the IUCN have been regularly sought by the CITES secretariat. NGOs play an important role here too in monitoring. The World Conservation Monitoring Unit has been responsible for computerized tracking of exports and imports and for maintaining the CITES trade database.[27] TRAFFIC, a joint program of the WWF and the IUCN, has also been very active and effective in monitoring trade in illegal wildlife.

Raustiala points out that although it was signed subsequent to CITES, the Convention on the Conservation of Migratory Species of Wild Animals (1979) allows only for the access of "national non-governmental bodies."[28] In contrast, the landmark Montreal Protocol on Substances That Deplete the Ozone Layer, negotiated in 1987, states:

> Any body or agency, whether national or international, governmental or non-governmental, qualified in fields relating to the protection of the ozone layer . . . may be admitted unless at least one third of the parties present object. The admission and participation of the observers shall be subject to the rules of procedure adopted by the Parties. (Article 11:5)

NGO participation, as Raustiala points out, is circumscribed here in particular ways. The first limitation is the criteria of inclusion—"qualified in fields relating to the protection of the ozone layer." The second limitation is the need for a super-majority if NGO participation is challenged. The Framework Convention on Climate Change (1992) contains wording almost identical to that in the Montreal protocol, as does the Convention on Biological Diversity (1992). The Basel Convention on Transboundary Trade in Hazardous Waste (1989) is similar, with NGO participation limited to those NGOs with "qualifications in fields relating to hazardous waste." The 1994 environmental side agreement to NAFTA— the North American Agreement on Environmental Cooperation (NAAEC)—goes further than most environmental treaties informally granting NGO access and participation. NGOs may submit claims to the secretariat asserting that an NAAEC party is failing to enforce its environmental law effectively and thereby potentially trigger a formal investigation. NGO members may also serve on the arbitration panels created to assess the merits of and actions addressing such submission.

Thus, NGOs are getting much wider access in environmental regimes. Language stipulating NGO participation is now a standard part of global environmental accords. At the same time, however, their participation is constrained by the willingness of treaty signatories to provide them a formal place in international environmental policymaking. As Table 10–1 makes clear, not all treaties are friendly to ENGOs. The International Tropical Timber Organization makes no reference at all to them, although NGOs have used the sustainable development clause in the 1994 revised treaty to advocate specific timber policies. Moreover, there is a range of what counts as NGO participation under the terms of the various treaties. CITES and the World Heritage Convention rely on monitoring by NGOs to ensure compliance with treaty provisions. The Kyoto Protocol, on the other hand, simply allows NGOs and other nonstate actors to observe formal negotiations. In all cases, decisions regarding basic management rules, including the participation of nonmembers, are the province of treaty parties, invariably states.

Summary

NGOs are active participants in creating, shaping, and implementing global environmental regimes. Their contributions are widely publicized and acknowledged. They play important roles in the creation of new treaties to protect the environment, in advocacy, in monitoring, in collecting and publicizing scientific knowledge, in developing awareness of sustainable development, and in changing social mores and attitudes.

We have seen that NGOs are not always successful in changing existing environmental policies or convincing states and IGOs to adopt new ones. What factors influence ENGO success? Three factors stand out. One is resources. There is a clear divide between large and small NGOs. Scarce resources constrain the long-term study of single environmental problems, the observation of international policymaking, and the accumulation of institutional competence and memory. These resource constraints account for some of the failures of ENGOs to influence policymaking on less prominent issues such as desertification.

A second factor is issue structure. Some kinds of environmental issues are easier to call to public attention, easier to organize around, and easier to access because they do not require specialized technical knowledge. Endangered animals and polystyrene containers are two examples of highly visible problems that NGOs can easily transmit information about. Other issue areas are more complex and require such levels of technical proficiency that NGOs have difficulty participating in their agenda setting and solution processes. Global warming is an example; there are vociferous arguments among technical experts as to whether global warming is occurring and, if so, why. The Montreal Protocol on Climate Change (the predecessor to Kyoto) has been harder for NGOs to organize around because global warming is such a contentious issue and its effects are hard to see concretely. The public is thus less easy to mobilize.[29]

A third factor is the receptivity of states and transnational actors to NGO influence. Some IGOs, for example, have recognized the importance of NGOs in environmental policymaking. Others have not. The World Bank has been willing to consult with NGOs about environmental issues, but many observers argue that NGOs have not convinced the bank to change its neoclassical economics biases.

Discussion Questions

1. What forces have been behind the expansion of ENGOs in the last fifty years?
2. What do ENGOs do? Are some roles and activities more prevalent than others?
3. Is there such a thing as a typical ENGO? Why or why not?
4. Have NGOs been successful in changing global environmental policies and practices? Are there notable instances of failure?

Suggestions for Further Reading

Thomas Princen and Matthias Finger, eds., *Environmental NGOs in World Politics* (London: Routledge, 1994); Paul Wapner, *Environmental Activism and World Civic Politics* (Albany: State Univ. of New York Press, 1996). To learn more about the ENGOs discussed in this chapter, visit their websites.

Notes

[1] Gareth Porter and Janet W. Brown, *Global Environmental Politics* (Boulder, CO: Westview Press, 1996), 1.

[2] Lorraine Elliot, *The Global Politics of the Environment* (New York: New York Univ. Press, 1998).

[3] David J. Frank, Ann Hironaka, L. Meyer, E. Schafer, and N. B. Tuma, "The Rationalization and Organization of Nature in World Politics," in *Constructing World Culture: International Nongovernmental Organizations,* ed. J. Boli and G. Thomas, 81–99 (Stanford, CA: Stanford Univ. Press, 1999).

[4] Walter Rosenbaum, *Environmental Politics and Policy* (Washington, DC: CQ Press, 1995).

[5] John McCormick, "The Role of Environmental NGOs in International Regimes," in *The Global Environment: Institutions, Laws, and Policy*, ed. Norman Vig and Regina S. Axelrod, 52–71 (Washington, DC: CQ Press, 1999).

[6] Matthias Finger, "Environmental NGOs in the UNCED Process," in *Environmental NGOs in World Politics: Linking the Local and the Global*, ed. Thomas Princen and Matthias Finger, 186–213 (New York: Routledge, 1994).

[7] Norman J. Vig and Regina S. Axelrod, eds., *The Global Environment: Institutions, Laws, and Policy* (Washington, DC: CQ Press, 1999).

[8] Sheila Jasanoff, "NGOs and the Environment: From Knowledge to Action," *Third World Quarterly* 18, no. 3 (1997): 581.

[9] Paul Wapner, "The Transnational Politics of Environmental NGOs: Government, Economic, and Social Activism," in *The Global Environment in the Twenty-first Century: Prospects for International Cooperation,* edited by Pamela Chasek (New York: The United Nations University, 2000), 102.

[10] Porter and Brown, *Global Environmental Politics.*

[11] Michael McCubbins and T. Schwartz, "Congressional Oversight Overlooked: Police Patrols v. Fire Alarms," *American Journal of Political Science* 28 (1984): 165–79.

[12] Kal Raustiala, "States, NGOs, and International Environmental Institutions," *International Studies Quarterly* 41 (1997): 719–40.

[13] Wapner, "The Transnational Politics of Environmental NGOs: Governmental, Economic, and Social Activism."

[14] Paul Wapner, *Environmental Activism and World Civic Politics* (Albany: State Univ. of New York Press, 1996).

[15] Ibid., 85.

[16] Mark Williams, "The World Bank, the World Trade Organization, and the Environmental Social Movement," in *Non-State Actors and Authority in the Global System,* ed. Richard Higgott, Gareth Underhill, and A. Bieler, 241–55 (New York: Routledge, 2000).

[17] Ibid.

[18] Gary Sampson, "The Environmentalist Paradox: The World Trade Organization's Challenges," *Harvard International Review* (Winter 2002), 56–61.

[19] Peter Newell, "Environmental NGOs and Globalization: The Governance of TNCs," in *Global Social Movements,* ed. Robin Cohen and Shirin M. Rai (London: The Athlone Press, 2000), 120.

[20] Wapner, "The Transnational Politics of Environmental NGOs."

[21] Newell, "Environmental NGOs and Globalization."

[22] Ibid., 125.

[23] Ibid.

[24] Steve Yearly and John Forrester, "Shell, a Sure Target for Global Environmental Campaigning?" in Cohen and Rai, *Global Social Movements*, 138.

[25] S. Caulkin, "Amnesty and WWF Take a Crack at Shell," *The Times* (May 11, 1997).

[26] United States General Accounting Office, *International Environmental Agreements Are Not Well-Monitored* (Washington, DC: GAO, 1992).

[27] Elizabeth Brown Weiss, "The Five International Treaties: A Living History," in *Engaging Countries: Strengthening Compliance with International Environmental Accords,* ed. Edith Brown Weiss and Harold Jacobson (Cambridge, MA: MIT Press, 1998).

[28] Raustiala, "States, NGOs, and International Environmental Institutions."

[29] Weiss, "The Five International Treaties."

Part III

Conclusion

P art III, Chapter 11, is the conclusion of the book. The concluding chapter first summarizes the main themes of the book and then discusses some major issues that NGOs need to address in order to continue to work effectively in this new millennium. Two crucial issues are raised in the chapter—legitimacy and performance. Legitimacy includes NGO representativeness and accountability. Increasingly, scholars, practitioners, and other stakeholders are questioning NGOs' legitimacy and their effectiveness. We explore these different issues and emphasize the reality that currently NGOs are not necessarily and automatically seen as "do gooders." They are now faced with some serious challenges—challenges that might shape their future growth and effectiveness.

Chapter 11

Conclusion

NGOs and international relations theory
NGO legitimacy
NGO performance

This book has surveyed NGO participation in defining today's international relations. Part I provided a picture of the nature of NGOs and their growth, followed by a description of their roles in international politics. Since NGOs work in a world polity fundamentally ordered by states, Chapter 4 discussed the range of relationships between the two. At the same time, NGO interactions with IGOs help sustain a global forum outside of a strict state-state diplomatic framework. From this broad context, the book moved on to five sets of cases: NGOs in foreign aid, their accountability in Bangladesh, their contributions to changing definitions of international security, their participation in advancing women's rights through the UN, and their roles in sustaining global environmental regimes.

One of the key objectives of this book is to emphasize not only the presence of a vibrant NGO sector in international relations but also its growing strength. States exist alongside transnational actors. We have to go beyond formal governments and analyze the role of the NGO sector to understand today's global governance. The transnational and constructivist approaches to international relations are useful because they alert us to non-state actors, in the first case, and to the way that beliefs and identity inform behavior, in the second. Transnationalism reinforces the point that global governance is informal and fluid, that states and non-state actors exist side by side, and that the distinction between the international and domestic arenas is increasingly blurred.

Constructivist international relations does not privilege NGOs especially, but its concern with how rules and norms lead international actors to define actions that conform to those rules and norms allows us to see how NGOs can shape international politics. NGOs have been instrumental in helping to define understandings of proper conduct in key areas: that there are alternatives to state-led models of economic and social development; that states and transnational actors have responsibilities to the victims of conflict and natural disaster; that certain kinds of warfare and weaponry are anathema despite their tactical utility; and development and codification of the idea that human rights are universal, and that women's rights are part and parcel of universal human rights.

Constructivism holds out the possibility that international politics can be transformed by changing basic understandings of how the international system operates and what actors do within it. To simplify, actors in the international system understand that the international system works in certain ways, perceive their interests in terms of that understanding, and then act in accordance with that understanding. In short, they construct international politics. This leads to the possibility that if international actors understood the structure of the international system differently, they would also understand their roles, rights, and responsibilities differently and act accordingly. If states, for example, see the international system as anarchical and composed of sovereign, independent nation-states (the realist understanding of international politics), they will act according to the principle of self-help and assume that conflict is a normal part of interstate relations. If, on the other hand, they understand international politics as composed of multiple actors (including but not limited to states) and governed by systematic transnational rules of behavior (international law, for example) that limit a state's rights to conduct its internal affairs according to its own lights, they might not act as if conflict and self-help were normal states of affairs.

This raises possibilities for thinking about NGOs in international politics. A great deal of what NGOs do involves trying to change how states and transnational actors behave. Basic to this process is the attempt to change understandings of appropriate behavior and identity. NGOs are, therefore, potential transformers of international politics. They potentially change the structure of the international system in two ways. First, they can alter understandings of who is a legitimate actor in international politics. Part of the reason that NGOs look new to many observers is that they have not always been included among the major players in international politics. Recognition by IGOs like the UN has provided them a defined place from which to carry out the roles discussed in Chapter 3. Such recognition has allowed them to press their claim for regular participation in international politics.

This is why the idea of global civil society is so important to NGOs. Recall that the argument for global civil society posits a range of transnational interactions outside of traditional interstate relations. Global civil society is domestic civil society writ large, and therefore it requires non-state actors like NGOs, MNCs, and so on. The movements to create and understand this global civil society highlight NGO activities and, in turn, strengthen their claim to a legitimate place in world politics.

Second, NGOs potentially transform state identities and expectations of what is proper state behavior. Martha Finnemore, for example, has argued that the Red Cross and other humanitarian agencies in the nineteenth century changed basic understandings of the conduct of interstate warfare by promoting the ideals of proper treatment of civilians and captured or wounded soldiers.[1] As Chapter 8 demonstrated, the ICBL and other NGO networks have extended this humanitarian principle to cover the use of certain conventional weapons. The long-term effect is to restrain the conduct of a basic instrument of interstate relations (war.) Fifty years of NGO advocacy on behalf of human rights have similarly altered systemic understandings of how governments should treat their citizens. While states continue to fight wars and abuse the rights of their citizens, international expectations that sovereign states are justified in these activities have changed. Even those governments that fail to live up to international expectations, and increasingly international law, are at pains to explain their policies.

NGOs *potentially* can change identities and expectations, therefore behavior. This does not mean, necessarily, that they succeed in these efforts. When are NGOs successful? In particular, what enables NGOs to translate their normative preferences into international laws, rules, and understandings? NGO have three advantages over states in the conduct of transnational relations. First, NGOs focus on single issues or sets of issues, while states must perform many functions, with national security as a top priority. Second, in taking up principle-based issues, NGOs commit themselves to causes that states frequently subordinate to other foreign policy interests or ignore completely. By involving domestic activists in their advocacy efforts, NGOs can bring pressure on states internally, based on domestic representation and legitimacy, as well as internationally, based on humanitarian principles and generalized public opinion. Third, in contrast to states, the commitment of NGOs to their issues is intense.[2]

Of course, we do not claim that NGOs are more important than governments and other non-state actors, like MNCs or IGOs. They cannot make international law or enforce law directly. And, of course, they do not possess the financial resources that global corporations command. The cases presented—foreign aid, landmines, humanitarian relief, women's rights, and environmental protection—suggest that effective rule making depends in no small part on the willingness of other transnational actors to abide by those rules. However, the fact is that states and other global actors have to learn not only to reckon with but also to develop effective partnerships with the NGO sector.

Issues

This book has taken up a number of issues that concern NGO activities, but it is important to appreciate the possibilities and the limitations of NGO participation in international politics. There are serious concerns among different stakeholders that NGOs have to deal with in order to continue playing an effective role in future. The following sections explore some of these key concerns. One has to do with legitimacy. The other concerns performance.

Legitimacy

Legitimacy is a crucial issue for NGOs. Legitimacy implies representativeness and trustworthiness. There are indications that NGOs are seen as legitimate actors in civil society. A 2003 poll conducted by the public relations firm Edelman, for example, found that opinion leaders in Europe and the United States view NGOs as trusted representatives of the public interest. European opinion leaders trust them more than they do business (the four top brand names identified by respondents were those of prominent INGOs); Americans trust them as much as they do business.[3] A Gallup poll on public trust in social and political institutions, conducted just prior to the 2003 World Economic Forum in Davos, Switzerland, found that NGOs were ranked second out of seventeen institutions. They ranked well ahead of government and international business.[4] These attitudes seem to persist. A 1997 poll demonstrated this when it found that young Germans placed more credibility in

Greenpeace than in any other institutional authority. Among fourteen to eighteen year olds, Greenpeace ranked higher than political parties, unions, television personalities, and politicians in terms of public interest.[5] Commenting on the results of his firm's poll, Richard Edelman observed, "NGOs are now firmly established as the Fifth Estate in global governance, rivaling the credibility of revered corporate brands and filling a trust vacuum in both the U.S. and Europe."[6]

That said, one needs to be cautious about whom NGOs actually represent. Governments, international organizations, and MNCs—some of which have been criticized by NGOs for their weak accountability to citizens—increasingly ask whether or why they should listen to NGOs. Several reasons have prompted these kinds of questions. First, there are some NGOs promoting agendas that most would consider as going against public interest. The Earth Society, for example, which is funded by the coal industry in the United States, argues that global warming is good because it enhances vegetation growth. Second, many NGOs are also viewed as political, meaning that their activities challenge prevailing relationships of social, economic, or political power. For example, as discussed in Chapter 7, in Bangladesh development NGOs are increasingly seen by government and others as political entities. Similarly, relief NGOs operating in civil conflicts cannot avoid political roles even as they strive to maintain their neutrality. Third, as they grow in confidence and experience, southern partners and supposed beneficiaries increasingly question the legitimacy of NNGOs' advocacy, supposedly in their behalf. In such a dynamic environment NNGOs are challenged to show that they have a valid role in processes of international development.

Representation conveys the ideas of transparency, accountability, and participation. The One World Trust, an NGO, recently studied the accountability mechanisms of NGOs, international businesses, and IGOs. The study found that IGOs such as the World Bank and WTO scored high in respect to online information sharing, while NGOs like the WWF and CARE got much lower marks. The study also found that many NGOs fail to furnish relevant information that is useful to stakeholders.[7]

Several factors can work against NGO representativeness, hence legitimacy. NNGOs can bypass existing local organizations when setting up their own organizations or choosing their partner agencies unilaterally. As Chapters 6 and 7 pointed out, pressure for upward accountability to donors instead of toward beneficiaries can also compromise NGOs' claim to represent local communities. It can also challenge NGOs' conceptions of themselves and their societal roles. NGOs have a reputation for volunteerism and dedication to the public interest, identities that distinguish them from other kinds of societal actors. Yet, these identities are often compromised to meet donors' expectations, the latter focusing more on outputs than on outcome.

There is also an ongoing debate about whether NGOs actually promote dependency on outside donors. Several concerns are raised by scholars and affected parties about the funding dependency between SNGOs and foreign donors. The supply of external funding can lead to the emergence of bogus NGOs. Cooptation of legitimate NGOs, short-term commitments to long-term needs, bureaucratization of NGOs, legitimization of donor policies and projects, and the development of barriers to self-reliance and empowerment of people are emerging concerns shared by different stakeholders.

One observation illustrates this issue of legitimacy:

> During an international conference on Third World development, a Latin American participant stood up and said: "Once upon a time, we were a free nation, with our own culture and development process. Then the Spanish came and conquered us. We were defeated because they had horses. Later, our people fought the Spanish until we gained independence. But are we really independent? Even now, foreign countries dictate us economically, culturally and politically. And they do not need horses to conquer us now because we have NGOs."[8]

This statement bears testimony to a growing concern regarding the role of NNGOs in promoting developing countries' welfare.

NGO participation is not always an unmitigated good. Enhanced participation by civil society in governance may enhance the power of self-interested groups that are already powerful—in resources, organization, political influence—and this may undermine the political processes and lead to low levels of regime effectiveness. Low-income populations may be at a disadvantage in the policy process because they may not have access to groups that can represent their interests. Some see an imperialistic attitude in the relationship between NNGOs and SNGOs. Like it or not, most international NGOs are Northern; they are more powerful and have more resources than their Southern counterparts, and they have easier access to developed country governments and the most important IGOs. Hence, in major areas of global crises (AIDS, global warming, sustainable development, for example) they are the ones that shape the transnational NGO policy agenda. "For some in developing countries, this is a new and subtle form of imperialism, as if the ability to raise thousands of dollars at New York fund raisers gives pressure groups the right to define the problems of poor people better than they can themselves."[9]

NGOs have also been criticized for using unrealistic information and inappropriate strategies to get media attention. In 1995 Greenpeace had to admit that its claim about the Royal Dutch Shell's planned disposal of the Brent Spar offshore drilling rig in the North Atlantic was inaccurate.[10] Such questionable strategies raise the issue of credibility and trust.

Cultural sensitivity is an important component of transnational development efforts because that sensitivity (or lack of it) will affect how beneficial NGO activities will be for their target populations. Yet, many NGOs have institutional and cultural styles that they cannot or will not shed. A recent external study of a Japanese NGO in Bangladesh suggests the depth of the problem. The study noted that despite twenty years of grassroots development work, the NGO was still viewed as a Japanese organization. A top-down management style, in which local Japanese staff responded to directives from headquarters either in Tokyo or Dhaka and in which local people themselves were instructed but not consulted, preserved the identity of an outside interloper. Moreover, it reinforced the prevailing political arrangement of passive citizenry receiving benefits from above, in this case the NGO.[11]

Many INGOs have come to understand that their most important contribution to democratization and social/economic development may result simply by not crowding out local NGOs. The latter, of course, are a prerequisite for the kind of open civil societies envisioned by donor governments and NNGOs alike when they engage in democracy assistance; it would be hard to imagine that strong democracies in the former communist states would develop simply because Western NGOs show up to carry out projects. The shift among the larger NNGOs from hands-on projects to financial support of counterpart organizations reflects this understanding. The trend is by no means universal, and project-centered work carried out by Northern volunteers, as is the case with CANHELP Thailand, remains the norm among NGOs.

Representation also concerns NGOs' political responsibilities in advocacy activities. Lisa Jordan and Peter van Tuijl define political responsibility as "a commitment to embrace not only the goals in a campaign but to conduct the campaign with democratic principles foremost in the process."[12] This does not necessarily happen in practice. The authors identify four kinds of transnational NGO campaign: cooperative, concurrent, dissociated, and competitive. Each has a different level of political responsibility to stakeholders. In a cooperative campaign the level of political responsibility toward the most vulnerable actors is optimal. Advocacy agendas and strategies are usually set in close consultation with groups who are supposed to benefit from the campaign, and risks are assumed only in regard to the burden that can be borne by the most vulnerable. The Narmada Dam campaign is a good example.

The concurrent campaign has coinciding representation of different but compatible objectives. It achieves a medium level of political responsibility, given that the objectives in various political arenas are different. However, there is frequent review of strategies and coexisting management of political responsibilities by varying combinations of NGOs involved at different levels.

The dissociated campaign manifests a low level of political responsibility, in which advocacy objectives represented by various NGOs in different political arenas begin to clash. There are occasional and unaffiliated reviews of strategies and management of political responsibilities among different NGOs involved.

The fourth type, the competitive campaign, is devoid of any political responsibility. In this situation, advocacy at one level may actually have an adverse or counterproductive impact at another level. The authors characterize the situation as one in which a parallel representation of opposing objectives by different NGOs operates in different political arenas. There is no joint review of strategies or management of political responsibilities that may result in human rights violations or other negative impacts on the interests of local communities.

Jordan and van Tuijl use the case of the Huaorani fight against the Conoco oil company to illustrate the pitfalls of a competitive transnational NGO campaign. The Huaorani are a group of forest-dwellers who live in the Amazon region of Ecuador. Since 1967, American oil companies have exploited oil resources in Ecuador: leaking pipelines, oil fires, and violence and intimidation have characterized that exploitation. In the 1970s the government of Ecuador began to invite other multinational oil corporations into the region to develop the country's oil reserves. The international campaign against Conoco ran from the late 1980s to the mid-1990s. US and European-based environmental and human rights groups took up the issue, with positions ranging from opposition to Conoco to support for the company as the best option in a bad situation. For the most part these positions were taken without consulting the Huaorani, who live deep in the forest. Some NGOs had no Ecuadorian contacts at all. Strategies were adopted based upon what was considered to be politically feasible, as opposed to what was requested by the affected communities. Deals were agreed to that undercut the rights of indigenous peoples to manage their own territories. According to Jordan and van Tuijl, the campaign against Conoco in Ecuador provides an example of the worst kind of campaign when measuring political responsibility. The authors argue that NGOs should begin to manage their relationships at least at the concurrent campaign level.

Sebastian Mallaby's account of the ill-fated World Bank project of promoting a dam in Bujagali, Uganda, speaks of another emerging problem in transnational networking of NGOs—NGO activists joining hands to form formidable blocks against projects that are otherwise supported by local residents. These activists engage in strategies of opposition without gathering adequate and valid information and with little or no consultation with the affected parties.[13] As Mallaby narrates, Western NGOs were in revolt once the World Bank made the proposal public. They argued that the Ugandan environmental movement was outraged at the likely damage to waterfalls at the site and that the poor who lived there would be uprooted from their land for the sake of electricity they could not afford. When Mallaby traced the activists of the Ugandan environmental movement, he eventually met the director of Uganda's National Association of Professional Environmentalists—a small group of twenty-five members—which was spearheading this opposition. His interviews with villagers gave a different picture. They actually supported the project because they were offered generous financial terms to relocate. "This story is a tragedy for Uganda. Clinics and factories are deprived of electricity by Californians whose idea of an electricity crisis is a handful of summer blackouts. But it is also a tragedy for the fight against poverty worldwide, because projects in dozens of countries are similarly held up for fear of activist resistance."[14]

Scholars are increasingly cautioning NGOs to guard against losing credibility. Margaret Gibelman and Sheldon Gelman's research on publicized NGO wrongdoing in different parts of the world found NGO scandals continuing into the new millennium.[15] Scandals include fraud, corruption, financial embezzlement, and mismanagement. These seriously affect NGO legitimacy.

One way for NGOs to gain more public confidence and trust is to develop and adopt codes of conduct. The NGO Code of Conduct in Disaster Relief is an example of attempts to develop appropriate procedures with universal application. Codes of conduct can enhance NGOs' legitimacy by demonstrating their accountability, openness to public scrutiny, and adherence to acceptable ethical standards.[16] The World Association of Nongovernmental Organizations has drafted a Code of Ethics and Conduct for NGOs that sets forth principles and standards to guide the management, operations, and behaviors of NGOs.[17]

Performance

Discussions of codes of conduct prompt questions about NGO performance. These questions are intimately related to issues of legitimacy and representation, of course, because development NGOs in particular claim that they deliver public goods better than states or MNCs. Effectiveness as a criterion of legitimacy cannot be overemphasized, because it is presumably the main reason for donors' attraction to the NGO sector.

Measuring how well NGOs perform depends on who is doing the measuring. NGO criteria of performance are increasingly under pressure to conform to those of Northern donor governments. First, public funds are accompanied by more stringent "contractual" demands for financial accountability and the realization of agreed-on results. Second, recent thinking in official development assistance has shifted donor priorities toward institutional restructuring of recipient countries, with corresponding pressure on NGOs by donor governments to alter their role in society. Third, NGOs tend to argue that they are more cost effective than governments in reaching and serving people who are poor or marginalized, and they are now being called upon to demonstrate that this is indeed the case. Fourth, there is a growing realization that organizational effectiveness is positively correlated with an ability to learn from experience. Learning requires performance assessment.[18]

The chapters on foreign aid and NGO accountability in Bangladesh address the problem of measuring NGO performance. This problem is compounded by the fact that NGOs often have controversial and vague roles; popular and official expectations about their roles can differ significantly from those that they actually perform. Identifying assessment criteria to measure NGO effectiveness is itself difficult. Where criteria have been developed and utilized, NGO success stories have been questioned. Claims about cost effectiveness, sustainability, and popular participation do not always bear up under scrutiny. Recent research argues that NGOs' effectiveness as agents of development has been largely exaggerated or is assumed rather than demonstrated. Empowerment may be the most difficult value to achieve in the NGO sector since self-help, collective decision making, and other genuine participatory methods are difficult to implement.[19] Many NNGOs are not democratically organized. In many there is a clear separation between activists and members whose participation may only be in the form of annual subscriptions. There is increasing evidence that NGOs do not perform as effectively as had been assumed in terms of reaching the poor.[20] Anecdotal evidence concerning the Grameen Bank suggests that SNGOs have as much trouble doing this as do their Northern counterparts.[21] Along with success stories, there are failures.

Using NGOs to promote development is attractive because they are assumed to be more flexible than government agencies. This assumes that NGOs can learn from experience easily. Alan Fowler echoes other scholars' concerns that this is not happening in the NGO sector,[22] at least not in the way one wants to see it being institutionalized. One main reason for this is that many official agencies are unwilling or unable to support the long-term horizons, careful nurturing, and gradual qualitative results that characterize successful institutional development. NGOs often chafe under the annual budgeting constraints imposed by ODA funding procedures, yet, as seen in Chapter 6, the lure of stable funding is a powerful incentive to adjust to donor-government aid criteria. This not only undercuts long-term development objectives, but also the capacity to adjust to past shortcomings or changing needs in counterpart communities.

Finally, the diversity of NGOs now operating in the international arena makes measuring effectiveness tricky. The three NGOs profiled in the introduction to this book possess quite different goals, resources, and capabilities. Standards of performance for one kind of NGO do not necessarily apply to another kind. For example, whether development NGOs should adhere to donor-government standards of performance concerning project design, implementation, and accounting does not apply to advocacy NGOs, which do not engage in that kind of work. Among advocacy NGOs the question of performance and effectiveness is not straightforward. To take the Huaorani case mentioned above, whether NGOs succeeded in their advocacy efforts depends on how far their policy positions were removed from the final outcome. To say that NGOs succeeded or failed in their attempts to oppose Conoco's oil-extraction practices ignores the fact that there was no unified position among NGOs themselves.

A similar problem arises in the case of NGO interactions with organizations like the World Bank and the IMF. NGOs are divided on the question of whether and how to reform these two organizations. Some wish to see minor changes made in order to facilitate operational cooperation with NGOs. Others, like the participants in the Jubilee 2000 campaign, want basic changes made in the multilaterals' policies toward developing-country debt. Yet others, like the Fifty Years Is Enough campaign, wish to see the World Bank and the IMF eliminated. Clearly, the multilaterals have responded to some NGO demands but not others. Effectiveness must necessarily be accounted in different ways.

Effectiveness also concerns NGOs' contribution to political change, democratization, and sustainable development. Writers offer contending positions. In his study of African NGOs Fowler argues that NGOs are more likely to maintain the status quo than to change it.[23] Gerald Clarke, in contrast, points out the important roles that NGOs have played in consolidating democratic reforms in countries such as Brazil, Chile, Thailand, and the Philippines.[24]

Concluding Comments

Michael Edwards and his colleagues state:

> At the start of the new millennium, nongovernmental organizations (NGOs), along with others, share a sense of excitement about new possibilities, tempered by widespread anxiety about the future. The excitement stems from the quickly expanding opportunities for civic action that global trends are creating; the anxiety arises from the increasingly critical questions being asked about the role development NGOs will play in this future.[25]

Along with the question of roles, NGOs will also have to address the concerns raised regarding the process of their operation. NGOs influence the course of international politics in part because they articulate democratic and participatory alternatives to the status quo. Legitimacy, representation, and a proven track record of performance are important resources that can help them make good on their claims.

In closing, we return to Marc Nerfin's metaphor, mentioned in Chapter 2, which points out that NGOs are neither princes (the state) nor merchants (businesses).[26] The growth of NGOs arises in part from demands by citizens for accountability from the prince and the merchant. Questions have been raised about the accuracy of this metaphor. Although recognizing the legitimacy of each sector of society, it tends to glorify NGOs at the expense of legitimate functions of states and markets.[27]

We conclude with the reminder that NGOs rarely work independently in international society. Transnational civil society, of which NGOs are a vital component, is part of a broader international society. Ignoring NGOs' activities in the transnational arena impoverishes our understanding of international politics. Placing too much emphasis on them runs the risk of assigning to them functions they are not equipped to carry out. NGOs act, often effectively, but they do not act alone.

NGOs engaging in international politics are rather like Woodrow Wilson going to the Versailles conference. Their motives are pure. For the most part they genuinely aspire to create a more just, more benevolent world. But they encounter players who are steeped in their own traditions and who pursue purposes that are more selfish. The challenge for them is to find a way to pursue their agendas without subverting their motives or marginalizing themselves. To compromise overmuch with the world view of the way things are is to risk the former; to stand on high principle, the option Wilson ultimately took, is to risk the latter.

Notes

[1] Martha Finnemore, "Rules of War and Wars of Rules: The International Red Cross and the Restraint of State Violence," in *Constructing World Culture,* ed. J. Boli and G. Thomas, 149–68 (Stanford, CA: Stanford Univ. Press, 1999).

[2] John Clark, "The State, Popular Participation, and the Voluntary Sector," *World Development* 23, no. 4 (1995): 593–601.

[3] Edelman Survey of Trust, "Global Trust Landscape Shifts Significantly in 2002," *CRS Wire,* January 22, 2003. Available online.

[4] "Philanthropy Measures Up: World Economic Forum Global Leaders Tomorrow Benchmarking Philanthropy Report, January 28, 2003. Available online.

[5] Paul Wapner, "The Transnational Politics of Environmental NGOs: Governmental, Economic, and Social Activism," in *The Global Environment in the*

Twenty-first Century: Prospects for International Cooperation, ed. Pamela Chasek, 87–108 (New York: The United Nations Univ., 2000).

[6] Edelman Survey of Trust, "Global Trust Landscape Shifts Significantly in 2002."

[7] Hetty Kovach, Carolina Neligan, and Simon Burall, "Power without Accountability?" One World Trust report, January 1, 2003. Available from the oneworldtrust.org website.

[8] Hira Jhamtani, "The Imperialism of Northern NGOs," *Earth Island Journal* 7, no. 3 (1996): 10–11.

[9] Michael Elliott, "NGOs: The Good, the Bad, and the Illegitimate," MSNBC, January 26, 2001. No longer available.

[10] Brijesh Nalinakumari and Richard Maclean, "NGOs: A Primer on the Evolution of the Organizations That Are Setting the Next Generation of 'Regulations,'" *Environmental Quality Management* (Summer 2005): 16.

[11] Hedayatul Huq, "Non-governmental Organizations Revisited: Rural Development by a Japanese NGO in Bangladesh," *University of Aizu Center for Cultural Research and Studies Annual Review* 3 (1997): 25–37.

[12] Lisa Jordan and Peter van Tuijl, "Political Responsibility in Transnational NGO Advocacy," *World Development* 28, no. 12 (2000): 2053.

[13] Sebastian Mallaby, "NGOs: Fighting Poverty, Hurting the Poor," *Foreign Policy* (September-October 2004): 50–58.

[14] Ibid., 52.

[15] Margaret Gibelman and Sheldon R. Gelman, "A Loss of Credibility: Patterns of Wrongdoing among Nongovernmental Organizations," *Voluntas: International Journal of Voluntary and Nonprofit Organizations* 15, no. 4 (December 2004): 355–81.

[16] Anthony Adair, "Codes of Conduct Are Good for NGOs Too," *IPA Review* 51 (March 1999): 26–27.

[17] The WANGO code is available online.

[18] See Alan Fowler, "Relevance in the Twenty-first Century: The Case for Devolution and Global Association of International NGOs," *Development in Practice* 9, no. 1–2 (February 1999): 143–51.

[19] Iain Atack, "Four Criteria of Development NGO Legitimacy," *World Development* 27, no. 5 (1999): 855–64.

[20] Syed M. Hashemi and S. Schular, *State and NGO Support Networks in Rural Bangladesh: Concepts and Coalitions for Control* (Copenhagen: Centre for Development Research, 1992); Anthony Bebbington, Graham Thiele, et al., eds., *NGOs and the State in Latin America: Rethinking Roles in Sustainable Agricultural Development* (London: Routledge, 1993).

[21] See David Bornstein, *The Price of a Dream: The Story of the Grameen Bank* (Chicago: Univ. of Chicago Press, 1996).

[22] Alan Fowler, "Distant Obligations: Speculations on NGO Funding and the Global Market" (paper presented to the annual conference of the Development Studies Association, Nottingham, September 1992).

[23] Ibid.

[24] Gerald Clarke, "Non-governmental Organizations (NGOs) and Politics in the Developing World," *Political Studies* 47 (1998): 36–52.

[25] Michael Edwards, David Hulme, and Tina Wallace, "Increasing Leverage for Development: Challenges for NGOs in a Global Future," in *New Roles and Relevance: Development NGOs and the Challenge of Change,* ed. D. Lewis and T. Wallace (West Hartford, CT: Kumarian Press, 2000), 1.

[26] Marc Nerfin, "Neither Prince nor Merchant—An Introduction to the Third System," *IFDA Dossier* 56 (1986): 3–29.

[27] Thomas Weiss and Leon Gordenker, eds., *NGOs, the UN, and Global Governance* (Boulder, CO: Lynne Rienner, 1996).

Bibliography

Aall, Pamela, Daniel T. Miltenberger, and Thomas G. Weiss. *Guide to IGOs, NGOs, and the Military in Peace and Relief Operations*. Washington, DC: United States Institute of Peace, 2000.

Abiew, Frances. *The Evolution of the Doctrine and Practice of Humanitarian Intervention*. The Hague: Kluwer Law International, 1999.

Abramson, Paul, and Ronald Inglehart. *Value Change in Global Perspective*. Ann Arbor: Univ. of Michigan Press, 1995.

Adair, Anthony. "Codes of Conduct Are Good for NGOs Too." *IPA Review* 51 (March 1999): 26–27.

Ahmed, Fauzia. "Beyond Beijing: Making Room for Feminist Men." *Sojourner: The Women's Forum* 22, no. 2 (1996): 18.

Ahmed, Shamima. "The Issue of NGO Accountability in Bangladesh: Perspectives and Perceptions of NGO Leaders." *Asian Thought and Society* 25, no. 75 (2000): 255–66.

Ahsan, E., and S. N. Muslim. *Accountability in the Bangladesh Civil Service*. Report presented at the ASEAN-SAARC Conference on Administrative and Financial Accountability. Dhaka: Bangladesh. January 16–20, 1994.

Akehurst, Michael. "Humanitarian Intervention." In *Intervention in World Politics*, edited by H. Bull, 95–118. Oxford: Clarendon Press, 1984.

Aminuzzaman, Salahuddin. "NGOs and the Grassroot Base Local Government in Bangladesh: A Study of Their Institutional Interactions." In *NGOs under Challenge: Dynamics and Drawbacks in Development*, edited by F. Hossain and S. Myllyla, 84–104. Helsinki: Ministry for Foreign Affairs of Finland, Department for International Development Cooperation, 1998.

Amnesty International. *Amnesty International Report*. New York: Amnesty International, 1991.

Anderson, Mary B. *Do No Harm: How Aid Can Support Peace—or War*. Boulder, CO: Lynne Rienner, 1999.

Anheier, Helmut, Marlies Glasius, and Mary Kaldor, eds. *Global Civil Society*. Oxford: Oxford Univ. Press, 2001.

Asia Watch and the Women's Rights Project. *A Modern Form of Slavery: Trafficking of Burmese Women and Girls into Brothels in Thailand*. New York: Human Rights Watch, 1993.

Atack, Iain. "Four Criteria of Development NGO Legitimacy." *World Development* 27, no. 5 (1999): 855–64.

Bebbington, Anthony, and Graham Thiele, with Penelope Davies, Martin Prager, and Hernando Riveros, eds. *NGOs and the State in Latin America: Rethinking Roles in Sustainable Agricultural Development.* London: Routledge, 1993.

Bebbington, Anthony, and John Farrington, eds. *Reluctant Partners? Non-governmental Organizations, the State, and Sustainable Agriculture Development.* London: Routledge, 1993.

Bebbington, Anthony, and Roger Riddell. "Heavy Hands, Hidden Hands, Holding Hands? Donors, Intermediary NGOs and Civil Society Organizations." In *NGOs, States, and Donors: Too Close for Comfort?* edited by David Hulme and Michael Edwards, 107–27. London: St. Martin's Press, 1997.

Bedont, Barbara. "Negotiating for an International Criminal Court: The Like Minded and the Non-governmental." *Peace Magazine* (September-October 1998), 21–24.

Beigbeder, Yves. *The Role and Status of International Humanitarian Volunteers and Organizations.* Dordrecht: Martinus Nijhoff Publishers, 1991.

Berkovitch, Nitza. "The Emergence and Transformation of the International Women's Movement." In *Constructing World Culture: International Nongovernmental Organizations since 1875,* edited by J. Boli and G. Thomas, 100–126. Stanford, CA: Stanford Univ. Press, 1999.

Berman, Maureen, and Joseph Johnson. *Unofficial Diplomats.* New York: Columbia Univ. Press, 1977.

Berry, Jeffrey. *The Interest Group Society.* New York: Scott Foresman, 1984.

————. *Lobbying for the People.* Princeton, NJ: Princeton Univ. Press, 1977.

Berry, Nicholas. *War and the Red Cross: The Unspoken Mission.* New York: St. Martin's Press, 1997.

Boli, John, and George Thomas, eds. *Constructing World Culture: International Nongovernmental Organizations since 1875.* Stanford, CA: Stanford Univ. Press, 1999.

Bolling, Landrum, with Craig Smith. *Private Foreign Aid: U.S. Philanthropy for Relief and Development.* Boulder, CO: Westview Press, 1982.

Bornstein, David. *The Price of a Dream: The Story of the Grameen Bank.* Chicago: Univ. of Chicago Press, 1996.

Boserup, Ester. *Women's Role in Economic Development.* London: Earthscan, 1998.

Bromley, Mark. "The International Human Rights Law Group: Human Rights and Access to Justice in Post Conflict Environments." In *NGOs and Human Rights: Promise and Performance,* edited by Claude Welch, 141–50. Philadelphia: Univ. of Pennsylvania Press, 2001.

Cameron, Maxwell, Robert Lawson, and Brian Tomlin. *To Walk without Fear: The Global Campaign to Ban Landmines.* Toronto: Oxford Univ. Press, 1998.

Caulkin, S. "Amnesty and WWF Take a Crack at Shell." *The Times,* May 11, 1997.

Cernea, Michael. *Nongovernmental Organizations and Local Development. World Bank Discussion Papers.* Washington, DC: World Bank, 1988.

Chatterjee, Pratap. "Fifty Years Is Enough" Launch. *Inter Press Service,* May 17, 1994. Available online.

Checkel, Jeffrey. "The Constructivist Turns in International Relations Theory." *World Politics* 50, no. 1 (1998): 324–48.

Chen, Martha A. "Engendering World Conferences: The International Women's Movement and the UN." In *NGOs, the UN, and Global Governance*, edited by Thomas Weiss and Leon Gordenker, 139–55. Boulder, CO: Lynne Rienner, 1996.

CIA. *World Fact Book*. July 2005.

Clark, Ann M. *Diplomacy of Conscience*. Princeton, NJ: Princeton Univ. Press, 2001.

——. "Non-governmental Organizations and Their Influence on International Society." *Journal of International Affairs* 48, no. 2 (1995): 507–26.

Clark, John. *Democratizing Development: The Role of Volunteer Organizations*. London: Earthscan, 1991.

——. "The State, Popular Participation, and the Voluntary Sector." *World Development* 23, no. 4 (1995): 593–601.

Clarke, Gerald. "Non-governmental Organizations (NGOs) and Politics in the Developing World." *Political Studies* 47 (1998): 36–52.

Cleary, Seamus. "The World Bank and NGOs." In *The Conscience of the World: The Influence of Non-governmental Organizations in the U.N. System*, edited by Peter Willetts, 63–97. London: Hurst and Company, 1996.

Commins, Steve. "World Vision International and Donors: Too Close for Comfort?" In *NGOs, States, and Donors: Too Close for Comfort?* edited by David Hulme and M. Edwards, 140–55. London: St. Martin's Press, 1997.

Connors, Jane. "NGOs and the Human Rights of Women in the United Nations." In *The Conscience of the World: The Influence of the Non-governmental Organisations in the UN System*, edited by Peter Willetts, 147–80. London: Hurst and Company, 1996.

De Waal, Alex. *Famine Crimes: Politics and the Disaster Relief Industry in Africa*. Bloomington: Indiana Univ. Press, 1998.

Diaz-Alberini, Jose. "Nonprofit Advocacy in Weakly Institutionalized Political Systems: The Case of NGDOs in Peru." *Nonprofit and Voluntary Sector Quarterly* 22, no. 4 (Winter 1993): 317–38.

Dorsey, Ellen. "The Global Women's Movement: Articulating a New Vision of Global Governance." In *The Politics of Global Governance: International Organizations in an Interdependent World*, edited by Paul F. Diehl, 335–59. Boulder, CO: Lynne Rienner, 1997.

Doyle, Michael, and John Ikenberry, eds. *New Thinking in International Relations Theory*. Boulder, CO: Westview Press, 1997.

Doyle, Michael, and Nicholas Sambanis. "International Peace Building: A Theoretical and Quantitative Analysis." *American Political Science Review* 94, no. 4 (2001): 779–802.

Durch, William, ed. *The Evolution of UN Peacekeeping*. Basingstoke: MacMillan, 1993.

Eade, Deborah, and Suzanne Williams. *The OXFAM Handbook of Development and Relief*. Vols. 1–3. Oxford: Oxfam (UK and Ireland), 1995.

Edelman Survey of Trust. "Global Trust Landscape Shifts Significantly in 2002." *CRS Wire*, January 22, 2003. Available online.

Edwards, Michael, and David Hulme. *NGO Performance and Accountability: Beyond the Magic Bullet*. London: Earthscan, 1995.

Edwards, Michael, and David Hulme. *Beyond the Magic Bullet: NGO Performance and Accountability in the Post–Cold War World.* West Hartford, CT: Kumarian Press, 1996.

Edwards, Michael, David Hulme, and Tina Wallace. "Increasing Leverage for Development: Challenges for NGOs in a Global Future." In *New Roles and Relevance: Development NGOs and the Challenge of Change,* edited by D. Lewis and T. Wallace, West Hartford, CT: Kumarian Press, 2000.

Edwards, Michael, and John Gaventa, eds. *Global Citizen Action.* Boulder, CO: Lynne Rienner, 2001.

Ehrenberg, John. *Civil Society: The Critical History of an Idea.* New York: New York Univ. Press, 1999.

Einhorn, Jessica. "The World Bank's Mission Creep." *Foreign Affairs* 80, no. 5 (September-October 2001): 22–35.

Elliott, Lorraine. *The Global Politics of the Environment.* New York: New York Univ. Press, 1998.

Elliott, Michael. "NGOs: The Good, the Bad, and the Illegitimate." MSNBC, January 26, 2001. No Longer Available.

Farrington, John, and Anthony Bebbington, eds. *Reluctant Partners: Non-governmental Organizations, the State, and Sustainable Agricultural Development.* London: Routledge, 1993.

Ferris, Elizabeth. "The Churches, Refugees, and Politics." In *Refugees and International Politics*, edited by G. Loescher and L. Monahan, 159–78. Oxford: Clarendon Press, 1990.

Findlay, Trevor. *Cambodia: The Legacy of UNTAC.* SIPRI Research Report, no. 9. Oxford: Oxford Univ. Press, 1995.

Finger, Matthias. "Environmental NGOs in the UNCED Process." In *Environmental NGOs in World Politics: Linking the Local and the Global,* edited by Thomas Princen and Matthias Finger, 186–213. New York: Routledge, 1994.

Finnemore, Martha. "Rules of War and Wars of Rules: The International Red Cross and the Restraint of State Violence." In *Constructing World Culture*, edited by J. Boli and G. Thomas, 149–68. Stanford, CA: Stanford Univ. Press, 1999.

Fisher, Julie. *Nongovernments: NGOs and the Political Development of the Third World.* West Hartford, CT: Kumarian Press, 1998.

Florini, Ann M., ed. *The Third Force: The Rise of Transnational Civil Society.* Tokyo: Japan Center for International Education; Washington, DC: Carnegie Endowment for International Peace, 2001.

Foreman, Shephard, and Abby Stoddard, "International Assistance." In *The State of Nonprofit America,* edited by Lester Salamon, 240–75. Washington, DC: Brookings Institute, 2002.

Forman, Lori. "NGOs as a Catalyst for Environmental Cooperation." *CGP Newsletter* 9 (Summer 1995): 5–6.

Forrester, Veronica. "The German Political Foundations." In *Pressure Groups, Policies, and Development: The Private Sector and EEC-Third World Policy,* edited by C. Stevens and J. V. Van Themaat, 40–60. London: Hodder and Staughton, 1985.

Fowler, Alan. "Distant Obligations: Speculations on NGO Funding and the Global Market." Paper presented to the annual conference of the Development Studies Association, Nottingham, September 1992.

———. "Relevance in the Twenty-first Century: The Case for Devolution and Global Association of International NGOs." *Development in Practice* 9, no. 1–2 (February 1999): 143–51.

Fox, Jonathan, and L. David Brown, eds. *The Struggle for Accountability: The World Bank, NGOs, and Grassroots Movements.* Cambridge, MA: MIT Press, 1998.

Frank, David J., Ann Hironaka, J. Meyer, E. Schafer, and N. B. Tuma. "The Rationalization and Organization of Nature in World Politics." In *Constructing World Culture: International Nongovernmental Organizations since 1875,* edited by J. Boli and G. Thomas, 81–99. Stanford, CA: Stanford Univ. Press, 1999.

Fruttero, Anna, and Varun Gauri. "The Strategic Choices of NGOs: Location Decisions in Rural Bangladesh." *Journal of Development Studies* 42, no. 5 (2005): 759–87.

Fukuyama, Francis. *Trust: The Social Virtues and the Creation of Prosperity.* New York: The Free Press, 1996.

Gaer, Felice D. "Reality Check: Human Rights NGOs Confront Governments at the UN." In *NGOs, the UN, and Global Governance,* edited by Thomas G. Weiss and Leon Gordenker. Boulder, CO: Lynne Rienner, 1996.

Gaimusho. *Waga Kuni No Seifu Kaihatsu Enjo.* Tokyo: Keizai Kyoryoku Suishinkyoku, 1999.

———. *Waga Kuni No Seifu Kaihatsu Enjo.* Tokyo: Keizai Kyoryoku Suishinkyoku, 2000.

Gerreffi, Gary, R. Garcia-Johnson, and E. Sasser. "The NGO-industrial Complex." *Foreign Policy* (July-August 2001): 56–65.

Gilbert, Christopher, and David Vines. *The World Bank: Structure and Policies.* Cambridge: Cambridge Univ. Press, 2000.

Gibelman, Margaret, and Sheldon R. Gelman. "A Loss of Credibility: Patterns of Wrongdoing among Nongovernmental Organizations." *Voluntas: International Journal of Voluntary and Nonprofit Organizations* 15, no. 4 (December 2004): 355–81.

Gilpin, Robert. *Global Political Economy.* Princeton, NJ: Princeton Univ. Press, 2000.

Goodhand, Jonathan, with Peter Chamberlain. "Dancing with the Prince: NGOs' Survival Strategies in the Afghan Conflict." In *Development, NGOs, and Civil Society,* edited by J. Pearce, 91–108. Oxford: Oxfam GB, 2000.

Granitsas, Alkman, and Deidre Sheehan. "Grassroots Capitalism." *Far Eastern Economic Review* 39 (July 12, 2001).

Halliday, Fred. *Rethinking International Relations.* London: MacMillan, 1994.

Hashemi, Syed M. "NGO Accountability in Bangladesh: Beneficiaries, Donors, and the State." In *Beyond the Magic Bullet: NGO Performance and Accountability in the Post–Cold War World,* edited by M. Edwards and David Hulme, 123–31. West Hartford, CT: Kumarian Press, 1996.

Hashemi, Syed M., and S. Schuler. *State and NGO Support Networks in Rural Bangladesh: Concepts and Coalitions for Control.* Copenhagen: Centre for Development Research, 1992.

Hastings, Sally. *Neighborhood and Nation in Tokyo, 1905–1937.* Pittsburgh: Univ. of Pittsburgh Press, 1995.

Helman, Gerald, and Steven S. Ratner. "Saving Failed States." *Foreign Policy* 89 (Winter 1992–93): 3–20.

Hermann, Charles, Charles Kegley, and James Rosenau, eds. *New Directions in the Study of Foreign Policy.* Boston: Allen and Unwin, 1987.

Higgott, Richard A., Geoffrey R. D. Underhill, and Andreas Bieler, eds. *Non-state Actors and Authority in the Global System.* London: Routledge, 2000.

Hilkka, Pietila, and Jeanne Vickers. *Making Women Matter: The Role of the United Nations.* London: Zed Books, 1994.

Hino, Toshiko. *NGO-World Bank Partnerships: A Tale of Two Projects.* Human Capital Development Working Papers 67. Washington, DC: World Bank, June 1996.

Holloway, Richard. *Supporting Citizens' Initiatives: Bangladesh's NGOs and Society.* Bangladesh: The Univ. Press Limited, 1998.

Holsti, K. J. *International Politics: A Framework for Analysis.* 6th ed. Upper Saddle River, NJ: Prentice Hall, 1992.

Howe, Florence. Editorial. *Women's Studies Quarterly* 1–2 (1996): 5–14.

Hoy, Paula. *Players and Issues in International Aid.* West Hartford, CT: Kumarian Press, 1998.

Hudock, Ann. *NGOs and Civil Society.* London: Polity Press, 1999.

Huq, Hedayatul. "Non Government Organizations Revisited: Rural Development by a Japanese NGO in Bangladesh." *University of Aizu Center for Cultural Research and Studies Annual Review* 3 (1997): 25–37.

Ihonvbere, Julius O. *Economic Crisis, Civil Society, and Democratization: The Case of Zambia.* Trenton, NJ: Africa World Press. 1996.

Indo-Asian News Service. "Clampdown on NGOs Could Cripple Bangladesh Development." *Yahoo India News* (February 14, 2004).

IOB Policy and Operations Evaluation Department. Ministry of Foreign Affairs. "Evaluation of Netherlands-Funded NGOs in Bangladesh." The Hague: Netherlands Ministry of Foreign Affairs, 1996.

Jacobson, Harold, and Edith Brown Weiss. "A Framework for Analysis." In *Engaging Countries: Strengthening Compliance with International Environmental Accords,* edited by Edith Brown Weiss and Harold Jacobson, 1–18. Cambridge, MA: MIT Press, 1998.

Jaquette, Jane S. "Losing the Battle/Winning the War: International Politics, Women's Issues, and the 1980 Mid-decade Conference." In *Women, Politics, and the United Nations,* edited by A. Winslow. Westport, CT: Greenwood Press, 1995.

Jarrar, Allam. "The Palestinian NGO Sector: Development Perspective." *Palestinian-Israel Journal of Politics, Economics, and Culture* 12, no. 1 (2005): 43–48.

Jasanoff, Sheila. "NGOs and the Environment: From Knowledge to Action." *Third World Quarterly* 18, no. 3 (1997): 579–94.

Jhamtani, Hira. "The Imperialism of Northern NGOs." *Earth Island Journal* 7, no. 3 (1996): 10–11.

Joachim, Jutta. "Framing Issues and Seizing Opportunities: The UN, NGOs, and Women's Rights." *International Studies Quarterly* 47, no. 2 (2003): 247–74.

Jordon, Lisa, and Peter van Tuijl. "Political Responsibility in Transnational NGO Advocacy." *World Development* 28, no. 12 (2000): 2051–65.

Kahler, Miles. "Inventing International Relations: International Relations Theory After 1945." In *New Thinking in International Relations,* edited by Michael Doyle and G. John Ikenberry, 20–53. Boulder, CO: Westview Press, 1987.

Kamaluddin, S. "Banking: Lending with a Mission." *Far Eastern Economic Review* 156 (March 18, 1993): 38–40.

Karim, Mahbubul. "NGOs, Democratization, and Good Governance: The Case of Bangladesh." In *New Roles and Relevance: Development NGOs and the Challenge of Change,* edited by David Lewis and Tina Wallace, 99–108. West Hartford, CT: Kumarian Press, 2000.

Karim, Mahbubul. "NGOs in Bangladesh: Issues of Legitimacy and Accountability." In *Beyond the Magic Bullet: NGO Performance and Accountability in the Post–Cold War World,* edited by Michael Edwards and David Hulme, 132–41. West Hartford, CT: Kumarian Press, 1996.

Karl, Marilee. *Women and Empowerment: Participation and Decision Making.* London: Zed Books, 1995.

Keck, Margaret E., and Kathryn Sikkink. *Activists beyond Borders.* Ithaca, NY: Cornell Univ. Press, 1998.

Keohane, R., and Nye, J. *Power and Interdependence.* 2nd ed. Glenview, IL: Scott Foresman, 1989.

Khan, Mohammed Mohabbat. "Accountability of NGOs in Bangladesh: A Critical Overview." *Public Management Review* 5, no. 2 (2003): 267–78.

Khandker, S., B. Khalily, and Z. Khan. *Is Grameen Bank Sustainable?* Washington, DC: Human Resources Development and Operations Policy Division, World Bank, 1994.

Kingdon, John. *Agendas, Alternatives, and Public Policy.* 2nd ed. New York: Harper Collins, 1995.

Klare, Michael, and Yogesh Chandrani, eds. *World Security: Challenges for a New Century.* 3rd ed. New York: St. Martin's Press, 1998.

Klein, Naomi. "Does Protest Need a Vision." *New Statesman* (July 3, 2000): 23–25.

Krasner, Stephen, ed. *International Regimes.* Ithaca, NY: Cornell Univ. Press, 1982.

———. "Sovereignty." *Foreign Policy* (January-February 2001): 21–29.

Lancaster, Carol. *Transforming Foreign Aid: United States Assistance in the 21ˢᵗ Century.* Washington, DC: Institute for International Economics, 2000.

Lewis, David J. "NGOs, Donors, and the State in Bangladesh." *Annals, AAPSS* 554 (November 1997): 33–45.

Lewis, David, and Babar Sobhan. "Routes of Funding, Roots of Trust? Northern NGOs, Southern NGOs, Donors, and the Rise of Direct Funding." *Development in Practice* 9, no. 1–2 (1999): 117–29.

Linden, Eugene. *The Alms Race: The Impact of American Voluntary Aid Abroad.* New York: Random House, 1976.

Linklater, Andrew. *International Relations: Critical Concepts in Political Science.* 5 vols. London: Routledge, 2000.

Long, David, and Laird Hindle. "Europe and the Ottawa Process." In *To Walk without Fear: The Global Movement to Ban Landmines,* edited by M.

Cameron, R. Lawson, and Brian Tomlin, 248–68. Ontario: Oxford Univ. Press Canada, 1998.

Mallaby, Sebastian. "NGOs: Fighting Poverty, Hurting the Poor." *Foreign Policy* (September-October 2004): 50–58.

Mama, Amina. "Strengthening Civil Society: Participatory Action Research in a Militarised State." In *Development, NGOs, and Civil Society,* edited by D. Eade, 175–89. London: Oxfam, 2000.

Maran, Rita. "The Role of Non-governmental Organizations." In *An End to Torture: Strategies for Its Eradication,* edited by B. Duner, 222–44. London: Zed Books, 1998.

Maren, Michael. *The Road to Hell: The Ravaging Effects of Foreign Aid and International Charity.* New York: The Free Press, 1997.

Martens, Kerstin. *NGOs and the United Nations: Institutionalization, Professionalization, and Adaptation.* New York: Palgrave MacMillan, 2005.

Maslen, Stuart. "The Role of the International Committee of the Red Cross." In *To Walk without Fear: The Global Movement to Ban Landmines,* edited by M. Cameron, R. Lawson, and Brian Tomlin, 80–98. Ontario: Oxford Univ. Press Canada, 1998.

Mathews, Jessica. "Power Shift." *Foreign Affairs* 76, no. 1 (1997): 50–66.

Maughan, Steven. "The Role of Environmental NGOs in International Regimes." In *The Global Environment: Institutions, Laws, and Policy,* edited by Norman Vig and Regina S. Axelrod, 52–71. Washington, DC: CQ Press, 1996.

———. "'Mighty England Do Good': The Major English Denominations and Organisation for the Support of Foreign Missions in the Nineteenth Century." In *Missionary Encounters: Sources and Issues,* edited by R. Bickers and R. Seton, 11–37. Richmond, Surrey: Curzon Press, 1996.

McCormick, John. "The Role of Environmental NGOs in International Regimes." In *The Global Environment. Institutions, Laws, and Policy,* edited by Norman Vig and Regina S. Axelrod, 52–71. Washington, DC: CQ Press, 1999.

McCubbins, M., and T. Schwartz. "Congressional Oversight Overlooked: Police Patrols v. Fire Alarms." *American Journal of Political Science* 28 (1984): 165–79.

Mendelson, Sarah. "Democracy Assistance and Political Transition in Russia: Between Success and Failure." *International Security* 25, no. 4 (2001): 68–106.

Mercy Corps. "Mercy Corps Is Launching a Program to Assist Approximately One Million People Living in 50 Communities in Iraq." *InterAction-Media*, July 10, 2003. Available online.

Metaka, Motoko. "Building Partnerships toward a Common Goal: Experiences from the International Campaign to Ban Landmines." In *The Third Force: The Rise of Transnational Civil Society,* edited by A. Florini, 143–76. Tokyo: Japan Center for International Exchange; Washington, DC: Carnegie Endowment for International Peace, 2001.

Meyer, Carrie. "Opportunism and NGOs: Entrepreneurship and Green North-South Transfers." *World Development* 23, no. 8 (1995): 1277–89.

Mingst, Karen A., and Margaret P. Karns. *The United Nations in the Post–Cold War Era.* Boulder, CO: Westview Press, 2000.

Miniter, Richard. "The False Promise of Slave Redemption." *Atlantic Monthly* 284, no. 1 (1999): 63–70.

Morgenthau, Hans. *Politics among Nations.* 5th ed. New York: Knopf, 1972.

Murphy, Gillian H. "The Seattle WTO Protests: Building a Global Movement." In *Creating a Better World: Interpreting Global Civil Society,* edited by Rupert Taylor, 28–42. Bloomfield, CT: Kumarian Press, 2004.

Najam, Adil. "NGO Accountability: A Conceptual Framework." *Development Policy Review* 14 (1996): 339–53.

Nalinakumari, Brijesh, and Richard Maclean. "NGOs: A Primer on the Evolution of the Organizations That Are Setting the Next Generation of 'Regulations.'" *Environmental Quality Management* 14, no. 4 (Summer 2005): 1–21.

Natsios, Andrew. *U.S. Foreign Policy and the Four Horsemen of the Apocalypse: Humanitarian Relief in Complex Emergencies.* Boulder, CO: Praeger, 1997.

Nelson, Paul J. *The World Bank and Non-governmental Organizations.* New York: St. Martin's Press, 1996.

Nelson, Paul. "Information, Location, and Legitimacy: The Changing Basis of Civil Society Involvement in International Economic Policy." In *Global Citizen Action,* edited by Michael Edwards and John Gaventa, 59–72. Boulder, CO: Lynne Rienner, 2001.

Nerfin, Marc. "Neither Prince Nor Merchant—An Introduction to the Third System." *IFDA Dossier* 56 (1986): 3–29.

Newell, Peter. "Environmental NGOs and Globalization: The Governance of TNCs." In *Global Social Movements,* edited by Robin Cohen and Shirin M. Rai, 117–33. London: The Athlone Press, 2000.

NGO Dairekutori—'94. Tokyo: NGO Katsudo Suishin Sentaa, 1994.

Noel, Alain, and J. P. Therien. "From Domestic to International Justice: The Welfare State and Foreign Aid." *International Organization* 49, no. 3 (1995): 523–53.

Nolan, Cathal. *Principled Diplomacy: Security and Rights in U.S. Foreign Policy.* Westport, CT: Greenwood Press, 1993.

O'Brien, Robert, A. M. Goetz, J. Aart Scholte, and M. Williams. *Contesting Global Governance: Multinational Economic Institutions and Global Social Movements.* Cambridge, MA: Cambridge Univ. Press, 2000.

Olson, Mancur. *The Logic of Collective Action.* New York: Schocken Books, 1971.

Onuf, Nicholas. *World of Our Making.* Columbia: Univ. of South Carolina Press, 1988.

Ottaway, Marina. "Reluctant Missionaries." *Foreign Policy* (July-August 2001): 44–54.

Oxfam GB. *A Short History of Oxfam.* Available online.

Palliser, Michael. "Diplomacy Today." In *The Expansion of International Society,* edited by H. Bull and A. Watson, 371–86. Oxford: Clarendon Press, 1984.

Patterson, Amy. "It's a Small World: Incorporating Service Learning into International Relations Courses." *PS* 33, no. 4 (2000): 817–22.

Perera, Jehan. "In Unequal Dialogue with Donors: The Experience of the Sarvodaya Shramadana Movement." In *NGOs, States and Donors,* edited by David Hulme and M. Edwards, 156–67. New York: St. Martin's Press, 1996.

Perkins, Wenchi Yu. "NGO Watch." *UN Chronicle* 1 (2005): 54–55.

"Philanthropy Measures Up: World Economic Forum Global Leaders Tomorrow Benchmarking Philanthropy Report." January 28, 2003. Available online.

Pietila, Hilka, and Jeanne Vickers. *Making Women Matter: The Role of the United Nations.* London: Zed Books, 1994.

Porter, Gareth, and Janet W. Brown. *Global Environmental Politics.* Boulder, CO: Westview Press, 1996.

Potter, David. "Assessing Japan's Environmental Aid Policy." *Pacific Affairs* 67, no. 2 (1994): 200–215.

Potter, David. Interview with Yasue Kuwahara, Cincinnati, Ohio, April 20, 1996.

———. *Japan's Foreign Aid to Thailand and the Philippines.* New York: St. Martin's Press, 1996.

———. "NGOs and Japan's Role in Post Cold War Asia." In *Weaving a New Tapestry: Asia in the Post–Cold War World,* edited by W. Head and E. Clausen, 189–208. Boulder, CO: Praeger, 1999.

———. "State and Local Government Negotiation with Japanese Multinational Corporations." In *Japan in the Bluegrass,* edited by P. P. Karan, 58–79. Univ. Press of Kentucky, 2001.

Price, Richard. "Reversing the Gun Sights: Transnational Civil Society Targets Landmines." *International Organization* 52, no. 3 (1998): 613–44.

Princen, Thomas, and Matthias Finger. *Environmental NGOs in World Politics.* London: Routledge, 1994.

Putnam, Robert. *Making Democracy Work: Civic Traditions in Modern Italy.* Princeton, NJ: Princeton Univ. Press, 1993.

Randel, Judith, and Tony German. "Germany." In *Stakeholders: NGO-Government Partnerships for International Development,* edited by Ian Smillie and Henny Helmich, 114–22. London: Earthscan, 1999.

Raustiala, Kal. "States, NGOs, and International Environmental Institutions." *International Studies Quarterly* 41 (1997): 719–740.

Reinicke, Wolfgang. "The Other World Wide Web: Global Public Policy Networks." *Foreign Policy* 117 (Winter 1999–2000): 44–57.

Risse, Thomas. "'Let's Argue!': Communicative Action in World Politics." *International Organization* 54, no. 1 (2000) 1–39.

———. "The Power of Norms versus the Norms of Power: Transnational Civil Society and Human Rights." In *The Third Force,* edited by A. Florini, 177–210. Tokyo: Japan Center for International Education; Washington, DC: Carnegie Endowment for International Peace, 2000.

Risse-Kappen, Thomas, ed. *Bringing Transnational Relations Back In.* Cambridge, MA: Cambridge Univ. Press, 1995.

Rix, Alan. *Japan's Foreign Aid Challenge: Policy Reform and Aid Leadership.* London: Routledge, 1993.

Romzek, Barbara, and M. Dubnick. "Accountability in the Public Sector: Lessons from the Challenger Tragedy." In *Current Issues in Public Administration,* edited by F. Lane, 158–76. New York: St. Martin's Press, 1994.

Rosenbaum, Walter. *Environmental Politics and Policy.* Washington, DC: CQ Press, 1995.

Rourke, John, and Mark Boyer. *World Politics: International Politics on the World Stage, Brief.* 2nd ed. New York: Dushkin/McGraw-Hill, 1998.

Rutherford, Kenneth. "The Evolving Arms Control Agenda: Implications of the Role of NGOs in Banning Antipersonnel Landmines." *World Politics* 53, no. 1 (2000): 74–114.

Ruttan, Vernon. *United States Development Assistance Policy.* Baltimore: Johns Hopkins Univ. Press, 1996.

Salamon, Lester. "The Rise of the Nonprofit Sector." *Foreign Affairs* 73, no. 4 (1994): 109–22.

Salamon, Lester, and Helmut Anheier. *The Emerging Nonprofit Sector: An Overview.* Manchester, NH: Manchester Univ. Press, 1994.

———, eds. *The Nonprofit Sector in Comparative Perspective.* Manchester, NH: Univ. of Manchester Press, 1997.

Salamon, Lester, and Wojciech Sokolowski, eds. *Global Civil Society: Dimensions of the Nonprofit Sector.* Bloomfield, CT: Kumarian Press, 2004.

Sampson, Gary. "The Environmentalist Paradox: The World Trade Organization's Challenges." *Harvard International Review* (Winter 2002): 56–61.

Scholte, Jan Aart. "The IMF and Civil Society: An Interim Progress Report." In *Global Citizen Action,* edited by Michael Edwards and John Gaventa, 87–103. Boulder, CO: Lynne Rienner, 2001.

Scott, James. *Seeing Like a State.* Princeton, NJ: Princeton Univ. Press, 2000.

Scott, Mathew J. O. "Danger—Landmines! NGO-Government Collaboration in the Ottawa Process." In *Global Citizen Action,* edited by M. Edwards and J. Gaventa, 121–34. Boulder, CO: Lynne Rienner, 2001.

Seelye, Katharine. "U.S. Is Said to Erode Rule of Law." *International Herald Tribune,* April 16, 2002, 3.

Shabecoff, Philip. *A New Name for Peace: International Environmentalism, Sustainable Development, and Democracy.* Hanover, NH: Univ. Press of New England, 1996.

Shinichi, Shigetomi, ed. *The State and NGOs: Perspectives from Asia.* Singapore: Institute of Southeast Asian Studies, 2002.

Sikkink, Kathryn. "Human Rights, Principled Issue Networks, and Sovereignty in Latin America." *International Organization* 47, no. 3 (Summer 1993): 411–41.

Simmons, Peter J. "Learning to Live with NGOs." *Foreign Policy* 112 (Fall 1998): 82–96.

Smillie, Ian. "At Sea in a Sieve? Trends and Issues in the Relationship between Northern NGOs and Northern Governments." In *Stakeholders: Government-NGO Partnerships for International Development,* edited by Ian Smillie, Henny Helmich, et al., 7–35. London: Earthscan, 1999.

Smillie, Ian. "The World Bank." In *Stakeholders: Government-NGO Partnerships for International Development,* edited by Ian Smillie, Henny Helmich, et al., 278–87. London: Earthscan, 1999.

Smillie, Ian, and Henny Helmich, in collaboration with Tony German and Judith Randel. *Stakeholders: Government-NGO Partnerships for International Development.* London: Earthscan, 1999.

Smith, Brian. *More Than Altruism: The Politics of Private Foreign Aid.* Princeton, NJ: Princeton Univ. Press, 1990.

————. "Nonprofit Organizations in International Development: Agents of Empowerment or Preservers of Stability?" In *Private Action and the Public Good,* edited by Walter W. Powell and Elisabeth S. Clemens, 217–27. New Haven, CT: Yale Univ. Press, 1998.

Sollis, Peter. "The Development-Relief Continuum: Some Notes on Rethinking Assistance for Civilian Victims of Conflict." *Journal of International Affairs* 47, no. 2 (1994): 451–71.

Stephenson, Carolyn. "Women's International Nongovernmental Organizations at the United Nations." In *Women, Politics, and the United Nations,* edited by A. Winslow, 135–53. Westport, CT: Greenwood Press, 1995.

Stern, Geoffrey. *The Structure of International Society.* 2nd ed. London: Pinter, 2000.

Stiles, Kendall. "International Support for NGOs in Bangladesh: Some Unintended Consequences." *World Development* 30, no. 5 (2002): 835–47.

Tarrow, Sidney. *Power in Movement: Social Movements and Contentious Politics.* 2nd ed. Cambridge, MA: Cambridge Univ. Press, 1998.

Technology Links Forum to the UN and the World. *NGO Forum on Women '95 Bulletin* (December 1995): 10.

Tendler, Judith. *Turning Private Voluntary Organizations into Development Agencies: Questions for Evaluation.* USAID Program Evaluation Discussion Paper no. 12. Washington, DC: USAID, 1982.

Terry, Fiona. *Condemned to Repeat? The Paradox of Humanitarian Action.* Ithaca, NY: Cornell Univ. Press, 2002.

Thakur, Ramesh. "Human Rights: Amnesty International and the United Nations." In *The Politics of Global Governance: International Organizations in an Interdependent World,* edited by Paul Diehl, 247–68. Boulder, CO: Lynne Rienner, 1997.

Tinker, Irene. "Nongovernmental Organizations: An Alternative Power Base for Women?" In *Gender Politics in Global Governance,* edited by Mary K. Meyer and Elisabeth Prugl, 88–104. Boulder, CO: Rowman and Littlefield, 1999.

Tvedt, Terje. *Angels of Mercy or Development Diplomats? NGOs and Foreign Aid.* Trenton, NJ: Africa World Press, 1998.

Udall, Lori. "The World Bank and Public Accountability: Has Anything Changed?" In *The Struggle for Accountability: The World Bank, NGOs, and Grassroots Movements,* edited by Jonathan Fox and David Brown, 391–436 (Cambridge, MA: MIT Press, 1998).

Union of International Associations, ed. *Yearbook of International Organizations: Guide to Global Civil Society Networks, 2000–2001.* Vol. 1B. Munich: K. G. Saur Verlag.

United Nations. *The United Nations and the Advancement of Women, 1945–1996.* Blue Book series, vol. 6, rev. ed. New York: United Nations Department of Public Information, 1996.

United Nations Development Program. *Human Development Report, 1993.* New York: Oxford Univ. Press, 1993.

United States General Accounting Office. *International Environmental Agreements Are Not Well-monitored.* Washington, DC: GAO, 1992.

Uvin, Peter. "From Local Organizations to Global Governance: The Role of NGOs in International Relations." In *Global Institutions and Local Empowerment: Competing Theoretical Perspectives,* edited by Kendall Stiles, 9–29. New York: St. Martin's Press, 2000.

Van Rooy, Alison, ed. *Civil Society and the Aid Industry.* London: Earthscan, 1998.

Vig, Norman J., and Regina S. Axelrod, eds. *The Global Environment. Institutions, Laws, and Policy.* Washington, DC: CQ Press, 1999.

Waltz, Kenneth. "Political Structures." In *Neorealism and Its Critics,* edited by R. Keohane, 70–97. New York: Columbia Univ. Press, 1986.

Wapner, Paul. *Environmental Activism and World Civic Politics.* Albany: State Univ. of New York Press, 1996.

Wapner, Paul. "The Transnational Politics of Environmental NGOs: Governmental, Economic, and Social Activism." In *The Global Environment in the Twenty-first Century: Prospects for International Cooperation,* edited by Pamela Chasek, 87–108. New York: The United Nations University, 2000.

Warkentin, Craig. "A New Politics of Multilaterism? NGOs, the WWW, and the Dynamics of Contemporary International Organization." Paper presented at the 41st annual convention of the International Studies Association, March 2000.

Waters, Tony. *Bureaucratizing the Good Samaritan.* Boulder, CO: Westview Press, 2001.

Weiss, Elizabeth. "The Five International Treaties: A Living History." In *Engaging Countries: Strengthening Compliance with International Environmental Accords,* edited by E. Weiss and H. Jacobson, 89–172. Cambridge, MA: MIT Press, 1998.

Weiss, Thomas, and Leon Gordenker, eds. *NGOs, the UN, and Global Governance.* Boulder, CO: Lynne Rienner, 1996.

Wendt, Alexander. "Anarchy Is What States Make of It: The Social Construction of Power Politics." *International Organization* 46, no. 2 (1992): 391–425. Reprinted in *International Relations: Critical Concepts in Political Science,* edited by A. Linklater, 2:615–51. London: Routledge, 2000.

White, Jerry, and Ken Rutherford. "The Role of the Landmine Survivors Network." In *To Walk without Fear: The Global Movement to Ban Landmines,* edited by M. Cameron, R. Lawson, and Brian Tomlin, 99–117. Ontario: Oxford Univ. Press Canada, 1998.

White, Sarah C. "NGOs, Civil Society, and the State in Bangladesh: The Politics of Representing the Poor." *Development and Change* 30, no. 2 (1999): 307–26.

Willetts, Peter, ed. *"The Conscience of the World:" The Influence of Non-governmental Organizations in World Politics.* Washington, DC: Brookings Institution, 1996.

———. "From 'Consultative' Arrangements to 'Partnership': The Changing Status of NGOs in Diplomacy at the UN." *Global Governance* 6, no. 2 (2000): 191–213.

Williams, Jody. "World Citizens and International Cooperation." Public address before the Campus Forum in Nagoya, Chukyo University, Nagoya, Japan, November 20, 1998.

Williams, Jody, and Stephen Goose. "The International Campaign to Ban Landmines." In *To Walk without Fear: The Global Movement to Ban Landmines,* edited by M. Cameron, R. Lawson, and Brian Tomlin, 20–47. Ontario: Oxford Univ. Press Canada, 1998.

Williams, Mark. "The World Bank, the World Trade Organisation, and the Environmental Social Movement." In *Non-state Actors and Authority in the Global System,* edited by R. Higgott, G. Underhill, and A. Bieler, 241–55. New York: Routledge, 2000.

Woods, Ngaire. "The Challenges of Multilateralism and Governance." In *The World Bank: Structure and Policies,* edited by J. Gilbert and D. Vines, 132–56. Cambridge: Cambridge Univ. Press, 2000.

Wood, Robert. *From Marshall Plan to Debt Crisis.* Berkeley and Los Angeles: Univ. of California Press, 1986.

World Bank. *Annual Report.* Washington, DC: International Bank for Reconstruction and Development, 1993.

———. *Economics and Governance of Nongovernmental Organizations in Bangladesh.* Development Series Paper no. 11. Bangladesh: World Bank Office, Dhaka, 2006.

———. *World Indicators 2005.* Washington, DC: World Bank, 2005.

World Trade Organization. "Agreement Establishing the World Trade Organization," Article V (Extract). 2000. Available online.

Yearly, Steve, and John Forrester. "Shell, a Sure Target for Global Environmental Campaigning?" In *Global Social Movements,* edited by R. Cohen and S. M. Rai, 134–45. London: The Athlone Press, 2000.

Yergin, Daniel, and Joseph Stanislaw. *The Commanding Heights: The Battle between Government and the Marketplace That Is Shaping the Modern World.* New York: Simon and Schuster, 1998.

Yunus, Muhammad. *Banker to the Poor: Micro-lending and the Battle against World Poverty.* New York: Public Affairs, 1999.

Zehfuss, Maya. "Constructivism in International Relations: Wendt, Onuf, and Kratchowil." In *Constructing International Relations: The Next Generation,* edited by Karin Fierke and Knud Jorgensen, 54–75. Armonk, NJ: M. E. Sharpe, 2001.

About the Authors

Shamima Ahmed is an associate professor in the Department of Political Science and Criminal Justice, Northern Kentucky University. Her teaching and research interests are in public administration, nonprofit management, and research methods. She has published in *Management Development Journal, International Journal of Public Administration, Asian Thought and Society, Public Personnel Management,* and *State and Local Government Review.*

David M. Potter is a professor of political science in the Faculty of Policy Studies, Nanzan University, Nagoya, Japan. He is the author of *Japan's Foreign Aid to Thailand and the Philippines* (St. Martin's Press, 1996) and co-author of *Media, Bureaucracies, and Foreign Aid* (Palgrave, 2004). He is the author of multiple articles and book chapters on Japan's foreign aid, foreign policy, and NGOs.

Index

Taratak Foundation, 45
Tarrow, Sidney, 26, 27
tax status: of MNCs, 72n6; of tax-exempt NGOs, 61, 72n6
Tendler, Judith, 120
Thailand: CANHELP Thailand for, 7, 20, 113, 247; women's restrictions from, 59
Thakur, Ramesh, 50
Thatcher, Margaret, 103
think tanks: from authoritarian governments, 65; entrepreneurs for, 49; public education from, 49; WRI as, 218
Third Conference on Population and Development (Cairo), 196–97
Third World: INGOs' for, 41–42; NGOs' economics for, 24; NGOs' numbers in, 20; NGOs' politics' restrictions in, 61; NGOs' withdrawal for, 115–16
Thomas, George, 21–22, 23
TNCs. *See* transnational corporations
trafficking, INGOs against, 43
transnational advocacy networks: NGO organization from, 27; politics of, 43–44; social movement leadership from, 27; for women, 201, 202
transnational civil society, within international society, 253
transnational corporations (TNCs): Coalition for Environmentally Responsible Economies for, 227; ENGOs on, 224, 227–29, 229–32; NGOs' environmental treaty monitors, 229–32; NGOs' public education about, 228; NGOs' surveillance of, 228; "shareholder activism" for, 228–29
transnationalism, for states with non-state actors, 12–13, 15, 241
transnational NGO campaigns; Huaorani v. Conoco in, 248–49, 251–52; NGOs' responsibilities in, 248
transnational NGOs, restrictions for, 61–62

transnational politics, for NGOs' accountability, 125–26
transnational relations, definitions of, 12, 13, 15
treaties: environmental, 229–32; monitors for, 229–32; NGOs' "treaties" as, 69; participation for, 230, 232
Trust (Fukuyama), 31
UN. *See* United Nations
UNCED. *See* United Nations Council on Economic Development
UN Conference on Human Rights (Vienna): Center for Women's Global Leadership for, 194; on gender-based violence, 194–96; Global Tribunal on Violations of Women's Rights at, 195–96; Sixteen Days of Activism against Gender Violence for, 195
UN Decade for Women, 189–91; CEDAW from, 191–92; GAD approach from, 193; networks from, 194; UN experience from, 193, 194; UNIFEM from, 193; WID from, 192–93
UNDP. *See* United Nations Development ment Program
UNDRO. *See* United Nations Disaster Relief Organization
UN Framework Convention on Climate Change (Kyoto Protocol): GCC v., 212; NGOs' treaty participation for, 230, 232
UNHCR. *See* United Nations High Commissioner for Refugees
UN High Commission for Refugees (UNHCR), 83
UNIFEM. *See* United Nations Development ment Fund for Women
United Nations (UN), 95n4. *See also* Economic and Social Council (UN)
United Nations Council on Economic Development (UNCED): from Brundtland Commission, 215, 216; creation of, 216, 217; for global